IRONIES OF HISTORY

Essays on
Contemporary Communism

ISAAC DEUTSCHER

London
OXFORD UNIVERSITY PRESS
NEW YORK TORONTO
1966

Oxford University Press, Ely House, London W. 1

GLASGOW NEW YORK TORONTO MELBOURNE WELLINGTON
CAPE TOWN SALISBURY IBADAN NAIROBI LUSAKA ADDIS ABABA
BOMBAY CALCUTTA MADRAS KARACHI LAHORE DACCA
KUALA LUMPUR HONG KONG

Printed in Great Britain by
Northumberland Press Limited
Gateshead on Tyne

IRONIES OF HISTORY

CONTENTS

PREFACE

THE main part of this book consists of articles and essays analysing social and political trends in the U.S.S.R., China, and Eastern Europe. This is in fact a selection from a much larger number of writings which I have devoted to these subjects in the last ten years or so. (Earlier essays of this series appeared in my *Heretics and Renegades*, an English edition of which was published in 1955, and in *Russia in Transition* brought out in the United States in 1957.) *Ironies of History* covers a significant period in Soviet and Communist affairs: Part I of this volume, 'Revisions and Divisions', begins with an examination of Khrushchev's 'secret speech' at the Twentieth Congress and with an exposure of the inconsistencies of his 'de-Stalinization'; it ends with a *post mortem* on Khrushchevism. The essays appear here in their original form, with the dates of writing or first publication clearly indicated. Readers who may feel confused by the vehement controversies aroused by some of my views may find these indications useful. I do not claim infallibility for my comments or for the predictions I have occasionally made; but I am entitled to be judged by the views I have expressed, not by those that others attribute to me.

I am including, in Part II, a retrospect on 'Twenty Years of Cold War'. This was the theme of speeches I made recently in the United States at 'Teach-Ins' on the war in Vietnam. I had the honour of being the only non-American invited by the American Inter-University Committee to speak as a critic of President Johnson's Administration at the great National Teach-In in Washington in May 1965. These meetings and debates were repeatedly broadcast and televised in full and gave rise to a wide movement of protest against the war in Vietnam and to a quite unprecedented demonstration of political non-conformism in the States.

Parts III and IV contain historical, biographical and literary essays, directly or indirectly related to my main political theme.

My thanks are due to the Editors of *The Times Literary Supplement*, the B.B.C. Third Programme, *The Listener*, *Socialist*

Register, Les Temps Modernes, New Left Review, The Nation, Partisan Review, Frankfurter Hefte, Chuo-Koron, and other periodicals where some of the essays of this volume first appeared. The first, third and fourth essays are reproduced here from my book *Russia in Transition* by permission of Coward-McCann Inc.

I.D.

London, April 1966

PART ONE

REVISIONS AND DIVISIONS

PART ONE

REVISIONS AND DIVISIONS

KHRUSHCHEV ON STALIN[1]

No one who has seen and heard N. S. Khrushchev speaking on a platform or arguing with people will doubt the authenticity of the text, published by the State Department, of his secret speech at the Twentieth Congress of the Soviet Communist Party. The text probably has its gaps, and here and there the transcript or the translation may not be quite accurate. Nevertheless this is the real stuff —genuine Khrushchev saying indirectly about himself almost as much as he says about Stalin.

The style, like the man himself, is untutored, impulsive, discursive, almost chaotic; yet at the same time it is peculiarly dynamic and down-to-earth. This is no theorist or historian producing a Marxist explanation of the Stalin era or offering analytical ideas and generalizations. In this respect Khrushchev is immeasurably inferior to the great Bolshevik critics who have exposed Stalin before him, to Trotsky, Bukharin, or Rakovsky. Yet he gives by far the most vivid image of the Stalin era, or, at any rate, of its final phase, and incidentally also of Stalin himself. He takes us into the dark corridors and galleries of Russia's recent past as a miner would take us, lamp in hand, down a coalpit; and with a miner's tough fist he puts dynamite under the rocks of Stalinism down below.

His performance must be something of a puzzle to the purveyors of clichés and simplifications about the Stalin era. How is it, one must ask, that a man of so sturdy a character, of a mind so inherently independent, and of so eruptive and untamable a temper could at all survive under Stalin, and survive at the very top of the Stalinist hierarchy? How did Khrushchev manage to control himself, to keep his thoughts to himself, and to hide his burning hatred from Stalin? How did he behave under the dictator's scrutinizing gaze when the dictator snarled at him: 'Why do your eyes look so shifty today?'

This is not the place to analyse the working of the minds of men

[1] Written and first published (in French, German, Italian, Japanese) in June 1956.

like Khrushchev during the Stalin era. I have attempted to do it elsewhere, for instance in my book *Russia After Stalin*. But this much can be said here: in this miner and miner's son risen to his present position one can still feel something of that tenacious, patient, yet alert and shrewd spirit which once characterized the old Russian worker when from the underground he bored under the Tsar's throne. To that spirit are now joined new mental horizons, a new capacity for organization, and an unwonted modernity. As one watches Khrushchev (even, as I have watched him, with a certain bias against him) one comes to think that he is probably still the Russian (or the Russo-Ukrainian) worker, writ large—the Russian worker who inwardly remained true to himself even in the Stalinist straitjacket, who has over the years gathered strength and grown in stature and grown out of the straitjacket. One might even say that through Khrushchev the old repressed socialist tradition of the Russian working class takes a long-delayed and sly revenge on Stalinism.

Yet Khrushchev also makes the impression of an actor who, while he plays his own part with superb self-assurance, is only half aware of his own place in the great, complex, and sombre drama in which he has been involved. His long, aggressive monologue is a cry from the heart, a cry about the tragedy of the Russian revolution and of the Bolshevik Party; but it is only a fragment of the tragedy. He himself did not expect to burst out with this cry. Only a few days before he made the secret speech, he did not know that he was going to make it; or, at any rate, he did not know what he was going to say. Even the composition of his speech shows that he spoke more or less impromptu: he dashes from topic to topic almost indiscriminately; he ventures spontaneously into the side lines; and he seems to throw out reminiscences and confidences and asides as they occur to him. By its irregularity this speech, delivered at the closing session of the congress on 25 February, contrasts curiously with his own formal address delivered at the inaugural session ten days earlier. The two speeches form a striking contrast in content as well. In his inaugural address Khrushchev said, for instance:

The unity of our party has formed itself in the course of years and tens of years. It has grown and become tempered in the struggle against many enemies. The Trotskyites, Bukharinites, bourgeois nationalists, and other most wicked *enemies of the people*, champions of a capitalist restoration, made desperate efforts to disrupt from the inside the Leninist unity of our party, and they all have smashed their heads against our unity.

The words might have come straight from Stalin's mouth. But ten days later Khrushchev argues thus:

It is Stalin who originated the concept *'enemy of the people'*. This term automatically rendered it unnecessary that the ideological errors of a man, or men, engaged in a controversy be proven; this term made possible the usage of the most cruel repression . . . against anyone who in any way disagreed with Stalin. . . .

Khrushchev then goes on to say that the Trotskyites, Bukharinites, and so-called bourgeois nationalists, whatever their faults, were not enemies of the people; that there was no need to annihilate them; and that they 'smashed their heads' not against the party's 'Leninist unity' but against Stalin's despotism.

The speaker to whom the congress listened on 25 February was a very different man from the one whom it heard ten days earlier. What happened during those ten days to change the man so radically? Clearly, some dramatic but as yet undisclosed event must have occurred in the meantime, an event which showed Khrushchev that it would not do to sit on the fence and that he had to come down on one side or the other in the conflict between Stalinism and anti-Stalinism. Did perhaps the small band of old Bolsheviks, wrecks from Stalin's concentration camps, who have been brought to the conference hall as guests of honour, stage some demonstration of protest which shook the assembly's conscience? Or were the young delegates, who had been brought up in the Stalin cult, so restive after Khrushchev's first ambiguous hints about Stalin (and even more so after Mikoyan's more outspoken remarks) that they forced him to come out into the open and take the bull by the horns?

Whatever happened, Khrushchev had to produce an answer on the spot; and the answer was an indictment of Stalin.[2] To justify his new attitude he ordered, no doubt with the Presidium's approval, that Lenin's testament be distributed among the delegates, that long-suppressed testament in which Lenin urged the party to re-

[2] Since these words were written we have learned that Khrushchev had for this the approval of the Central Committee, or rather of its majority—a large minority, consisting of Stalinist die-hards, was opposed to his coming out with the revelations.

move Stalin from the post of General Secretary, the testament for the publication and execution of which the anti-Stalinist opposition once clamoured for years and in vain.

To the student of Soviet affairs Khrushchev's disclosures bring little that is really new. A biographer of Stalin finds in them at the most a few more illustrations of familiar points. Khrushchev confirms in every detail the account of the relations between Lenin and Stalin towards the very end of Lenin's life which Trotsky gave. Stalin's old critics are also proved right in what they have said about his method of collectivization, about the purges, and about the Trotskyite and Bukharinite 'fifth columns', in the reality of which not only Communists but conservatives, liberals, and socialists in the West once preferred to believe. Nor is there anything surprising to the historian in Khrushchev's revelations about Stalin's role in the last war and about his miscalculations and mistakes.[3]

But it is not from the historian's viewpoint that Khrushchev's performance should be judged. He spoke not to scholars, but to men and women of a new Communist generation; and to them his words have come as a Titanic shock, and as the beginning of a profound mental—and moral—upheaval.

Consider only how Khrushchev's character-sketch of Stalin, drawn haphazardly yet extremely vividly, must affect Communists brought up in the Stalin cult. There they see him now, the 'Father of the Peoples', immured as he was in the Kremlin, refusing over the last twenty-five years of his life to have a look at a Soviet village —at the new collectivized village; refusing to step down into a factory and face workers; refusing even to cast a glance at the army of which he was the Generalissimo, let alone to visit the front; spending his life in a half-real and half-fictitious world of statistics and mendacious propaganda films; planning unleviable taxes; tracing front-lines and lines of offensives on a globe on his desk; seeing enemies creeping at him from every nook and cranny; treating the members of his own Politbureau as his contemptible lackeys, denying a Voroshilov admission to sessions, slamming the door in Andreyev's face, or upbraiding Molotov and Mikoyan; 'choking' his interlocutors 'morally and physically'; pulling the wires behind the great purge trials; personally checking and signing 383 black lists with the names of thousands of doomed party members; order-

---

[3] See, for instance, my *Stalin*, pp. 453-9.

ing judges and N.K.V.D. men to torture the victims of the purges and to extract confessions; 'planning' the deportations of entire peoples and raging impotently at the size of the Ukrainian people too large to be deported; growing sick with envy at Zhukov's military fame; 'shaking his little finger' at Tito and waiting for Tito's imminent fall; surrounded by dense clouds of incense and, like an opium eater, craving for more; inserting in his own hand passages of praise to his own 'genius'—and to his own modesty!—into his official adulatory biography and into history textbooks; himself designing huge, monstrously ugly, elephantine monuments to himself; and himself writing his own name into the new national anthem which was to replace the Internationale. Thus did Khrushchev expose before his party the huge, grim, whimsical, morbid, human monster before whom Communists had lain prostrate over a quarter of a century.

And yet Khrushchev adds that 'Stalin was convinced that all this was necessary for the defence of the interests of the working class against the plotting of the enemies and against the attack of the imperialist camp.' When he surmised that even those who stood closest to him did not share his phobias and suspicions, Stalin wrung his hands in despair: 'What will you do without me?' he growled. 'You are blind like chicken!' 'He saw this,' Khrushchev assures the congress again, 'from the position of the interest of the working class . . . of socialism and communism. We cannot say that these were the deeds of a giddy despot. . . . In this lies the whole tragedy!'

Yet the mainspring of the tragedy remains hidden from Khrushchev. His whole speech is full of the denunciation of the hero cult; yet it is nothing but inverted hero cult. Its one and only theme is the power, the superhuman power, of the usurper who 'placed himself above the party and above the masses'. In passage after passage Khrushchev argues that all the evil from which the Communist Party, the Soviet people, and the international labour movement have suffered for so long sprang from this one 'individual'. And then he tells us in quite as many passages that it is utterly wrong to imagine that one man could exercise so much influence on history, for the real makers of Soviet history have been the masses, the people, and the 'militant Bolshevik Party' bred and inspired by Lenin.

Where then was that 'militant party' when Stalin 'placed himself above it'? Where was its militancy and its Leninist spirit? Why and how could the despot impose his will on the masses? And why did 'our heroic people' submit so passively?

All these questions, which have so close a bearing on the Marxist *Weltanschauung*, Khrushchev leaves unanswered. Yet, if one agrees that history is made not by demigods but by masses and social classes one has still to explain the rise of this particular demigod; and one can explain it only by the condition of Soviet society, the interests of the Bolshevik Party, and the state of mind of its leadership. But no sooner have we descended with Khrushchev to this depth of recent Soviet history than his lamp is blown out, and we are once again enveloped by dark and impenetrable fumes.

The political evolution of the Soviet régime falls broadly into three chapters. In the first the Bolsheviks under Lenin established their monopoly of power, the single-party system, in which they saw the only way to preserve their government and to safeguard the October Revolution against domestic and foreign foes. But having suppressed all other parties, the Bolshevik Party itself split into several factions which confronted one another in utter hostility. The single-party system turned out to be a contradiction in terms: the single party was breaking up into at least three parties.

In the second chapter the rule of the single party was replaced by the rule of a single Bolshevik faction, the one led by Stalin. The principle of the 'monolithic' party was proclaimed. Only a party which does not permit diverse currents of opinion to emerge in its midst, Stalin argued, can safeguard its monopoly of power. However, the rule of the single faction also proved to be chimerical. Once it had gained complete mastery, the victorious faction, like the victorious party before it, was torn by internal rivalries and divisions.

In the third and final chapter the rule of the single faction gives way to the rule of the single leader, who by the nature of the whole process had to be intolerant of any potential challenge to his authority, constantly on his guard, constantly suspicious, and constantly bent on enforcing his will. The monopoly of power reached its culmination.

The Bolshevik Party, while it was suppressing all other parties, up to the year 1921, was still innerly free and democratically ruled. But having deprived others of freedom, it could not help losing its own freedom. The same then happened to the Stalinist faction. Between 1923 and 1930 it destroyed 'inner party democracy' for its opponents; but it was itself still more or less democratically ruled. In the end, however, it had to surrender all its freedom to its own leader.

From stage to stage the monopoly of power grew ever narrower. The narrower it was, the more fiercely and the more unscrupulously it had to be defended, and the fewer and the weaker were the inhibitions and restraining influences. The early Bolsheviks cherished controversy in their own ranks too much to be able to enforce the ban on controversy outside their ranks by anything like the Stalinist violence. Even the Stalinist faction, before it succumbed to Stalin, only expelled its opponents and exiled them; it could not even contemplate the bloody *dénouement* of the great purge trials. Stalin had to suppress his own faction before he could stage the holocaust.

Each phase of this evolution followed inexorably from the preceding one; the rule of the single leader from that of the single faction, and the rule of the single faction from that of the single party. What gave to the whole development its momentum and its convulsive and cruel character were the social tensions in a nation which was first ruined and famished after seven years of war, revolution, and civil war, and which was then rushed through forced industrialization and collectivization and drawn into devastating war and armament races, all calling for heavy sacrifice, rigid discipline, and massive coercion, and all providing Stalin with the justifications and pretexts for his use and abuse of the monopoly of power.

Stalin did not, thus, appear as a *diabolus ex machina*. Yet it is as a *diabolus ex machina* that Khrushchev presents him. It is not difficult to grasp why he views Stalin in this way. Khrushchev and his colleagues represent the Stalinist faction, or, rather, what has remained of it more than twenty years after its suppression. This is a different faction from that of twenty years ago. It rules a different country—the world's second industrial power. It leads a different 'socialist camp'—a camp containing one-third of mankind. It is richer in experience and in dearly bought insights. It is anxious to understand what has happened to it, and it is probing restlessly into its own mysterious past. But this is still the Stalinist faction, trying to grind its old axe and caught up in the tangle of its own experiences and of its traditional but now untenable viewpoints.

Khrushchev has described how the members of the Presidium,

B

the men who rule the Soviet Union and manage its vast, national-
ized economy (the world's greatest single industrial concern!)
spend their days and weeks poring over the archives of the
N.K.V.D., questioning the officials, who once conducted purges and
extracted confessions, and reliving in their thoughts the long nightmare of the past. Yet the understanding of which the members of
this Presidium, especially the older ones, are capable, has its historically formed limitations, which they cannot easily transcend.
They cannot see where and why things had 'gone wrong'. They
would like to cross out, if this were possible, the last chapter of their
story, the one in which Stalin oppressed and 'betrayed' his own
followers. They would still like to think that what was done in the
earlier chapters was justified and beneficial and need not have led
to the final débâcle and shame.

They denounce after the event the rule of the single leader but
see nothing wrong in the rule of the single faction, which in its
turn was rooted in the rule of the single party. They would like to
remain Stalinists without and against Stalin, and to recapture the
spirit of the 'sane' and 'innocent' Stalinism of the 1920s, of that
Stalinism which had not yet soaked its hands in the blood of the
Old Bolshevik Guard and in the blood of masses of peasants and
workers. They do not realize that the latter-day 'insane' Stalinism
had sprung from the earlier 'sane' Stalinism; and that it was not
only Stalin's whimsical and cruel character that was responsible
for it.

This approach governs all of Khrushchev's reasoning. It dictates
the range and the nature of his disclosures. Because Khrushchev
pleads the case of the old Stalinist faction 'betrayed' by Stalin, his
evidence against Stalin shows huge gaps and is all too often ambiguous, despite the bluntness of the language he uses and the
shocking character of the facts he relates.

Khrushchev builds his case against Stalin on three sets of facts:
on Lenin's denunciation, in his testament, of Stalin's 'rudeness and
disloyalty'; on Stalin's role in the purges; and on the faults of
Stalin's leadership in the war. Under each count of the indictment
he treats the facts selectively so as to turn the evidence against
Stalin rather than against the Stalinist faction.

He conjures up Lenin's ghost, because only with this ally at his
side can he, after thirty years of Stalin worship, hope to lay Stalin's
ghost. He quotes from Lenin's testament the passages aimed

directly against Stalin, but he passes over in silence all that Lenin said in favour of Trotsky and Bukharin. He assures us that he now views 'objectively and with detachment' the old party feuds, but he still labels Trotsky and Bukharin 'enemies of Leninism', although they are no longer 'enemies of the people'. In the light of Lenin's testament, Trotskyism and Bukharinism may be seen as offsprings of Leninism at least as legitimate as even the early Stalinism. The testament was therefore at first not published in Russia—it was only distributed to the delegates at the Twentieth Congress.[4] And even in his secret speech Khrushchev is afraid of making too extensive use of it.

Even more eloquent are the gaps in Khrushchev's story of the purges. He begins with dark hints about the assassination of Kirov in 1934, the event which set in motion the avalanche of the terror. He alludes to Stalin's connivance at the crime but adds that nothing is certain; and he leaves the mystery as deep as ever. Then he gives a more or less detailed and horrifying account of the secret purges of Eikhe, Postyshev, Kossior, Chubar, Mezhlauk, and Rudzutak, who perished between 1937 and 1940, and of the purge of Voznessensky in 1950. But he has nothing explicit to say about the purge trials of 1936-38, which shocked the world and in which the defendants were men of world fame, the recognized leaders of Bolshevism, of the Red Army, of Soviet diplomacy, and of the Communist International. He reveals nothing of the inner story of the purges of Zinoviev, Kamenev, Bukharin, Radek, Rakovsky, Pyatakov, Tukhachevsky. He is silent on Trotsky's assassination which was instigated by Stalin and Beria. Eikhe, Postyshev, and Chubar were by comparison insignificant figures: their names meant little or nothing not only to the outside world, but even to the young Soviet generation. But they were men of the Stalinist faction; and through Khrushchev the faction honours in them its martyrs.

That the Stalinist faction should rehabilitate its men, that it should pay tribute to its martyrs and that it should show up the cup of misery which its own leader made it drain is understandable. Only the meanest of its enemies can give themselves to *Schadenfreude* over this spectacle, or make light of the tragic note which reverberates through Khrushchev's speech. Khrushchev has revealed the enormity of the pogrom which Stalin inflicted on his own followers. Not for nothing did he dwell so much on the for-

---

[4] It has since been published in *Komunist* and in Lenin's *Works*.

tunes of the delegates to the Seventeenth Congress, which was held in 1934. At that assembly the Stalinist faction celebrated its final triumph over all its adversaries, and in party annals the congress is referred to as the 'Victors' Congress'. Of nearly 2,000 of those 'victors', delegates present at the congress, about 60 per cent. were, according to Khrushchev, 'arrested on charges of counter-revolutionary crimes (most in 1937-38)'. Of the 139 members of the Central Committee then elected '98 persons, i.e. 70 per cent., were arrested and shot (mostly in 1937-38)'. Thus, in those years alone Stalin annihilated 60 per cent. to 70 per cent. of the leading cadres of his own faction; and there were uncounted victims among the rank and file.

Public opinion outside Russia has in recent years been aware of the fate of the anti-Stalinist victims of the terror. It is only right that it should also be aware of the fate of the Stalinist victims. But do not Khrushchev and his associates feel the indecency of their exclusive concentration on their own Stalinist martyrs? Do they really think that a Trotsky, a Zinoviev, a Bukharin, a Tukhachevsky, or a Rakovsky, not to speak of others, will be forgotten while an Eikhe and a Postyshev are not?

Throughout Khrushchev's indictment of Stalin runs the motif of self-exculpation. We feel as if we sat in court and listened to a counsel for the prosecution who, while heaping accusations on the man in the dock, must remember all the time that he has also to prove that he, the prosecutor, and his friends, have had no share in the defendant's crimes. We readily believe in the defendant's guilt, but we wonder whether the prosecutor has not gone too far in self-exculpation. We even feel a sneaking suspicion that in order to exonerate himself he may have painted, here and there, the defendant's character just a shade too black.

'Everything depended on the wilfulness of one man,' Khrushchev repeats again and again. But if so, 'comrades may ask us: where were the members of the Political Bureau . . . ? Why did they not assert themselves . . . why is this being done only now?' These whys buzz in Khrushchev's ear like hateful wasps, and somewhat angrily he tries to chase them away. Unwittingly he only demonstrates that much more was at play than the 'wilfulness of one man'. Stalin had so much scope for his wilfulness only because Khrushchev and his like acknowledged him as their leader and accepted his will.

Khrushchev recalls how at first they all trusted Stalin and zealously followed him in the struggle against the other Bolshevik factions until they made him so powerful that they themselves became powerless. He shows that even when they might have been able to act against him they did not wish to act. He relates that in 1941, when the Red Army reeled under Hitler's first onslaught, Stalin's nerve snapped; he was despondent and sulked in his tent. It might seem that this was an opportunity for the party leaders to get rid of him. Instead they sent a deputation to Stalin to beg him to seize the reins again; and so they condemned themselves and the country to another twelve years of terror and degradation. None of them had the confidence and courage of Trotsky, who as early as 1927 foresaw such a turn of events and said (in his famous 'Clemenceau Thesis') that in such a crisis it would be the duty of party leaders to overthrow Stalin in order to wage war more efficiently and to a victorious conclusion.

The Politbureau of 1941 was afraid that a change of leadership in the middle of war would produce too dangerous a shock to morale; and it rallied to its oppressor. It should be noted that this was not the first situation of this kind. In exactly the same way the Politbureau had hoisted a dejected and sulking Stalin back into the saddle nine years earlier, at the height of collectivization. In every major emergency the Politbureau felt the need of the 'strong arm', and it turned to Stalin only to groan under his strong arm years thereafter. They had puffed up his authority sky high and so in a crisis they felt that they had not enough authority to take his place. As the history of the Soviet Union was one sequence of emergencies and crises, the Stalinist faction was all the time in an impasse, from which it was unable to get out even if for so many of its leaders and members the impasse was the grave.

The question inevitably arises whether during all those years any members of the ruling group made an attempt to destroy the incubus. It would have been unnatural if no plots at all had been hatched against Stalin in his own entourage. If Khrushchev and his colleagues really thought that 'it all depended on the wilfulness of one man' (which Trotsky, Zinoviev, and Kamenev never thought), might not some of them have concluded that the way out was to eliminate that one man? Khrushchev tells us that Postyshev, Rudzutak, and other leading Stalinists did indeed come into opposition to Stalin. But here, too, he leaves many things unsaid; and so the story of the Stalinist opposition to Stalin remains to be disclosed. The historian finds a further contradiction in Khrushchev's testimony, one which it has in common with Trotsky's appraisal of Stalin, although in Khrushchev the contradiction is, of course, far cruder. Khrushchev stresses the achievements as well as the failures of the Stalin era. For the achievements—industrial advance, educational progress, planned economy, victory in war—he praises the masses, the people, the party, the Leninist doctrine, and even the Central Committee, the cowed and docile Central Committee of the Stalin era! For the failures he blames Stalin alone. This distribution of praise and blame is too neat to be convincing. That Stalin's personal contribution to the black sides of Soviet life was exceptionally heavy goes without saying. But surely the backwardness and apathy of the masses and stupidity and blindness in the party also had something to do with the failures?

If the qualities of one man were responsible, say, for the Soviet military disasters of 1941-42, were they not also in some measure responsible for the victories of 1943-45? If all major decisions on policy and strategy were taken by Stalin alone, as Khrushchev says, then it is at least illogical to deny Stalin all credit for the results.

At times Khrushchev's argument savours of Tolstoy: in *War and Peace* Tolstoy argues that all ideas, plans, and decisions conceived by emperors, generals, and 'great men' are meaningless and worthless; and that only the innumerable, spontaneous, and uncoordinated actions of nameless masses of people shape history. But Tolstoy is consistent: he attributes to 'great men' no special influence on history, for evil any more than for good, whereas the present Soviet ruling group seems to play heads-I-win-tails-you-lose with Stalin's ghost.

As a reaction against the Stalin cult this is inevitable and perhaps even healthy. Not the first time in history is an orgy of iconolatry followed by a bout of iconoclasm. In a sense the man who smashes his idol stands above the one who prostrates himself before it; his understanding comes closer to truth. Yet his is still only a negative and limited understanding. The higher comprehension of her past which post-Stalinist Russia has yet to reach will surely transcend both iconolatry and iconoclasm.

No matter how vigorously Khrushchev pleads the alibi for himself and the present ruling group, he proves a semi-alibi only. This particular prosecutor cannot convince us that he has not been the defendant's accomplice—at best he persuades us that he was an accomplice under duress. He speaks of Beria as that 'villain who climbed up the government ladder over an untold number of corpses'. How true! But was Beria alone? Who of those who mounted the ladder of government under Stalin did not climb over his comrades' corpses? One wonders whether Beria, if he had been given the benefit of a public trial, would not have used in self-defence the same arguments that Khrushchev uses. Did he not use them at the secret trial?

However, we need not go so far. Khrushchev describes with horror the character of a former official who took part in preparing the purges of 1937-38 and in extracting confessions—the official was brought before the Presidium and questioned. He is, says Khrushchev, 'a vile person, with the brain of a bird, and morally completely degenerate'. Again, we need not doubt the truth of the description: the man's qualities evidently suited his function. But what does this repulsive character claim in his defence? His plea, as reported by Khrushchev, is that he acted on higher orders which he understood it to be his duty as a party member to carry out; and that he could do nothing else. Khrushchev indignantly rejects this apology as worthless. Yet almost in the same breath he uses the same apology for himself and the other members of the Politbureau: Under Stalin, he says, 'no one could express his will'.

The tragedy of contemporary Russia is that the whole *élite* of the nation, its intelligentsia, its civil service, and all its politically minded elements share in one degree or another in Stalin's guilt. Probably no one in Moscow who would set himself up today as Stalin's accuser and judge could prove his own alibi. Stalin made of the whole nation, at any rate of all its educated and active elements, his accomplices. Those who refused to do his bidding perished, with very, very few exceptions, long ago.

This is the unpropitious background against which de-Stalinization is now carried out. That it is being carried out at all shows to what extent it has become a national necessity for the Soviet Union. But the initiators and the agents of de-Stalinization are themselves inevitably tainted with Stalinism—no other human material is or can immediately be available. To paraphrase a famous Bolshevik saying, the edifice of post-Stalinist society has to be built with the bricks left over from Stalinist Russia.

Whatever is said against Khrushchev and his associates, the blow he has struck against Stalinism is much more than a tactical manoeuvre, and much more than the move of a dictator anxious to elevate himself at his predecessor's expense. Khrushchev has exposed not only Stalin but Stalinism, not only the man but his method of government; and this renders the continuation or revival of the method nearly impossible. He set out to state only the case of the Stalinist faction against Stalin; and he has destroyed the case of the Stalinist faction. He has, after all, been unable to confine himself to the rehabilitation of the Stalinists only. The logic of his argument led him to rehabilitate, reluctantly and half-heartedly, the martyrs of anti-Stalinism as well. He read out Lenin's and Krupskaya's letters from which the party learned that not Stalin and Molotov but Kamenev and Zinoviev (whom Khrushchev himself had described as 'enemies of the people' only a few days earlier) were the men who had stood closest to the founder of Bolshevism. He added that if the party had managed its affairs in the Leninist and not in the Stalinist manner, it would have worked tolerantly with those 'enemies of the people', even if it disagreed with them.

These were not just bygones. Nor was Khrushchev merely crying over spilled blood. Willy-nilly, he has exploded the idea of the monolithic party and of the monolithic state in which all must think alike. In terms of a historical revision he has proclaimed a new principle legalizing a plurality of views, differences of opinion, and controversy. He further justified and enhanced this new attitude by rejecting emphatically Stalin's theory which had served as the moral excuse for government by terror, the theory that as Russia advances along the road to socialism class conflicts grow sharper and 'class enemies' become more dangerous. Against this, Khrushchev insisted that the class conflicts grow milder, and the class enemies become fewer, less malignant, and less offensive; and that there is no need therefore to fight them in the manner in which they have been fought hitherto.

In acclaiming this view the Twentieth Congress has shattered the system of terroristic rule bequeathed by Stalin. It has also given a new impulse to the reversal of the trend that had led from the single party to the single leader, and from the monopoly of power to the monopoly of thought.

Having produced the shock, Khrushchev is anxious to soften its impact. 'We cannot let this matter get out of the party, especially not to the press', he warned his listeners. 'It is for this reason that we are considering it here at a closed Congress session. We should know the limits; we should not give ammunition to the enemy; we should not wash our dirty linen before their eyes.'

It was, however, hardly of the anti-Communist world, the 'enemy', that Khrushchev and the other party leaders were afraid in this case. One may even suspect that the indiscretion which has allowed the State Department to act as Khrushchev's first publisher, was not unwelcome to Moscow. It is from the mass of the Soviet people that his speech has been kept secret so far. To them the truth is conveyed only in carefully weighed and carefully graded doses.

It may be that the Soviet people would have reacted nervously or even morbidly to this awakening from the Stalin era, if it had been too rude. But it is just as possible that they would have shown the gratitude which people usually feel when they are awakened from a nightmare—and the ruder the awakening from a nightmare the better. However, an outsider cannot easily appraise the position in the Soviet Union. It may be that those in charge of this difficult and salutary operation judge the psychology of their own people correctly.

All the same, the 'washing of the dirty linen' can hardly be carried on behind the back of the Soviet people much longer. It will presently have to be done in front of them and in broad daylight. It is, after all, in their sweat and blood that the 'dirty linen' was soaked. And the washing, which will take a long time, will perhaps be brought to an end by hands other than those that have begun it—by younger and cleaner hands.

THE MEANING OF
DE-STALINIZATION[1]

'Is de-Stalinization a sign of a liberal trend in Soviet society or is it only a temporary expedient?' This is probably the question most frequently debated by the intelligentsia nowadays. I shall perhaps be forgiven for saying that behind the mere formulation of the question one can feel an extraordinary remoteness from the realities of the issue. The view that de-Stalinization is only a 'temporary expedient' or a slick manoeuvre, carried out by a few men in the Kremlin in the course of a narrow personal struggle for power, had perhaps a semblance of plausibility in the year 1953 or 1954, before the full force of the reaction against Stalinism had become apparent. In 1956 this view is patently anachronistic and untenable. The break with Stalinism is now felt in every aspect of Soviet activity and thought: in domestic and foreign policies, in education, in philosophical writing, in historical research, and indeed, in the whole atmosphere of Soviet life. The scale and range of the changes taking place indicate that what we are witnessing is a many-sided organic, and at times convulsive, upheaval in the existence of a huge segment of humanity.

I shall not dwell here on such recent events as the Twentieth Congress and Khrushchev's speech, the importance of which is obvious. What these and similar events show is that even if Stalin's successors had originally been guided by mere tactical considerations, the effects of their moves have by far transcended all tactics. The autocratic system of government, bequeathed by Stalin, is shattered. The backbone of the M.V.D., the political police, is broken. The *univers concentrationnaire* is dissolving. Stalinist monolithic uniformity is slowly, painfully, yet unmistakably beginning to give way to a certain diversity of outlook. If the 'liberal trend' is defined as a radical lessening of governmental

[1] Reply to questions posed by *Partisan Review*, fall 1956.

coercion and a striving for government by consent then this trend has been obviously and even conspicuously at work in Soviet society.

More important perhaps than the political trend is, to my mind, its social undercurrent, which Western commentators and experts have so far hardly noticed. After thirty years of the most ruthless and savage suppression by Stalinism, egalitarian aspirations are coming back into their own, regaining strength, and even exercising a direct influence on official policy. Lack of space does not allow me to summarize here, let alone to analyse, recent developments in Soviet labour and wages policy. Their cumulative effect has been to reduce the grotesque inequalities of the Stalin era. Stakhanovism, in which those inequalities were epitomized, has been given a quiet burial. The 'progressive piece rate' (a method of payment under which a worker producing above his norm earns rates rising in ever higher progression with the additional output) has been declared to be obsolete in most cases and socially harmful. (In Stalin's days the 'progressive piece rate' was sacrosanct!) The new wage system which is now being worked out is to be based on the time-wage rather than on the piece-wage, which Marx had described as a typically capitalist form of payment and which Stalin proclaimed as the quintessence of a socialist system of incentives. Twenty years ago Trotsky described, in *The Revolution Betrayed* and other writings, the crucial role of the piece wage in the Stalinist anti-egalitarian policy. Trotsky's argument has since been vulgarized and repeated *ad nauseam* by all leftish and many not so leftish critics of Stalinism. It is therefore strange that the same critics have failed to notice that Stalin's policy is being reversed in this vital point, too. Similarly, anti-Stalinists have invariably, and rightly, pointed to the introduction, in the thirties, of fees for secondary and higher education as a measure promoting social inequality—some have even seen in it the decisive act of a social 'counter-revolution' in the U.S.S.R. It is therefore at least illogical on their part not to recognize that with the abolition of *all* fees for education Stalin's successors have struck a momentous blow against inequality. (No nation in the West, not even the wealthiest, as yet provides its citizens with free education in all grades!)

De-Stalinization and 'liberalization' would indeed be frauds if they were confined merely to politics, and if they were not backed by a resurgent socialist egalitarianism. Freedom in the U.S.S.R. shrank and was suppressed as inequality grew; it can grow again only if inequality shrinks. To be sure, Soviet society is, and will remain for some time, highly stratified. Privileges and social differences which have grown up over the lifetime of a generation are not going to vanish and cannot vanish all at once. The struggle against inequality is likely to be hard and long. But what is for the time being of the greatest significance is that after so long a pause that struggle has begun anew, and that the egalitarian trend has already made—with surprising ease!—its first, and rather impressive conquests. This fact outweighs in importance volumes of abstract political theorizing about the 'impossibility of reform in a totalitarian system'.

It goes without saying that three decades of totalitarianism press heavily upon the present situation. The social background in which Stalinism was rooted has been greatly but not completely transformed. De-Stalinization proceeds in dialectical contradictions. The rule of the single Leader has been repudiated; but not the rule of the single faction (let alone of the single party), out of which Stalin's autocracy had sprung. The principle of the infallibility of the party leadership has been abandoned; but party members and non-party men alike are still denied the freedom to criticize and remove the fallible leaders. The ruling men proclaim the need for free and open controversy within a Marxist framework of thought; yet as such controversy develops they are seized with fright and not averse to cutting it short by administrative order. (This has happened in the important debate between the 'consumptionist' and 'productionist' schools of thought.) On the other hand, the controversies over the conduct of Soviet affairs in the last war and over the restitution of truthful history writing, controversies which have a close bearing upon present and future policies, are still in progress. The revulsion against Stalinist discipline and mental uniformity is universal and irrepressible; but it has not been positive enough and inspired by sufficiently great and clear ideas to be able to impart to society a real and fruitful diversity of outlook and to make society politically articulate. The principles and practices of the Stalinist theocracy are deeply discredited; but its mental habits again and again assert themselves. The cult of Stalin is dead; but the cult of Lenin, however more rational in both content and form, continues to obscure political thought.

It is enough to list these contradictions—and there are many more—to demonstrate once again not the spuriousness, as some think, but precisely the reality of the whole process. Without such contradictions de-Stalinization would have been sheer make-believe, stage-effect and hocus-pocus, or the lifeless concoction of an obtuse 'political scientist'. With them, it is what it is—an authentic historic development.

Stalinism represented an amalgamation of Marxism with the semi-barbarous and quite barbarous traditions and the primitive magic of an essentially pre-industrial, i.e., not merely pre-socialist but pre-bourgeois, society. Yet it was under Stalinism that Russia rose to the position of the world's second industrial power. By fostering Russia's industrialization and modernization Stalinism had with its own hands uprooted itself and prepared its 'withering away'. But here again the complex dialectics of the situation mock at the logical abstractions and simplifications of the 'political philosopher' and moralist. It is, broadly speaking, the rapid development of its productive forces that both enables and compels Soviet society to free itself from the shackles of Stalinism. But it is also the relative underdevelopment of the same productive forces that keeps the heavy residuum of Stalinism in being.

A nation, the urban population of which has grown by as many as fifty-five to sixty million people in only thirty years, the annual steel output of which has risen from five to fifty million tons in the same time, and the industrial apparatus of which has successfully coped with the problems of nuclear technology well ahead of all the old industrial nations of Europe—such a nation can no longer be ruled by a 'rising Sun' and a 'Father of the People' and held in awe by the whole set of Stalinist totems and taboos which belonged essentially to a much earlier and lower phase of civilization. With public ownership of the means of production firmly established, with the consolidation and expansion of planned economy, and—last but not least—with the traditions of a socialist revolution alive in the minds of its people, the Soviet Union breaks with Stalinism in order to resume its advance towards equality and socialist democracy.

This advance, however, finds an immediate obstruction in the relative inadequacy of the Soviet productive forces, which have not been developed sufficiently or have been developed too one-sidedly to secure for the bulk of the people a standard of living much higher than at present, a standard of living at which human relations could cease to be a constant competition and struggle of all against all and could become permeated by the spirit of socialist co-operation and association. The relative scarcity of consumer goods (especially of housing!) is the decisive *objective* factor which sets limits to egalitarian and democratic reform.

That scarcity should not be viewed merely in the context of the domestic economic situation of the U.S.S.R. It must be seen against the background of the world situation which imposes upon the U.S.S.R. an economic and power-political race with the United States and up to a point compels the Soviet rulers to press on with the development of heavy industry at the immediate expense of consumer interests. The needs of the industrialization of China and partly of Eastern Europe, too, have the same effect. The Soviet worker has begun to 'finance' in all earnestness the industrialization of the underdeveloped Communist countries; and he 'finances' it out of the resources which might otherwise have been used to raise his own standard of living. This, incidentally, is another usually overlooked yet extremely important aspect of de-Stalinization. (Stalin, at least in the first post-war years, compelled other communist countries to 'finance' Russia's economic recovery!) Here indeed two aspects of de-Stalinization—Russian domestic reform and reform in Russia's relationship with the entire Soviet bloc— can be seen in actual conflict with each other. (The fact that the Soviet worker 'finances' at his own immediate expense the industrialization of underdeveloped communist countries is, of course, an historic innovation of the greatest possible consequence. It contrasts sharply with the practice of imperialism which has secured surplus profits to capitalists but has also raised the standards of living of the workers of imperialist nations at the expense of colonial subjects. An exactly opposite development is taking place within the Soviet bloc. This explains perhaps why Western talk about Point Four programmes has become the laughing-stock of Asia. However, Russia's new commitments towards other communist countries act also as a brake on the reformist trend inside Russia.)

The contradictory character of the *subjective*, human and psychological, factors of de-Stalinization is not less striking. The force of inertia which keeps alive Stalinist habits of action and thought must not be underrated even after the check it has received since the Twentieth Congress. It has certainly not spent itself. A privileged minority is bound to defend its privileges. A bureaucracy accustomed to rule in the absolutist manner exerts itself to preserve its preponderance. The labour aristocracy, or a section of it, may not favour policies which narrow the social gap between that 'aristocracy' and the mass of workers. Yet the resistance of all these groups to the new policies has so far proved to be weaker, far weaker, than might have been expected. The worst crucial contradiction lies in the character of the chief agents of de-Stalinization who are none other than the former guardians of Stalinist orthodoxy. (How much ink my critics, especially in the U.S.A., have spilled to declare me an 'incurable wishful thinker', or even a 'Stalinist apologist', when three years before Khrushchev's secret speech I forecast this paradoxical development!)

The paradox is not accidental. De-Stalinization has become a social necessity; and necessity works through such human material as it finds available. Had any of the old Bolshevik Oppositions—Trotskyist, Zinovievist, and Bukharinist—survived till this day, Messrs. Khrushchev, Bulganin, Voroshilov and Co. would surely have long since been removed from power and influence, and anti-Stalinists would have carried out the de-Stalinization wholeheartedly, consistently, rationally, and with complete frankness. But the old Oppositions have been totally exterminated, and new ones could not form themselves and grow under Stalin's rule. The job which it should have been the historic right and privilege of authentic anti-Stalinists to tackle has thus fallen to the Stalinists themselves who cannot tackle it otherwise than halfheartedly and hypocritically. They have to undo much of their life's work in such a way as not to bring about their own undoing. Circumstances have forced Malenkov and Khrushchev to act *up to a point* as the executors of Trotsky's political testament. The wonder is not that they act these roles awkwardly, badly, and even monstrously badly, but that they act them at all!

How long can their performance last? How far can the epigones of Stalinism go on liquidating the Stalinist legacy? Can 'reform from above' abolish the totalitarian system, or what is left of it, and replace it gradually by a socialist democracy? Or is the development of such a democracy inconceivable without a revolutionary upheaval from below, at the mere threat of which, however, the present ruling group would retreat in panic from the road of reform?

The answer to this question is not a matter of theoretical preference either for 'reform' or for 'revolution' (as those of my critics seem to suppose who charge me with preaching a sort of an 'inevitability of gradualness' for post-Stalinist Russia) but of the facts of the situation. The break with Stalinism has so far been carried out by the way of reform from above. The whole record to date of the post-Stalin years is one of an astoundingly intense reformist initiative coming from the ruling group. No doubt, this initiative must have been stimulated by a variety of pressures from below, which have made the ruling group aware of the incompatibility of the new structure of Soviet society with the Stalinist 'superstructure'. But the pressures from below have been only semi-articulate, at best. So much so that no one outside the Soviet ruling group has been in a position to measure them or even to define them with any degree of precision. In any case, no conscious and effective political initiative has so far come from below—no spontaneous mass movement, no new political organization, programme, idea, or even slogan. (I am, of course, dealing with U.S.S.R. only; I cannot analyse here the different and in some respects more complex state of affairs in Eastern Europe.) True, political prisoners in the Vorkuta camps and elsewhere have struck to defend their rights; and Georgian students have demonstrated to defend . . . Stalin's memory. But these and possibly other similar and divergent manifestations of political action 'from below', however significant as symptoms, have been confined to the fringes of political life and do not as yet add up to any national political movement from below, 'reformist' or 'revolutionary'. The apparent absence of any such movement throws into even sharper relief the phenomenon of reform from above.

This state of affairs, too, has not been accidental. It reflects the gap which events of more than thirty years have created in the political consciousness of the nation. That Stalinism has 'atomized' and reduced to amorphousness the political mind of the Soviet people is an oft-repeated truism. However, it is easier to repeat the truism than to draw the consequences which inevitably follow from it. In a society whose political consciousness has been atomized or reduced to amorphousness any major political change, if there is an overwhelming social need for it, can come only from the ruling group. This is precisely what has happened in Russia. No matter how much one may dislike Stalin's epigones, one must acknowledge that they have proved themselves capable of a much more sensitive response to the need for reform than was generally expected of them.

However, the present phase is one of transition. It can last only as long as it takes to bridge or fill the historically formed gap in the political consciousness of the Soviet people. The present degree of liberalization is probably just sufficient to allow some scope for new processes of political thought and opinion-formation to develop in the intelligentsia and the working class. By their nature these are molecular processes, which require time to mature. But once they have matured they are certain to transform profoundly the whole moral and political climate of communism, and to transform it in a spirit of socialist democracy.

Only when the gap in the political consciousness of the Soviet masses and of the Soviet intelligentsia has been eliminated can de-Stalinization be brought to that ultimate conclusion to which Stalin's epigones can hardly carry it. To some extent, the change in the political climate is bound to coincide with a change of generations. It must take a few years more before the results of post-Stalinist opinion-formation show themselves and before new men come forward to expound new ideas and to formulate new programmes. By that time the generation of Khrushchev, Bulganin and Co. will, in any case, be making its exit; and it may well be replaced at the head of affairs not by the men of the middle generation who have spent, and in part wasted, their best years under Stalinism, but by much younger people who are only now growing to political maturity.

Whether the change and replacement of ruling groups and generations will proceed gradually and peacefully or through violent convulsions and irreconcilable conflict is a question which need hardly and can hardly be resolved *a priori*. The whole development is quite unprecedented; and there are too many unknowns in the equations. One can at the most analyse the conditions under which the change, or the series of changes, can run its course in a relatively peaceful and reformist manner; and those under which the reformist phase would prove to be a mere prelude to violent upheaval. The subject is too large, complex, and speculative to be tackled in this contribution. Moreover, whatever the variant of the historic development, the essential prerequisite for it is the same : the emergence

c

of a new and genuine political consciousness, which will be neither crippled by the imposition of any monolithic pattern nor falsified by totalitarian myths. De-Stalinization makes possible and even inevitable the crystallization of such a consciousness. Therein lies its progressive significance.

RUSSIA IN TRANSITION[1]

I

W HO would still maintain nowadays that Soviet society has emerged from the Stalin era in a state of petrified immobility, decayed and incapable of inner movement and change? Yet, only a short time ago this was the opinion commonly accepted; and a writer who defied it and claimed that, despite all appearances to the contrary, the Soviet universe did move seemed to argue from mere faith or wishfulness. Yes, the Soviet universe does move. At times it even looks as if it were still a nebula unsteadily revolving around a shifting axis—a world in the making, rumbling with the tremor of inner dislocation and searching for balance and shape.

It is the twilight of totalitarianism that the U.S.S.R. is living through. Again, how many times have 'political scientists' told us that a society which has succumbed to totalitarian rule cannot disenthrall itself by its own efforts, and that such is 'the structure of Soviet totalitarian power' (the like of which, it was said, history has never seen before!) that it can be overthrown only from the outside by mighty blows delivered in war. Yet it is as a result of developments within the Soviet society that Stalinism is breaking down and dissolving; and it is the Stalinists themselves who are the subverters of their own orthodoxy.

It is nearly four years now since the U.S.S.R. has ceased to be ruled by an autocrat. None of Stalin's successors has 'stepped into Stalin's shoes'. Government by committee has taken the place of government by a single dictator. A French writer, still somewhat incredulous of the change, recalls that in Rome, when a Caesar died or was assassinated, his head was struck off the public monuments but 'Caesar's body' was left intact until another head was put on it. Yet in Moscow not one but many heads have been put

[1] Written in December 1956 for the first issue of *Universities and Left Review*.

on Caesar's body; and perhaps even the 'body' is no longer the same. It is pointless to argue that it makes no difference for a nation whether it lives under the tyranny of an autocrat or under that of a 'collective leadership'. The essence of collective leadership is dispersal, diffusion, and therefore limitation of power. When government passes from one hand into many hands it can no longer be exercised in the same ruthless and unscrupulous manner in which it was exercised before. It becomes subject to checks and balances.[2]

It is not only Caesar's head that has vanished. What used to be his strong arm, the power of the political police, is broken. The people are no longer paralysed by fear of it. The stupendous machine of terror which overwhelmed so many people with so many false accusations and extorted so many false confessions of guilt, the machine which looked like an infernal *perpetuum mobile* at last invented by Stalin, has been brought to a standstill. Stalin's successors themselves have stopped it, afraid that even they would be caught by it; and they can hardly bring it back into motion, even if they wished to do so—the rust of moral opprobrium has eaten too deep into its cogs and wheels.

Nearly dissolved also is the Stalinist *univers concentrationnaire*, that grim world of slave labour camps which in the course of several decades sucked in, absorbed, and destroyed Russia's rebellious spirits and minds, leaving the nation intellectually impoverished and morally benumbed. Rehabilitated survivors of the Great Purges of the 1930s have returned from places of exile. There are, unfortunately, few, all too few, of them; and some may be broken and exhausted men. Yet, few as they are and such as they are, they are a leaven in the mind of post-Stalinist society—a reproach and a challenge to its disturbed conscience. Multitudes of other deportees have been allowed to leave concentration camps and to settle as 'free workers' in the remote provinces of the north and the east. Temporarily or finally, the nightmare of mass deportations has ceased to haunt Russia.

The mind of the nation has stirred to new activity. Gone are the days when the whole of the Soviet Union was on its knees before

[2] Since the time of writing Khrushchev has successfully asserted himself against his opponents and rivals and has eliminated them from the Presidium. But although government appears to have thus passed 'from many hands' back into one, Khrushchev's rule can hardly be described as a new 'tyranny of the autocrat'. Nor can his rule be expected to last very long: the 'Khrushchev era' cannot be anything like the Stalin era; it can only be an interregnum. [Note added in 1959]

the Leader and had to intone the same magic incantations, to believe in the same bizarre myths, and to keep its thoughts tightly closed to any impulse of doubt and criticism. To be sure, it is only slowly and painfully that people recover in their minds from monolithic uniformity and relearn to think for themselves and express their thoughts. Yet, a diversity of opinion, unknown for decades, has begun to show itself unmistakably and in many fields. A fresh gust of wind is blowing through the lecture halls and seminars of universities. Teachers and students are at last discussing their problems in relative freedom from inquisitorial control and dogmatic inhibition. The Stalinist tutelage over science was so barbarous and wasteful, even from the State's viewpoint, that it could no longer be maintained; and so it is perhaps not surprising that scientists should have regained freedom. What is more startling and politically important is the freedom for people to delve into the Soviet Union's recent history—a freedom still limited yet real. In Stalin's days this was the most closely guarded taboo, because the Stalin legend could survive only as long as the annals of the revolution and of the Bolshevik Party remained sealed and hidden away, especially from the young, who could find in their own memories no antidote to it.

Even now the annals have not been thrown open indiscriminately. They are being unsealed guardedly, one by one. The historians reveal their contents only gradually and in small doses. (The history of the October Revolution is still told in such a way that the giant figure of Trotsky is kept out of it—only his shadow is allowed to be shown casually, on the fringe of the revolutionary scene. But if Hamlet is still acted without the Prince of Denmark, the text of the play is becoming more and more authentic, while in Stalin's days the whole play, with the Prince cast as a villain, was apocryphal.) Every tiny particle of historical truth, wrested from the archives, is political dynamite, destructive not only of the Stalin myth proper, but also of those elements of orthodoxy which Stalin's epigones are anxious to conserve. The old-Bolshevik heresies, of which even the middle-aged Russian of our days has known next to nothing, and the authors of those heresies, the ghostly apostates and traitors of the Stalin era, are suddenly revealed in a new light: the heresies can be seen as currents of legitimate Bolshevik thought and as part and parcel of Russia's revolutionary heritage; and the traitors—as great, perhaps tragic, figures of the revolution.

The rehabilitation, even partial, of past heresy militates against wholesale condemnation of present and future heresy. It corrodes the very core of orthodoxy to such an extent that the ruling group shrinks from the consequences. But the ruling group is no longer in a position to stop the process of Russia's historical education which forms now the quintessence of her political education.[3]

This is not the place to discuss further the intellectual ferment of the post-Stalin era.[4] Suffice it to say, that in its initial phases de-Stalinization has been or was primarily the work of the intelligentsia. Writers, artists, scientists, and historians have been its pioneers. Their demands have coincided, at least in part, with the needs and wishes of the managerial groups and of influential circles in the party leadership. This accounts for the peculiarly limited, administrative–ideological character of the reforms carried out. Yet, as at the turn of the century, the intelligentsia has acted once again as the *burevestnik*, the storm finch. Its restlessness augurs the approach of an upheaval in which much wider social forces are likely to come into play.

II

The new working class which has emerged from the melting-pot of forced industrialization is potentially a political power of a magnitude hitherto unknown in Russian history. There are now in the U.S.S.R. four to five times as many industrial workers as there were before the revolution and even in the late 1920s. Large-scale industry then employed not much more than three million wage labourers. It now employs at least fifteen million (not counting transport workers, state farm labourers, the medium and higher technical personnel, etc.). The working class has not only grown in size; its structure and outlook, too, have changed. These are not the old Russian workers who combined exceptional political *élan* with

[3] It is difficult to find an analogy in any other nation at any time for so close an interdependence of history and politics as that which exists in the U.S.S.R. at present. The controversies of Soviet historians which preceded the 20th Congress foreshadowed Khrushchev's and Mikoyan's revelations at the Congress; and it was no matter of chance that even before Khrushchev, at the Congress itself, Professor Pankratova, an historian, made one of the most startling pronouncements.

[4] See the essay 'Post-Stalinist Ferment of Ideas' in my *Heretics and Renegades* (1955).

technological backwardness and semi-illiteracy. This, in its main sections, is a highly advanced working class which avidly assimilates skills and absorbs general knowledge. Among the young who now enter industry many have gone through secondary education. The change may be illustrated by the following comparison: about a quarter of a century ago as many as 75 per cent. of the workers employed in engineering were classed as unskilled and only 25 per cent. as skilled. In 1955 the proportion was exactly reversed: 75 per cent. were skilled men and only 25 per cent. remained unskilled. The relation is certainly not the same in other industries: engineering represents the most progressive sector of the economy. But the situation in this sector is highly significant, if only because engineering employs about one-third of the industrial manpower and accounts for about one-half of the total gross industrial output of the U.S.S.R.

The power of the Soviet bureaucracy was originally rooted in the weakness of the working class. The Russian proletariat was strong enough to carry out a social revolution in 1917, to overthrow the bourgeois régime, to lift the Bolsheviks to power, and to fight the civil wars to a victorious conclusion. But it was not strong enough to exercise actual proletarian dictatorship, to control those whom it had lifted to power, and to defend its own freedom against them. Here is indeed the key to the subsequent evolution or 'degeneration' of the Soviet régime. By 1920-21 the small working class which had made the revolution shrank to nearly half its size. (Not more than 1½ to 2 million men remained then in industrial employment.) Of the rest many had perished in the civil wars; others had become commissars or civil servants; and still others had been driven by famine from town to country and never returned. Most factories were idle. Their workers, unable to earn a living by productive work, traded in black markets, stole goods from the factories, and became *déclassés*. As the old landlord class and the bourgeoisie had been crushed, as the peasantry was inherently incapable of assuming national leadership, and as the industrial working class was half dispersed and half demoralized, a social vacuum arose in which the new bureaucracy was the only active, organized, and organizing element. It filled the political vacuum and established its own preponderance.

Then, in the course of the 1920s, the working class was reassembled and reconstituted; and in the 1930s, the years of forced industrialization, its numbers grew rapidly. By now, however, the workers were powerless against the new Leviathan state. The bureaucracy was firmly entrenched in its positions, it accumulated power and privileges and held the nation by the throat. The working class could not at first derive strength from its own growth in numbers. That growth became, on the contrary, a new source of weakness. Most of the new workers were peasants, forcibly uprooted from the country, bewildered, lacking habits of industrial life, capacity for organization, political tradition, and self-confidence. In the turmoil of the Second World War and of its aftermath, society was once again thrown out of balance. It is only in this decade, in the 1950s, that the vastly expanded working class has been taking shape and consolidating as a modern social force, acquiring an urban industrial tradition, becoming aware of itself, and gaining confidence.

This new working class has so far lagged behind the intelligentsia in the political drive against Stalinism, although it has certainly had every sympathy with the intelligentsia's demand for freedom. However, the workers cannot possibly remain content with the administrative–ideological limitations of the post-Stalinist reform. They are certain to go eventually beyond the intelligentsia's demands and to give a distinctive proletarian meaning and content to the current ideas and slogans of democratization. Their thoughts and political passions are concentrating increasingly on the contradiction between their nominal and their actual position in society. Nominally, the workers are the ruling power in the nation. In the course of forty years this idea has been ceaselessly and persistently instilled into their minds. They could not help feeling edified, elevated, and even flattered by it. They cannot help feeling that they should, that they ought, and that they must be the ruling power. Yet, everyday experience tells them that the ruling power is the bureaucracy, not they. The bureaucracy's strong arm has imposed on them the Stalinist labour discipline. The bureaucracy alone has determined the trend of economic policy, the targets for the Five-Year Plans, the balance between producer and consumer goods, and the distribution of the national income. The bureaucracy alone has fixed the differential wage scales and wage rates creating a gulf between the upper and the lower strata. The bureaucracy has pulled the wires behind the Stakhanovite campaigns and, under the pretext of socialist emulation, set worker against worker and destroyed their solidarity. And under Stalin's orders, it was the bureaucracy, aided by the labour aristocracy, that conducted a frenzied and relentless crusade against the instinctive egalitarianism of the masses.

Until recently the bureaucracy itself was subject to Stalin's whimsical terror and suffered from it even more than the working class did. This veiled, up to a point, the contrast between the theoretical notion of the proletarian dictatorship and the practice of bureaucratic rule. In their prostration before the Leader, worker and bureaucrat seemed to be equals. All the stronger did the beginning of de-Stalinization expose the contrast in their real positions. De-Stalinization was, at first, an act of the bureaucracy's self-determination. The civil servant and the manager were its first beneficiaries: freed from the Leader's despotic tutelage they began to breathe freely. This made the workers acutely aware of their own inferiority. However, the bureaucracy could not for any length of time reserve the benefits of de-Stalinization exclusively for itself. Having emancipated itself from the old terror, it willy-nilly relieved of it society as a whole. The workers, too, ceased to be haunted by the fear of the slave labour camp. Since that fear had been an essential ingredient of the Stalinist labour discipline, its disappearance entailed the end of that discipline. Malenkov's government proclaimed the obsolescence of the Stalinist labour code. That Draconic code had played its part in breaking the masses of the proletarianized peasantry to regular habits of industrial work; and only to those masses, bewildered and helpless, could it be applied. *Vis-à-vis* the new working class it was becoming increasingly useless and ineffective. A freer climate at the factory bench had indeed become the prerequisite for a steady rise in labour productivity and higher industrial efficiency.

Nor could the worker remain content merely with the relaxation of factory discipline. He began to use his freshly won freedom to protest against the pre-eminence of the managerial groups and of the bureaucracy. By far the most important phenomenon of the post-Stalin era is the evident revival of the long-suppressed egalitarian aspirations of the working class.

From this point the workers' approach to de-Stalinization begins to diverge from that of the intelligentsia. The men of the intelligentsia have been intensely interested in the political 'liberalization', but socially they are conservative. It is they who have benefited from the inequalities of the Stalin era. Apart from individuals and small groups, who may rise intellectually above their own privileged position and sectional viewpoint, they can hardly wish to put an end to those inequalities and to upset the existing relationship between various groups and classes of Soviet society. They are inclined to preserve the social *status quo*. For the mass of the workers, on the other hand, the break with Stalinism implies in the first instance a break with the inequalities fostered by Stalinism.

It should not be imagined that the renascent egalitarianism of the masses is politically articulate. It has not yet found any clear and definite expression on the national scale. We know of no resolutions adopted by trade unions or by workers' meetings protesting against privilege and calling for equality. The workers have not yet been free enough to voice such demands or to make their voices heard. They may not even have been capable of formulating demands as people accustomed to autonomous trade-union and political activity would do. It is more than thirty years since they ceased to form and formulate opinions, to put them forward at meetings, to stand up for them, to oppose the views of others, to vote, to carry the day, or to find themselves outvoted. It is more than thirty years since as a class they ceased to have any real political life of their own. They could hardly recreate it overnight, even if those in power had put no obstacles in their way. Consequently the new egalitarianism expresses itself only locally, fitfully, and incoherently. It is only semi-articulate. It works through exercising pressure at the factory level. Its manifestations are fragmentary and scattered. Yet it makes itself felt as the social undertone to de-Stalinization, an undertone growing in volume and power.

Many recent acts of official policy have clearly reflected this egalitarian pressure from below. For the first time since 1931 the government has tackled a basic reform of wages; and although the reform has not yet taken final shape, the reversal of the anti-egalitarian trend is already clearly discernible. Hitherto the piece rate has formed the basis of the whole wages system: at least 75 per cent. of all industrial wages were, until quite recently, made up of piece rates, because these lend themselves much more easily than time rates to extreme differentiation. Within this system the so-called progressive piece rate was favoured most of all, a method of payment under which the Stakhanovite producing 20, 30, and 40 per cent. above the norm of output earned not just 20, 30, and 40 per cent. more than the basic pay, but 30, 50, 80 per cent. or even more. This method of payment, glorified in Stalin's days, as the supreme achievement of socialism, has now been declared as harmful to the interests of industry and workers alike. The grossly over-advertised Stakhanovite 'movement' has been given a quiet burial. The time wage has again become the basic form of payment. It would be preposterous to see in this a triumph of socialism. Both the piece wage and the time wage—but the former much more than the latter—are essentially capitalist forms of payment; and it is only a measure of the retrograde character of some aspects of Stalin's labour policy that the return to the time wage should be regarded as progress. Yet progress it marks. It shows that workers no longer respond to the crude Stalinist appeal to their individual acquisitiveness which disrupted their class solidarity and that the government has been obliged to take note of this.

The year 1956 brought two further significant acts of labour policy: a rise by about one third in the lower categories of salaries and wages; and a new pension scheme with rates of pensions drastically revised in favour of workers and employees with low earnings. While in the Stalin era the purpose of almost every government decree in this field was to increase and widen the discrepancies between lower and higher earnings, the purpose of the recent decrease has been to reduce such discrepancies.

The reawakening egalitarianism has likewise affected the government's educational policy. Beginning with the school year 1956-57, all tuition fees have been abolished. It should be recalled that these had first been abolished early in the revolution, when Lenin's government pledged itself to secure free education for all. Poverty, cultural backwardness, and extreme scarcity of educational facilities made universal free education unattainable. The pledge remained nevertheless an important declaration of purpose. Stalin then reintroduced fees for secondary and academic education. Only the bureaucracy and the labour aristocracy could afford to pay; and so education was almost defiantly reserved as a privilege for the children of the privileged. The tuition fee extended to the ranks of the young generation the social differences which Stalin's labour policy fostered among their parents. It tended to perpetuate and deepen the new stratification of society. On this ground Stalin's communist critics, especially Trotsky, charged him with paving the way for a new bourgeoisie. All the more significant is the present

abolition of all fees. This renewed pledge of universal free education, given by Stalin's successors, is of far greater practical value
than was Lenin's pledge, because it is backed up by a tremendously
expanded and still expanding school system. Even so, Soviet society
has still a long way to go before it achieves genuine equality in
education. Only in the towns are there enough secondary schools
to take in all children—in the country there will not be enough of
them before 1960 at the earliest. Universal academic education is
Zukunftsmusik. All the same, the abolition of school fees is the
rulers' tribute to the new egalitarianism.

Odd episodes from everyday life and street scenes described in
the Soviet press allow sometimes even the outsider to watch this
new mood as it surges momentarily, in quite unexpected ways, to
the surface.

Recently, for instance, *Trud* related an incident that occurred at
the Red Square in Moscow. A worker accosted a member of the
Supreme Soviet and rudely chided him for 'wearing such fine
clothes' as no worker could afford. 'I can see at once', the worker
said, 'that never in your life have you done a day's work at the
factory bench.' *Trud*, indignant at this example of 'hooliganism',
tells its readers that the member of the Supreme Soviet had in fact
been a factory worker most of his life; and that the man who
accosted him behaved cowardly for he withdrew and disappeared
in the crowd before his identity could be established.

There is hardly a detail in this seemingly irrelevant episode
which does not have almost symbolic eloquence. It was unthinkable in Stalin's days that a worker should dare to accost a member
of the Supreme Soviet; and that he should do so at the Red Square
of all places, just outside the Kremlin wall. This used to be the
most heavily guarded spot in the whole of the Soviet Union—it
swarmed with police agents and was usually shunned by the ordinary citizen who had no business to be there. But the worker's new
daring still has its well-defined limits. Having chided the dignitary,
he prefers to keep his anonymity, to withdraw, and to plunge into
the crowd. Times have changed, but not enough for a worker to
believe that he may vent with impunity his feelings at 'their' fine
clothes and 'their' privileges. That many of 'them' had risen from
the working class is true, of course; but this does not make the
underdog feel less of an underdog. The peculiar form of protest

he chose may have savoured of 'hooliganism'. But, as a rule, men express their feelings in this way when they cannot easily express them in more legitimate forms. Yet how much resentment at inequality must have been pent up in the man, and how bitter must it have been, to explode in this way!

Among his workmates the protester certainly feels on much safer ground than at the Red Square; and there, at the factory bench or at the canteen, the privileges of the bureaucracy and of the labour aristocracy have become the recurrent theme of daily conversation. It is the oldest of themes; yet how novel it is after the long and sullen silence of the Stalin era. There, among themselves, the workers are pondering anew their position forty years after the revolution and groping for new collective action. The day may not be far off when the anonymous man returns to the Red Square but not to accost a bigwig and vent resentment furtively. He will come back, head uplifted, and surrounded by multitudes, to utter anew the old and great cry for equality.

III

Of Stalin I once said that like Peter the Great he used barbarous means to drive barbarism out of Russia. Of Stalin's successors it may be said that they drive Stalinism out of Russia by Stalinist methods.

The procedures of de-Stalinization are characterized by ambiguity, tortuousness, and prevarication. At first it was allegedly only a matter of doing away with the 'cult of the individual', the grotesque adulation of the Leader. When the issue was first posed, in the spring of 1953, even the name of the 'individual' who had been the object of the cult was not mentioned; and up to the Twentieth Congress, up to February 1956, the press still extolled the great Apostolic succession of 'Marx–Engels–Lenin–Stalin'. The cult was abandoned, yet it was kept up. But having made this first step, Stalin's successors could not help making the next one as well. They had to denounce the Leader's 'abuses of power'. They denounced them piecemeal and shrunk from saying frankly that these were Stalin's abuses. They found a scapegoat for him. As Beria had for fourteen years been Stalin's police chief, the responsibility for many of Stalin's misdeeds could conveniently be placed on him.

For a time this particular scapegoat was constantly held before the eyes of Russia and the world—until it refused to do service. For one thing, Stalin could not be dissociated from the man who had for so long been his police chief. For another, many of the worst 'abuses', to mention only the Great Purges of 1936-38, had occurred before Beria took office in Moscow. The denunciation of Beria implied the denunciation of Stalin himself; and it led directly to it. It was as if the scapegoat had returned from the wilderness to drag the real and the chief sinner down the steep slope. It threatened to drag others as well. Malenkov, Khrushchev, Kaganovich, Molotov, Voroshilov, had all been Beria's close colleagues and associates. The more they revealed of the horrors of the past, the stronger grew their urge to exonerate themselves and to find a new scapegoat—this time for themselves. That new scapegoat was none other than Stalin. 'It was all his fault, not ours' was the *leitmotif* of Khrushchev's secret speech at the Twentieth Congress. 'It was all his fault', *Pravda* then repeated a hundred times, 'but nothing has ever been wrong with our leading cadres and with the working of our political institutions.'

It was a most hazardous venture for Stalin's ex-associates to try and acquit themselves at his expense. This scapegoat too—and what a giant of a scapegoat it is!—is returning from the wilderness to drag them down. And so they are driven to try to re-exonerate Stalin, at least in part, in order to exonerate themselves.

Such attempts at 'tricking history' and playing blindman's buff with it are all in good Stalinist style. In effect, Stalin's successors avoid telling the truth even when, on the face of it, truth should reflect credit on them. Their first move on their assumption of power was to repudiate the 'doctors' plot'. Yet, to this day they have not told the real story of that last great scandal of the Stalin era. What was hidden behind it? Who, apart from Stalin, staged it? And—for what purpose? Khrushchev's 'secret' speech has not yet been published in the Soviet Union, a year after it was made; and this despite the fact that its contents have in the meantime been shouted from the housetops outside the Soviet Union. Special commissions have been at work to review the many purges and trials and to rehabilitate and set free innocent victims. But their work has remained a secret. Not even a summary account of it has been published to explain officially the background, the motives, the dimensions, and the consequences of the purges. Masses of slave labourers have been released from concentration camps; and many prisoners have regained freedom under a series of amnesties. Yet not a single announcement has been made to say how many convicts have benefited from the amnesties and how many have left the concentration camps. The present rulers are so afraid of revealing the real magnitude of the wrongs of the Stalin era, that they dare not even claim credit for righting the wrongs. They must behave like that 'honest thief' who cannot return stolen goods to their owner otherwise than stealthily and under cover of night.

How many of the 'stolen goods' have in fact been returned?

The break with Stalinism was initiated under the slogan of a return to the 'Leninist norms of inner party democracy'. The Twentieth Congress was supposed to have brought about the practical restitution of those norms. Yet to anyone familiar with Bolshevik history it is obvious that this was far from being true. The Congress adopted all its resolutions by unanimous vote, in accordance with the best Stalinist custom. No *open* controversy or *direct* clash of opinion disturbed the smooth flow of its monolithic 'debates'. Not one in a hundred or so speakers dared to criticize Khrushchev or any other leader on any single point. Not a single major issue of national or international policy was in fact placed under discussion.

The change in the inner party régime has so far consisted in this: major decisions of policy are taken not by Khrushchev alone and not even by the eleven members of the Presidium but by the Central Committee which consists of 125 members (or 225 if alternate members are included). Inside that body free debate has apparently been restored; and differences of opinion have been resolved by majority vote. Only to this extent have 'Leninist norms' been re-established. But under Lenin the differences in the Central Committee were, as a rule, not kept secret from the party or even from the nation at large; and the rank and file freely expressed their own views on them. The post-Stalinist Central Committee has never yet aired its differences in the hearing of the whole party. Thus, only the upper hierarchy appears to be managed more or less in the Leninist way. The lower ranks are still ruled in the Stalinist manner, although far less harshly. In the long run the party cannot remain half free and half slave. Eventually the higher ranks will either share their newly won freedom with the lower ranks, or else they themselves must lose it.

IV

Within the Soviet Union de-Stalinization has so far been carried out as a reform *from above*, a limited change initiated and controlled at every stage by those in power. This state of affairs has not been accidental. It has reflected the condition of Soviet society both *'above'* and *'below'*, in the first years after Stalin.

Above—powerful interests have obstructed reform, striving to restrict it to the narrowest possible limits, and insisting that the ruling group should in all circumstances hold the initiative firmly and not allow its hands to be forced by popular pressure. The attitude of the bureaucracy is by its very nature contradictory. The need to rationalize the working of the state machine and to free social relations from anachronistic encumbrances has induced the bureaucracy to favour reform. Yet, at the same time the bureaucracy has been increasingly afraid that this may imperil its social and political preponderance. The labour aristocracy has been troubled by a similar dilemma: It has been not less than the rest of the workers interested in doing away with the old terroristic labour discipline; but it cannot help viewing with apprehension the growing force of the egalitarian mood; and it resents the changes in labour policy which benefit the lower-paid workers without bringing compensatory advantages to the higher-paid. The various managerial groups and the military officers' corps are guided by analogous considerations; and they are, above all, anxious to maintain their authority. The attitude of these groups may be summed up thus: Reform from above? Yes, by all means. A revival of spontaneous movements from below? No, a thousand times no!

Below—everything has so far also favoured reform from above. Towards the end of the Stalin era the mass of the people craved for a change but could do nothing to achieve it. They were not merely paralysed by terror. Their political energy was hamstrung. No nation-wide, spontaneous yet articulate movements rose from below to confront the rulers with demands, to wrest concessions, to throw up new programmes and new leaders, and to alter the balance of political forces. In 1953-55 political prisoners and deportees

struck in the remoteness of sub-polar concentration camps, and
these strikes led to the eventual dissolution of the camps. This was
a struggle on the submerged fringe of the national life; but whoever
has any sense of Russian history must have felt that when political
prisoners were in a position to resume, after so long an interval, the
struggle for their rights, Russia was on the move. Then the year
1956 brought much agitation to the universities of Leningrad, Moscow, and other cities. However, these and similar stirrings, symptomatic though they were, did not as yet add up to any real revival of
the political energies in the depth of society.

It is not only that the working class had lost the habits of independent organization and spontaneous action. Stalinism had left a
gap in the nation's political consciousness. It takes time to fill such
a gap. It should be added that the gap is only relative. It is not by
any means a vacuum. By spreading education, by arousing the
people's intellectual curiosity, and by keeping alive the socialist
tradition of the revolution, be it in a distorted and ecclesiastically
dogmatic version, Stalinism has in fact accumulated many of the
elements that should eventually go into the making of an extraordinarily high political consciousness. But Stalinism also forcibly
prevented these elements from coalescing and cohering into an
active social awareness and positive political thought. It increased
enormously the potential political capacities of the people and systematically prevented the potential from becoming actual. Stalinist
orthodoxy surrounded the nation's enriched and invigorated mind
with the barbed wire of its canons. It inhibited people from observ-
ing realities, comparing them, and drawing conclusions. It inter-
cepted inside their brains, as it were, every reflex of critical thought.
It made impossible the communication of ideas and genuine political intercourse between individuals and groups. De-Stalinization has
given scope to these constrained and arrested reflexes and has
opened for them some channels of communication. This does not
alter the fact that the people entered the new era in a state of political disability, confusion and inaction; and that any immediate
change in the régime, or even in the political climate, could come
only through reform from above.

Reform from above, let me repeat, could be the work of Stalinists
only. Had any of the oppositions—Trotskyist, Zinovievist, and Bukharinist—survived till this day, Khrushchev, Bulganin, Voroshilov
and Company would surely have long since been removed from

D

power; and anti-Stalinists would have carried out de-Stalinization wholeheartedly and consistently. But the old oppositions had been exterminated; and new ones could not form themselves and grow under Stalinist rule. Yet the break with Stalinism had become a social and political necessity for the Soviet Union; and necessity works through such human material as it finds available. Thus, the job which it should have been the historic right and privilege of authentic anti-Stalinists to tackle has fallen to the Stalinists themselves, who cannot tackle it otherwise than halfheartedly and hypocritically. They have to undo much of their life's work in such a way as not to bring about their own undoing. Paradoxically, circumstances have forced Malenkov and Khrushchev to act, *up to a point*, as the executors of Trotsky's political testament. Their de-Stalinization is like the 'dog's walking on his hinder legs'. It is not done well; but the wonder is that it is done at all![5]

[5] History knows quite a few instances in which necessity worked through the most unsuitable human material when none other was available. Of course, whenever conservative rulers had to carry out progressive reforms, their work was self-contradictory and patchy; and it accumulated difficulties for the future. In my *Russia After Stalin* (1953), analysing the social circumstances which would drive Stalin's successors to break with Stalinism, I compared their position with that of Tsar Alexander II, the First Landlord of All the Russias, who, in conflict with the feudal landlord class and with himself, emancipated Russia's peasants from serfdom. Another example is Bismarck, the leader of the Junker class who transformed and adapted feudal Germany to the needs of bourgeois development. One might go much further back into the past and compare de-Stalinization to the reform which, early in the sixteenth century, was carried out in the Church of Rome as a prelude to the Counter-Reformation. The Church had been left by the Borgia Popes in a state of utter corruption and discredit; and it was by cardinals who had themselves been the Borgias' servants that it was reformed and raised up. The reformers first of all restricted the 'cult of the individual' in the Vatican and limited the Pope's powers. Then they revealed to the faithful the crimes the Borgias had committed. Cardinal Gaspar Contarini, one of the most famous reformers, wrote to Alexander Farnese, Pope Paul III: 'Can that be called a government whose rule is the will of one man, by nature prone to evil? . . . A Pope ought to know that those over whom he exercises power are free men.' Counsels in the Vatican were divided on this issue as much as they have been in the Kremlin of our days. Some prelates objected to de-Borgiazation fearing that discredit thrown on the memory of the deceased Pontiff would rebound upon the Church and sap its authority. Cardinal Contarini met their objections with this argument: 'How? Shall we trouble ourselves so much about the reputation of two or three Popes and not rather try to restore what has been defaced, and to secure a good name for ourselves?' The words might have been uttered by Khrushchev himself before he proceeded to unmask Stalin at the Twentieth Congress. However, in playing with such analogies one must not forget about the decisive differences in the character of rulers, in institutions, and in social backgrounds. The Church of Rome was not in charge of the affairs, and did not plan and manage the publicly owned economy, of a modern and expanding industrial society.

V

Leon Trotsky once made the prediction that Stalinism *in extremis* would place Russia before the danger of a 'Thermidorian counter-revolution'. It will be remembered that in France the *coup d'état* of 9 Thermidor (27 July, 1794) brought about the downfall of Robespierre, the collapse of the Jacobin Party, the transfer of government from the Convention to the Directory, and the final ascendancy of the wealthy bourgeoisie over the revolutionary plebs. Although the *coup* looked at first like an episode in the internal struggles of the Jacobin Party, it did not, as its initiators had hoped, merely replace in government one set of Jacobins by another; it entailed a fundamental change in the balance of social forces and spelled the doom of Jacobinism. Trotsky was convinced that Stalinism would lead towards a similar crisis in consequence of which a struggle beginning inside the Bolshevik Party might transcend its initial limits and, after the bourgeoisie and the *kulaks* had intervened in it, end in the restoration of the bourgeois order.

The notion of the 'Soviet Thermidor' was not one of Trotsky's most lucid ideas—he himself was aware of this and repeatedly revised and modified it.[6] However, in the 1920s, when he first expounded the idea, the N.E.P. bourgeoisie and the *kulaks* still existed in Russia; and they had to be reckoned with as inherently counter-revolutionary forces capable of arousing the mass of the small-holding peasantry against Bolshevism and the weak 'socialist sector' of the economy. Thirty years later the possibility of a Soviet Thermidor, as Trotsky first visualized it, appears to be very remote or altogether unreal. The N.E.P. bourgeoisie has disappeared; and it is difficult to see how the collectivized peasantry can ever gain ascendancy over the urban proletariat and restore the bourgeois order. Not only the old possessing classes have vanished. The political parties of the old Russia are also dead and beyond resurrection.

[6] Trotsky made the original predictions in 1926-29. In the 1930s he redefined Thermidor as being not a counter-revolution proper but a 'reaction within the revolution' and argued that Stalin had accomplished his Thermidor as early as 1923. A critical survey of this problem will be found in the second and third volumes of my Trotsky trilogy. In this essay the term 'Thermidor' is used as Trotsky used it at first to signify a veiled counter-revolution, the originators of which belong to the party of the revolution and are unaware of the consequences of their action. Although Trotsky's historical analogy is partly erroneous, the idea itself offers a clue to some recent events.

It is nearly forty years—and what years!—since they were driven from the political stage. They have since been uprooted from the nation's memory. What is even more important, their programmes and ideas have lost all relevance to the new structure and problems of Soviet society. The few *émigré* Mohicans—Monarchist, Cadets, Social Revolutionaries, and Mensheviks—if they returned to Russia, would appear incomparably more archaic to the present generation than the returning Bourbons appeared to the French or the restored Stuarts to the English; they would seem as ancient as the phantoms of the Wars of the Roses were to the England of the machine age. Any new political movements which may spring into being can hardly be of a 'Thermidorian' character. They are bound to seek to achieve their aims within the framework of the institutions created by the October Revolution and falsified by Stalinism.

However, if the Soviet Union need no longer be afraid of the spectre that once haunted Trotsky, in Eastern Europe the chances of a 'Thermidorian counter-revolution' are very real indeed. The communist régime there is not even ten years old. Its foundations are not consolidated. The *kulaks* and even the urban bourgeoisie are still there. The peasantry as a whole has preserved private property and clings to it tooth and nail. The traditions of the old anti-communist parties are still alive and potent. Some of the old cadres of those parties are still there and have not by any means lost contact with the masses. The masses have not lost their capacity for spontaneous political action. Moreover, in most of these countries communist rule has been associated with Russian conquest and domination; and outraged national dignity and the longing for independence turn automatically against communism as well as Russia.

Consequently, the break with Stalinism has had a very different impact on Eastern Europe than on the Soviet Union. A momentous conflict has, in fact, arisen, between the logic of de-Stalinization in the U.S.S.R. and its logic in Poland, Hungary, and Eastern Germany. In the latter countries de-Stalinization is no longer the carefully calculated reform from above controlled at every stage by those in power. There, on the contrary, the explosive anti-Stalinism of the masses has tended to control those in power. Reform from above has led to the revival of movements from below. No sooner had Moscow begun to move away from the Stalin cult, in the spring of 1953, than Berlin rose in revolt. After the Twentieth

Congress Poznan and Warsaw rose, and Budapest took to arms. All over Eastern Europe the communist parties have been torn between Stalinists and anti-Stalinists; and everywhere social and political forces have been present, ready to intervene in the internecine communist struggle and to turn it into a Thermidor, a Thermidor which in appearance is also, or even primarily, a war of national liberation.

In the aftermath of the Second World War Stalin exported revolution to Eastern Europe on the point of bayonets. He then used the hidden but all-pervading police terror to keep that revolution in being. Now, when his police terror has gone or has ceased to terrorize, the great question has arisen whether a revolution begotten by foreign conquest can ever acquire an independent existence of its own and redeem itself. Can it ever be accepted by the people on the spot and gain their wholehearted support and devotion? Or must such a revolution collapse the moment the conqueror has withdrawn his bayonets?

There is perhaps no single answer to these questions. At any rate, the October upheavals in Poland and Hungary gave two different answers, perhaps neither of them final. Poland rebelled against Russia but remained communist. She retained the revolution and rejected the bayonets. Moreover, something like a proletarian revolution from below developed there, which adopted the communist régime in order to free it from the Stalinist stigma, to transform it, and to shape it in its own political image. It was this proletarian movement from below which kept the Thermidorian forces at bay in October. In Hungary the position was different. There, too, the insurrection was at first communist-inspired in its anti-Stalinism and sought to regenerate the revolution, not to overthrow it. Then Hungarian Stalinist provocation and Soviet armed intervention infuriated the insurgents, drove them to despair, and enabled anti-communist forces to gain the initiative. Thus a Thermidorian situation arose: What had begun as an internecine communist conflict and looked at first only like a shift from one communist faction to another, from Gerö to Nagy, developed into a fully-fledged struggle between communism and anti-communism.[7] Hungary, in effect, rejected Russian bayonets together with the revolution which was originally brought to that country on those bayonets. This was not

[7] Nagy and his faction played the role which Trotsky at one time assumed Bukharin and Rykov would play in Russia but which they did not play.

a counter-revolution carried out by a hated and isolated possessing class defending its dominant position against the masses. It was, on the contrary, the ardent work of a whole insurgent people. It may be said that in October–November, the people of Hungary in a heroic frenzy tried unwittingly to put the clock back, while Moscow sought once again to wind up with the bayonet, or rather with the tank, the broken clock of the Hungarian Communist revolution. It is difficult to say who it was who acted the more tragic, and the more futile or hopeless role.

It may not be out of place to recall here that thirty-five years before these events Trotsky warned the Russian Communist Party against the monstrosity of a communist rule imposed upon a foreign people by force of arms. 'He who wants to carry revolution abroad on the point of bayonets,' Trotsky then said, 'it were better for him that a millstone were hanged about his neck, and he cast into the sea.' Stalin did not heed the warning, and he bequeathed the millstone to his successors. Ever since his death, the millstone has been 'hanging about their necks'.

VI

De-Stalinization in Russia had provided the decisive impulse for the upheavals in Poland and Hungary; and now these upheavals inevitably sent their tremors into Russia. At once all the dilemmas inherent in de-Stalinization were aggravated to the utmost. The threat to Russia's strategic interests and her international position was obvious. The die-hards of Stalinism could not but blame the reformers for provoking it by the encouragement they had given to 'Titoism' and every variety of anti-Stalinism. The reformers replied that it was precisely the sluggish tempo of de-Stalinization that had driven Poland and Hungary to revolt. However, the first reaction of the Soviet ruling group in the face of peril was to close their ranks and to call a halt to de-Stalinization. Yet, they could not make any serious attempt to resuscitate the old orthodoxy. Twice such attempts had been made, first after the Berlin rising in June 1953, at the time of Beria's fall; and then at the beginning of 1955, when Malenkov was dismissed from the post of Prime Minister. Both attempts failed and only served to stimulate the reformist trend. A new attempt could have no other result—it could only intensify the disintegration of Stalinism. The desecration of the old orthodoxy had made too deep an impression on the mind of the people to be effaced. It was too late to put the broken idols together again.

More important than the effect of the crisis on the ruling group was its impact on the Soviet masses. The predicament in which Soviet policy found itself could not be concealed from them. Voices of communist critics abroad could not be silenced. The Soviet press had to reproduce wholly or in parts the arguments of Tito, Kardelj, Togliatti, Gomulka, and others. The Polish press, momentarily in the vanguard of anti-Stalinism, was avidly read in Russia; and it played its part in stimulating 'ideological revision'. The ferment reached a new pitch of intensity; and this time it spread from the intelligentsia to the working class. The rulers unwittingly helped to spread it. Khrushchev publicly threatened to expel from universities the most vocal of the 'heretical' students and to send them, as a punishment, to work at the factory bench. The expelled students could only carry the germs of the heresies to the factories and infect the workers. (It is strange that this should not have occurred to Khrushchev: the Tsars used similarly to punish rebellious students: they drafted them into the army as privates, with the result that the regiments where the students served became centres of revolt.)

The Polish–Hungarian drama has thus opened a new phase in the internal development of the U.S.S.R. If until now the pressure which on the factory level the workers exercised against the bureaucracy was 'economist' in character, and if they were not animated by any clear political idea, the development now probably reached a point at which the intelligentsia, or rather its ideologues and theorists, began to politicize the consciousness of the working class and to inject into it their own ideas—just as sixty years earlier Social Democratic intellectuals had carried the notions of political socialism 'from the outside' into the spontaneous movement of the workers. At any rate, the first stirrings of a movement from below made themselves felt; and this may bring to a close that chapter of history in which de-Stalinization was a matter exclusively of reform from above.

At present, at the beginning of the year 1957, two distinct yet interconnected processes seem to be developing: the formation of a new political consciousness; and the inception or regeneration of a spontaneous mass movement. It is a question fateful for Russia's and the world's future at what pace these two processes will evolve and how they will react upon one another. It is possible for a spontaneous mass movement to acquire suddenly a very stormy momentum and to outstrip the growth of political consciousness. Such a movement may well upset the nation's political balance before it has itself acquired a clear awareness of aims, a positive political programme, and a firm and confident leadership. Such a movement may be guided only by its own impetus and express only the pent-up resentments of the workers (and/or the peasants). It may, in particular, raise the cry for equality in an extreme, uncompromising and Utopian manner while the nation's economic resources are insufficient for the extreme egalitarian demands to be met even halfway, especially after a long period during which consumer industries were underdeveloped. Should such a disproportion arise between consciousness and spontaneity, and should it become very acute, then the revived mass movement may well suffer shipwreck. Instead of achieving genuine and lasting democratization it may become a factor of social disruption and chaos. The present rulers would probably try to deal with the situation by means of a combination of concessions and repression. But they would hardly go far enough in meeting popular demands. Nor would they be in a position to use the Stalinist organs of suppression against the bursting energy of the masses : they could hardly bring back to the scene the political police in the full panoply of Stalinist 'efficiency'. Their last resort would be to appeal for help to the army, as they did in Berlin in June 1953 and in Budapest in October–November 1956.

The assumption by the Soviet marshals and generals of the role of the guardians of 'order' not only in satellite countries but within the Soviet Union itself would create a new situation. It should be remarked that Stalin never had the need to use his marshals and generals in this way—he did not send his armoured divisions to crush popular uprisings—because he could rely on his infallible, invisible, and all-pervading police terror. This enabled him to keep the army leaders in a politically subordinate position. But should the latter, under Stalin's successors, come to act regularly as the guardians of order, an important shift of power would necessarily follow. Sooner or later the army leaders would say to themselves that instead of guarding order on account of and for the benefit of the party leaders, they could as well do it on their own account and for their own benefit. In other words, the strains and stresses caused by a stormy revival of mass movements lacking leadership and clear political purpose, may lead to the establishment of a military dictatorship of the Bonapartist type. All the more so as the military could hardly view with indifference a situation in which they must see a threat to Russia's positions of power and to all the strategic gains she won in the last world war.

What Karl Marx wrote in *The 18th Brumaire* about how the various factions of the French bourgeoisie by calling repeatedly on the army to 'save society' set the stage for military dictatorship is well worth quoting here, for despite all the differences of time and place (and despite Marx's somewhat old-fashioned imagery), his words may still apply:

> When barrack and bivouac were periodically thrown upon the head of French society to oppress its brain and keep it quiescent; when sword and musket periodically functioned as judge, administrator, guardian and censor, gendarme and night-watchman; when military moustache and tunic were periodically acclaimed as the tutelary deities of society —was it not inevitable that it should eventually occur to barrack and bivouac, sword and musket, moustache and tunic, to save society once for all on their own initiative, by declaring their own rule supreme and by saving . . . society the trouble of self-government? . . . Barrack and bivouac, sword and musket, moustache and tunic would be only more apt to hit upon this idea, seeing that they might then expect higher pay for more exalted service.

Fortunately, 'military moustache and tunic' have not yet been periodically acclaimed as the tutelary deities of the Soviet Union— although they may still gain that acclaim.[8] Nor is it inevitable or even probable that the formation of a new political consciousness should lag so dangerously behind the revival of mass movements. The gap in consciousness created by Stalinism, it should be repeated, is relative only. Most of the elements needed to fill it are there. Under the shocks of the Twentieth Congress and of the events in Poland and Hungary, and amid an intense moral–political ferment, it may be filled much more rapidly than it would be otherwise. The

---

[8] I wrote about the 'Bonapartist' ambition of Marshal Zhukov, and in its light analysed his political conduct, well before he was officially charged with harbouring that ambition. In the summer of 1957, after he had used his influence to oust Molotov and Kaganovich, Zhukov tried to obtain 'acclaim for military moustache and tunic' but failed. An implicit and anticipatory explanation of the reasons for his failure can, I trust, be found in these pages.

great heart-searching and transvaluation of values, of which the
Soviet press offers only minute and purely negative reflections, is
going on. The Soviet peoples take the measure of their problems,
view critically themselves and the world around them, and are
getting ready for another world-shaking historic experience.

A society which has gone through as much as Soviet society has
gone through, which has achieved so much and suffered so much,
which has seen, within the lifetime of one generation, its whole
existence repeatedly shattered, re-made, and transformed to its very
foundations, and which has again and again ascended the highest
peaks of hope and heroism and descended to the lowest depths of
misery and despair—such a society cannot fail to draw from its
rich and uniquely great experience equally great generalizing ideas
and practical conclusions and to embody these in programmes of
action worthy of itself. Nor can it fail to produce sooner or later the
men and women strong enough in mind and character—a new
'phalanx of heroes reared on the milk of the wild beast'—to transform ideas into deeds.

No one, however, can foresee the actual rhythm of historic developments. In moments of great crises spontaneous mass movements *do* run ahead of all political groups, even the most radical
ones, and of their programmes and methods of action. So it was in
Russia in February 1917. The workers then found in the Soviets, the
Councils of *their* deputies, the institutions within which they
learned to harmonize impulse and thought, to test conflicting programmes, and to choose leaders. Of those institutions Stalinist
Russia preserved no more than the name and the dead shells. Yet
in the memory of the working class the Soviets have survived as *the*
instruments of socialist government and self-government, *the* organs
of a 'workers' state'. Even in Hungary, amid all the confusion of
revolution and counter-revolution, the insurgent workers hastily
formed their Councils. Any political revival in the working class of
the U.S.S.R. is almost certain to lead to a revival of the Soviets
which will once again become the testing ground of political programmes, groups, and leaders, and the meeting place of spontaneous
movements and political consciousness.

Whatever the future holds in store, a whole epoch is coming to
a close—the epoch in the course of which the stupendous industrial
and educational advance of the U.S.S.R. was accompanied by
deep political lethargy and torpor in the masses. Stalinism did not

and could not create that state of torpor; it spawned on it and sought to perpetuate it but was essentially its product. Basically, the apathy of the masses resulted from the extraordinary expenditure of all their energies in the great battles of the revolution. The aftermath of the French revolution was likewise one of a deadening lassitude in which the people 'unlearned freedom', as Babeuf, who was so close to the masses, put it. Christian Rakovsky, recalling in his exile at Astrakhan in 1928 Babeuf's remark, added that it took the French forty years to relearn freedom. It has taken the Soviet people not less time—but there is no doubt that they are at last relearning freedom.

FOUR DECADES
OF THE REVOLUTION[1]

THE Soviet Union has marked the fortieth Anniversary of the October Revolution by sending the first artificial satellite to circle round Earth. The 'Soviet man' has thus been the first to reach out into the interplanetary space; and now he is dreaming aloud of the time, which he believes to be very near, when he himself may be able to ascend high enough to overcome the earth's gravitation, and soar in a cosmic vehicle towards the moon and the stars.

The Soviet people undoubtedly see a profound and real connexion between the latest triumphs of their technology and the revolution which took place in Petrograd forty years ago. Forty (and even twenty-five) years ago Russia was industrially one of Europe's most backward nations. 'Dubinushka', the famous folksong, which grimly contrasted the 'clever Englishman who invented machine after machine' and the Russian *muzhik* who, sighing and groaning, wielded only 'the wooden club', was something like Russia's genuine national anthem. The October Revolution was, in one of its aspects, a protest against inherited poverty and an archaic way of life. Bolshevism instilled in the people the aspiration to 'catch up with the advanced West and to surpass it'. Now the Muscovites, as they watch the passage of the man-made satellite, read in it the message of fulfilment.

The October Revolution, it might be said, defied in its own way history's 'law of gravitation'. Its enemies at first saw it as a grotesque and ephemeral episode. Even Marxists had long thought it impossible that Russia, barely emerged from feudalism, destitute and illiterate, should shake off capitalism before any other country had done so and act as pioneer of socialism. Generations of socialists, Western and Russian, had grown up in the belief that the industrialized and advanced nations of Europe would be the first to accomplish this, and that Russia could only follow in their foot-

[1] First published in *The New Statesman*, November 1957.

steps. Lenin himself had shared this belief until shortly before the revolution, and had regarded it as one of the laws and axioms of Marxism. When he finally abandoned it and took power, he still looked forward to revolution in western Europe to help to raise Russia from her poverty and backwardness. He used to say that 'Socialism is already a material reality in our days, but its two halves are torn asunder: one half, the political conditions for it, has been created in Russia, while the other, the industrial and cultural prerequisites, exists in Germany'.

To the end of his days Lenin expected that the victory of communism in Germany would bring the 'two halves' together. When this hope was dashed, the Bolshevik Party set out, under Stalin, to create 'the German half of socialism' within Russia's own boundaries and by Russia's own efforts. This again seemed a hopeless undertaking, in the light of statistical comparisons and economic axioms. There followed the sombre, heroic, and cruel drive of industrialization, in the course of which the Soviet people, oppressed by Stalin's despotism, found themselves politically and morally as far from socialism as ever. Indeed, much of the 'Russian half' of socialism, the rough plebeian democracy of the early Leninist years, had been destroyed or debased, even though social ownership of the means of production had been firmly consolidated. Yet around 1940 the Soviet Union was winning the race with Germany in heavy and armament industries. Then the Second World War inflicted the prodigious losses which threatened to throw it a long, long way back; and in the aftermath of the war came chaos and famine.

However, the Soviet Union resumed the industrial drive. The Western power against which it now had to match its strength was no longer Germany but the United States. The 'two halves' of socialism were still 'torn asunder'—the industrial half was in America. To build up that 'half' within the Soviet Union has ever since been the over-riding purpose of Soviet policy.

These forty years of Soviet history are made of the most dynamic interplay of backwardness and progress. In more than one field, extreme and desperate backwardness has driven the U.S.S.R. to adopt the most desperate and extreme forms of progress. Capitalism could not achieve stability in the old Russia because of the nation's obsolete and irrational social structure. The October Revolution smashed that structure and gave Russia a tremendous impulse which carried her beyond all the stages of bourgeois development that European society had to traverse towards publicly owned and planned economy.

Handicapped industrially and militarily by the illiteracy of its masses, the Soviet Union was then driven to develop what is today the world's most extensive and modern educational system. Consequently, Soviet universities train at present more technicians and engineers than do all the universities of the West taken together, and the young Soviet factory worker or miner is, as a rule, a man with secondary education. It is arguable that the Russians are already the most educated of all nations. The paradox is that their educational system was built up together with the medieval Stalinist inquisition, with police rule and concentration camps. This paradox shows itself in the psychological formation of the Soviet people: in some ways they are the most inarticulate and the meekest of all peoples; yet in others they are the most ambitious, the most aspiring, and the most independent-minded. At times the modern Russian appears to be an unexampled combination of slave and Promethean hero.

The latest Soviet feats underline the pattern of contrasts even more sharply. The Russians are the first to revolt effectively against man's earthboundedness and to spread out into outer space; yet in their mass they dwell in slums so overcrowded that the living-space of an individual is no more than seven or eight square yards. Constriction within the tiny cage of daily existence and the lure of infinite space and freedom seem to be the two equally real elements of Russian life. Further, the nation whose scientists and engineers have opened for mankind the way to the moon and are already thinking in terms of astronautics still suffers from the want of ordinary means of transport: Russian passenger trains are too few, too primitive, and too slow, motor traffic is negligible; and country roads, muddy or ice-bound, are impassable throughout a great part of the year.

Here too, however, backwardness may provide the Soviet Union with the strongest motive and also with the widest opportunities for progress. The cities of the West are labouring under the conflict between their inherited architecture and their constantly expanding traffic, a conflict which seems insoluble and tends to reduce the traffic to an absurdity. The Russians may be able to avoid this predicament. They are driven by their very plight to adopt the most modern ideas of city planning and to develop ultra-modern forms of transport. They may yet replace the droshka by the helicopter rather than by the ordinary motor-car, and the train by the transport plane.

The Russians are, of course, not the first nation that has managed in its striving for progress to turn backwardness into a decisive advantage. The Germans did the same in the second half of the last century, when from being one of Europe's economically underdeveloped nations they rose to the rank of its leading industrial power. As a late-comer to the industrial world, Germany had no need to go through all the phases of development which the British and the French had passed gradually, slowly, over the lifetime of many generations. Assimilating the latest, ready-made achievements of British technology and organization, making their start from this high level, and being free from the ballast of obsolescent equipment and methods of work, the Germans presently excelled the British in efficiency and modernity of organization. In Asia, Japan repeated the same experience even more rapidly but far less thoroughly and extensively. Finally, the United States found in its backwardness *vis-à-vis* Europe a blessing in disguise—its very backwardness enabled it to take over the best of the Old World, and to secure technological supremacy. It is striking that the remarkable progress of these nations from industrial backwardness to maturity was in every case preceded and prepared by political or social revolutions (the War of Independence and the Civil War in the U.S., Bismarck's 'revolution from above' in Germany, and the Meiji revolution in Japan). None of these however, had the depth, the force, the blood-soaked momentum, and the continuously widening scope of the Russian revolution.

The U.S.S.R. is now just beginning to benefit from the advantages of the late-comer, advantages which may enable it to gain eventually the same sort of industrial ascendancy over the United States that the United States has had over Europe. To be sure, this late-comer has still a long and uphill road to climb. In most sectors of its economy the U.S.S.R. is at present far behind the U.S. In some it is even behind western Europe. But in a few, strategically decisive sectors it is already outstripping the United States. The discrepancy between the backward and the advanced parts is still enormous. But it should not be imagined that it can be overcome only by slow degrees. With atomic energy being harnessed to production, with automation embracing ever wider areas of industry, with electronics opening up new vistas, and, last but not least, with the machinery of planning being overhauled so as to allow more scope for the producers' social initiative, further Soviet progress, if it is not impeded by war or grave disturbances in domestic politics, may be much quicker than Western, or even Soviet, opinion anticipates.

Technologically the U.S.S.R. has hitherto served an apprenticeship with the U.S., imitating and assimilating American achievements. It will still go on imitating and assimilating; but the appearance of the Russian sputnik over our planet heralds the approaching end of the apprenticeship. Soviet progress is now likely to proceed by leaps and bounds, and this new level of technology and industrial wealth is bound to affect both the political climate of the Soviet Union itself and the prospects of international communism—both of which have in these forty years been decisively affected by Russian backwardness.

Classical Marxism had based its case for socialism on the argument that, compared with capitalism, socialism would represent superior economic efficiency and a higher form of social organization. The Bolshevik leaders accepted this as an axiom. Yet, the régime they founded could not claim such merits. True enough, its economic efficiency was, in any case, superior to that of Tsarist Russia, and this enabled Bolshevism to survive against all odds; but survival was only part of the test to which the régime which issued from the October Revolution was subjected. The other and the more difficult part lay in the relations between the Soviet Union and the industrial West. The decisive question has been: How does Soviet efficiency compare with that of the West?

This question has been of crucial importance for the whole evolution of communism both within the Soviet Union and without. The October Revolution had survived, but its claims and title-deeds were in doubt, to say the least. The Bolshevik Party responded to this predicament differently in different periods. Its history in these forty years falls into three chapters, each characterized by a different type of response: the Leninist period, with its active revolutionary internationalism; the early and middle parts of the Stalin era, with their ideological isolationism; and lastly, the close of the Stalin era and the post-Stalin years, with the sporadic breakdown of that isolationism.

The Leninist attitude towards Russia's inferiority *vis-à-vis* the West was wholly dictated by the Marxist tradition. Lenin him-

self never wavered in the view that the congenial ground for socialism was in the 'highly advanced and civilized' West; and in
international revolution he saw Russia's escape from her own backwardness. True, Lenin and Trotsky had even before Stalin called
upon Russia to 'catch up with the West.' But they did not expect an
isolated Russia to be able to raise herself by her own efforts to the
height of Western technology and industrial organization. They
based their policies in the main on the anticipation of a 'German
October', a 'French October', and even an 'English October'. They
brought to life the Communist International to direct and co-
ordinate the struggle in various countries; but they imagined the
process of international revolution as a series of national revolutions, each developing of its own accord and by its own momentum,
as the Russian revolution had developed. They were convinced that,
with the spread of communism, Russia's weight in the whole movement would be greatly reduced and that, even if China or India, of
whose revolutionary potentialities they were fully aware, were to
join Russia, the movement of all these nations towards socialism
would still require the industrial and cultural leadership of a communist West.

This scheme of things foundered on the failure of communism in
Europe which had become manifest in the early 1920s. 'The Comintern will not carry out a single revolution even in 90 years' was the
conclusion Stalin drew at a session of the Politburo. The Soviet
Union was isolated and thrown back on its own resources. The new,
Stalinist, response to the predicament consisted in the determination
to overcome Soviet inferiority at any cost and by the Soviet Union's
own efforts—with all that this implied in coercion and myth-making,
in low standards of living and human misery. The Stalinist isolationism was, in fact, a desperate striving to avoid and postpone that
decisive test of efficiency to which contact with the outside world
would have subjected the Soviet Union—a test at which the Soviet
Union would have inevitably failed. The Iron Curtain succeeded
for a time in concealing Soviet inferiority from the Soviet masses. It
did not, however, conceal it from the outside world—and this contributed to the further paralysis of communism in the West.
German and British, not to speak of American, workers, could not
be attracted by a 'socialism' which represented lower productivity,
far lower standards of living, and far less political freedom, than
they had attained under capitalism.

E

The Second World War drew the U.S.S.R. out of its shell and brought it back to the arena of world politics as both a great power staking out national claims, and as the head of the international communist interest. Stalin's armies carried revolution on the point of their bayonets into Eastern and Central Europe. Moreover, the international impetus of revolution, which had seemed extinct during a quarter of a century, came back into its own in Asia; the Chinese revolution was no mere by-product of the victory of Russian arms, but a gigantic social upheaval in its own right. Thus Russia's isolation was broken at a time when she was rapidly shortening her industrial lag behind the West.

Clearly, the political evolution within the Soviet Union, and the prospects of international communism depend now on the pace at which the Soviet Union continues to shorten the lag. So far the U.S.S.R. has achieved its industrial progress at the consumers' expense. Yet, superior efficiency necessarily translates itself, albeit with a delay, into higher standards of living. These should lead to the softening of social tensions, the weakening of antagonisms between bureaucracy and workers, and workers and peasants, to the further lessening of terror, and to the further growth of civil liberties. This trend may be complicated, blurred, or periodically halted by the inertia of Stalinism, by war panics, and, more basically, by the circumstance that the Soviet Union still remains in a position of overall economic inferiority *vis-à-vis* its American antipode.

The impact of the new situation upon world communism will make itself increasingly felt in coming years. Already it is obvious that a satellite over Earth is worth much more for the Soviet Union than many a satellite on Earth. The U.S.S.R.'s dramatic demonstration of its new technological power tends to re-establish its leadership in the communist camp, just after the leadership had been morally shaken. The message of the satellite to all Communist Parties is that things may be very different for them in the second half of the century from what they were in the first; that the epoch during which their cause has been discredited or at least handicapped by the poverty, backwardness, and oppressiveness of the first workers' state is drawing to a close; and that they may look forward to a time when the appeal of Communism may be as much enhanced by Soviet wealth and technological progress as the attraction of bourgeois democracy has in our days been enhanced by the fact that it has behind it the vast resources of the

United States. More than ever is the world-wide 'contest of the two systems' bound to centre on the technological and industrial duel of the two giants, a duel for which the earth is becoming too small.

The historian of the future will perhaps say that, forty years after the October revolution, man set out to conquer the moon and the planets before he had set his own planet in some sort of order; and so he projected his earthly follies into interplanetary space. But will the historian ponder this merely as one of the paradoxical curiosities of an age of transition, or will he see in it the tragedy of our time?

KHRUSHCHEV AT HOME[1]

. . . AND so the peripatetic Soviet Prime Minister is back home, for a short stay before the Summit meeting. On his return, he once again shook hands with the elders who came to greet him at Vnukovo Airport and once against he reported on his journey to crowds of Muscovites who had packed the Lenin Stadium to overflow. His latest series of cavalcades took him to countries as far apart as France and Indonesia; and the tour included two visits to India and a few joy-rides to Burma, Kashmir, and Afghanistan. He must have traversed at least two-thirds of the world in the last few years; and it will be surprising if he does not try to cover the last third too.

What sends him on all these tours and expeditions? The hope to win some political prizes? The belief in personal diplomacy? The confidence that he can through personal contacts with heads of foreign governments influence their attitude towards the Soviet Union and the state of world affairs? Or the ambition to act as propagandist *in partibus infidelium*?

No doubt all these motives play their part, but they are hardly decisive. For anyone brought up in the Marxist school of thought, as, after all, Khrushchev has been, it is the height of *naïveté* to believe that with smiles, handshakes, tirades, and *tête à tête* talks it is possible to effect any significant change in relations between great powers and power blocs, relations which are determined by class and group interests, imperialist ambitions, national rivalries, etc. We know, of course, that Nikita Khrushchev is a pragmatist and likes to 'see things for himself'. But even if one does not take too high a view of his intellectual stature one need not belittle it so much as to suppose that he seriously believes that it is necessary for the leader of the Soviet Union to see for himself the bazaars of Kabul, the temples of Kashmir, the dancers of Bali, or even the housing estates of Rouen and the film studios of Hollywood. The prizes with which he usually returns home, such as the 'Geneva

[1] Written in 1960.

spirit' or the 'Camp David spirit', are either very elusive or altogether illusory. There is nothing that he gains on his trips that he could not get by action through ordinary diplomatic channels: and often it amounts to far less. What remains are his supposed propagandist successes. Even about these I have my doubts, of which I will not unburden myself at the moment. But is it not strange that the head of so big a concern as the U.S.S.R. should spend nearly half of his working time abroad as his own itinerant publicity agent?

Evidently the question lends itself little to the routine analysis of the diplomatic commentator. It is a psychological question, on the face of it almost non-political, yet politically important. I suggest that what sends the Soviet Prime Minister on his curious treks is the *Wanderlust* of a lifelong prisoner who has at last found himself at large. He is seized by a restless curiosity for the world, a huge appetite for unfamiliar horizons and crowds, an obsessive craving for open spaces. This seems to be Nikita Sergeyevich's personal reaction to a lifetime spent in the strictest isolation from the outside world and in utter estrangement from all things foreign. Even as one of Stalin's highest dignitaries he was in fact his master's prisoner. The prison was inordinately spacious—it covered one-sixth of the globe—but prison it still was.

Anyone who knew the old-type, politically-minded Russian worker—and much of that type is still alive in Khrushchev—knows that curiosity for the world was one of his strongest passions. When he overthrew the Tsar and made the October revolution, one of his high hopes was that the revolution would bring him nearer to the world and the world nearer to him. Stalin knew that; and this is why he treated curiosity for the world as a mortal sin and punished it mercilessly. He watched even his *Soratniks* and Viceroys to see whether any of them was affected by the vice. They had constantly to prove to him that they were not. They had to show him that they lived with their eyes and ears piously averted from, or shut to, all things foreign, that they were immune to all the attractions of the Orient and the Occident and safely submersed in his 'Single Country Socialism'. One may well imagine how much curiosity for the world became pent up in many a Soviet breast. Whoever cannot imagine it needs only to look at Khrushchev—in him the pent-up emotion has burst.

The thousands of Muscovites who at the Lenin Stadium listen

to him as he reports on his journeys feel as if every one of them had been abroad with Nikita Sergeyevich. The whole of Russia, the whole of the Soviet Union, is vicariously going on these journeys.

At heart the Russians are perhaps the least self-sufficient of nations. Long ago 'Westernizing' dreamers and Marxist agitators had kindled in them a flame of internationalism which, although it was smothered and almost put out so many times, is still flickering and may yet blaze forth. At the moment that internationalism has taken on the most elementary form: it shows itself in the eagerness of the people to acquaint or re-acquaint themselves with the world in the simplest terms. In his travelogues Khrushchev speaks to them not only about his talks with Eisenhower, Nehru, or de Gaulle; he talks at length and with gusto about the landscapes he has seen, the climate and the vegetation of remote lands, the kind of people he has met, the edifices, the traffic problems, and the eating and drinking habits of foreigners. His audiences listen somewhat tensely to what he says about Summit meetings and disarmament and matters of war and peace that matter; but by now they know what to expect from him and become bored when they hear the same speech over and over again. But they awaken to him, and he himself seems to awaken, when the gad-about comes out on top of the summit-man, and shares with them his impressions of outlandish parts, when, for instance, he describes rapturously the marvels of the Indonesian landscape and says that if the authors of the Bible had known them, they would have located Paradise in Indonesia, and not anywhere else; or when he compares the fields of central France to the steppes of the Ukraine. Then the multitudes hang on his lips and really enjoy him—he is their walkie-talkie Baedeker in their imaginary peregrinations across the world. He expresses a national emotion, Russia's claustrophobic yearning to get out of her national shell.

However, for the time being, only very few and privileged Soviet citizens are allowed (or can afford) to go on the tours which their Prime Minister describes so glowingly. But how long will the Soviet people be contented with travelling by proxy? The more Khrushchev advertises the joys of globe-trotting, the more does he whet their appetite for it. As the appetite grows, and the means to satisfy it become available, it will sweep away all obstacles; and then the mass of Russians will flood into foreign countries in waves and tides such as have not been seen since the migration of peoples. They will then dispense with the Baedeker-Khrushchev. Let the tourist industries of all continents prepare for that day well in advance, for if they do not they will be hopelessly swamped. Let them not forget that there lives a Khrushchev in every Russian.

In his zest for talking Khrushchev is also profoundly representative of Russia today. For a nation which has suffered thirty years under the most taciturn of tyrants it is a positive relief to be ruled by a chatterbox for a change. Stalin was not only himself secretive and silent; he turned the most emotional and communicative of peoples into the most self-controlled and mute. He sealed two hundred million lips. If it had been given to him to rule Russia for another twenty years, taciturnity and reserve would have so much become the Russian's second nature that by comparison the most reserved Englishman would have looked like an exhibitionist. In Khrushchev, Russia's suppressed garrulity now celebrates its triumphant comeback. He symbolizes the great national unbuttoning that has been going on since 1953. His speech may be repetitive, rambling, or even incoherent; his views may be crude or flippant; he may speak as the Artful Dodger or as the clown. All this does not matter. The very flow of his words is balsam to Russian hearts. His magic lies in the profusion and the pell-mell of his speechifying, for as he wags his tongue two hundred million tongues lose their numbness.

With his speechifying, however, it is as with his travelling. Through him multitudes speak by proxy, but they have not yet spoken up themselves. True, Russia is no longer quite mute. There is much more free speech over there than foreigners think; and at all levels of society many more audacious ideas are expressed than the Sovietologists can imagine. But the ideas are expressed in low voices or whispers. They are not making themselves heard from the public platform, which Khrushchev has monopolized for himself. His stump oratory drowns all the off-noises and whispers. He perorates breathlessly and endlessly as if he feared that if he paused for a moment other voices might become audible.

Can this state of affairs last? Khrushchev's talkativeness only intensifies Russia's yearning for self-expression. He is both the mouthpiece of that yearning and its sworn enemy; and this double role involves him in no end of contradictions. In a way Stalin was more sophisticated: he knew that to keep the whole nation mute, he himself had to give it an example. Khrushchev imagines that the Russians will agree to be a silent nation led by a chatterbox.

II

As one listens to Khrushchev or watches him, one senses the *samouchka*, the self-taught man in him. Strictly speaking, he is not self-taught, for although he started out as a shepherd and miner and owed his first successes to self-education, he eventually sat at the feet of professors and scientists at Moscow's Industrial Academy. Yet, he is still full of the *samouchka*'s self-consciousness. More knowledgeable than most Western statesmen, he has not yet learned, and will never learn, to take his education for granted. He seems to be full of wonder at his own intellectual attainments, as if he were saying to himself: 'It is *me*, Nikita, the shepherd and the miner, who has read all these books and has learned all these difficult things'; and he must have been saying this to himself for thirty or thirty-five years now!

He loves to display erudition; and whenever an opportunity offers itself, he throws at you his clusters of facts and data, as if he were reciting, without a hitch, a freshly learned textbook lesson. Apart from this foible, he also has a valuable quality which is sometimes found in the self-educated: the conviction that education is a never ending labour. At the age of sixty-seven he is still trying to absorb new facts and data and is busy collecting crumbs of novel knowledge. From his journeys he brings back bagfuls of such crumbs and unpacks them with a flourish before his audiences.

In this, too, he is up to a point typical, for Russia today is still the eager *samouchka*, both sublime and ridiculous in her craving for education, her serious concern with self-improvement, her thrill and crude pride in achievement, her inability to take herself for granted, her need to draw self-assurance from self-display and self-advertisement, and her touchiness and emotional vulnerability.

Scratch many a Sputnik-conscious Russian and you will find the old *muzhik*. This is not surprising. Only a short time ago the barefoot, bearded, and illiterate peasant represented the true image of Russia; it was him that Stalin had pressed into the industrial Marathon race that was to usher us into interplanetary space. Now the engineer and the student are the representative national types. But it is precisely because the transformation has been accomplished at such breathtaking speed that the old national character is so strong in the new.

Russia remains a complex combination of backwardness and progress, although the proportion of these elements has vastly changed. Of this, too, Khrushchev is to some extent representative. You need not even scratch him to get at the *muzhik*. He has the peasant's sturdiness, stubbornness, and calculating and distrustful mind, but also the peasant's folklore and wit and *bonhomie*. He comes from that stock of Russo-Ukrainian workers who never strayed far away from their native rural parish pump, and wherever he is, in Kiev or Moscow, in Philadelphia or Versailles, the smell of his Kalinovka pump is with him.

Watch him on any of his trips abroad, when he is invited to inspect a shiningly modern industrial plant. More often than not his face gets tired and bored; his eyes have an uncomprehending look; and his talk with managers and engineers is perfunctory or impatient. He will say frankly that amid the complexities of modern technology he (the graduate of Moscow's Industrial Academy!) is out of his depth; and he will relate that when he was shown the first Sputnik, he could not make head nor tail of what his scientific advisers were telling him about it. But follow him when he is taken out to a farm and inspects cornfields and cowsheds. Then he regains his verve, and his eyes light up as he samples lumps of soil, corn-ears, and milky udders; he praises or finds fault with the way his host does the planting and the threshing; he drinks, he jests, and he pats the farmer's big belly. He is back in his element.

It is the same with him in Russia. On those infrequent occasions when he speaks on industrial affairs, he boringly reads his speech from a paper prepared for him by an industrial brains trust. It is when he finds himself on the fields of a *kolkhoz* that he has his field day. He likes to be thought of as the Soviet Union's Agronomist-in-Chief, though one suspects, of course, that his agricultural expertise is that of the shrewd peasant, not of the agronomist. As he never stops urging farmers to grow maize, the popular wit has given him the untranslatably comic nickname *Kukuruznik* (the maize boy). Maize is probably very important for Russia, for feeding her cattle, increasing her meat supplies, and improving nutritional standards. Still, his maize-mania is too much even for the most patient and the most mule-like of his compatriots . . .

I have said that one can see in Khrushchev the interplay of Russian backwardness and progress. Therein lies a great part of his strength, but also his weakness. Despite all his dynamic and reformist activity, he represents more the backwardness than the progress; and the balance between the two is changing rapidly all the time. The majority of the Soviet population consists already of urban workers and intelligentsia; and the proportion of the town dwellers is constantly rising. So is the proportion of the educated people: already now there are about fourteen million graduates of universities and colleges, and nearly forty-five million graduates of secondary schools. More and more people are growing up with a thoroughly modern outlook. You may scratch them as much as you like, and you will not find the *muzhik* any longer. To these people Khrushchev is already a clumsy anachronism. They would like to see at the head of the party and state a man, or rather men, far more expressive than he is of the needs and desires of an industrial society living under a planned economy.

Recently *Pravda*—or was it *Izvestia?*—admitted that only a couple of years ago the intelligentsia were 'prejudiced' against Khrushchev; but now, the paper assured us, the prejudice has been dispelled. Has it really? The intelligentsia have not been allowed to have their say about this. Probably some of Khrushchev's domestic reforms and moves in foreign policy have softened the 'prejudice'. But the intelligentsia would still prefer the national leadership to be more 'liberal', more up to date, and more intelligent than it is.

Nor is the great mass of the skilled and advanced workers overimpressed with the *Kukuruznik*. They are just a bit too mature for his artful dodging and clowning; and they dislike his pro-*muzhik* bias. It was no matter of chance that at the last session of the Central Committee (in December 1959) Khrushchev's policy was criticized on the ground that it offered the farmers benefits denied to workers and state employees, and Khrushchev had to promise solemnly that he would not allow this to go on. By the same token he is certainly the hero of the *kolkhozniki* and of the unskilled and semi-skilled workers (whose earnings he has been raising systematically), and of all those, even among the intelligentsia, whose ties with rural Russia are close and strong. This is quite enough to give him wide support at present and probably also in the next few years.

But with Khrushchev nearing the close of the biblical span of life, Russians are already beginning to think of the new problem of succession. No one can foresee who exactly his successor or successors will be. They may come from outside the present official hierarchy, or from those teams of relatively unknown men who make policy and take important decisions during the many weeks and months of Khrushchev's journeys abroad. (It is, in fact, these men who even now rule the country in a way they could not do under Stalin, for Stalin never left Russia lest anyone should take any decision or 'plot' against him behind his back.)

Whoever comes after Khrushchev will belong to a generation different from his and will be of quite a different outlook. The new crisis of succession will therefore pose as many problems as Stalin's death posed; and it will lead to no fewer, and to even more startling, changes. If today the Russians think of Stalin with a shudder of revulsion and awe, in ten years' time they will probably think of Khrushchev with a condescending smile as of the last *muzhik* who spoke on behalf of Russia to the world.

THREE CURRENTS
IN COMMUNISM[1]

HEGEL says somewhere that any party is real only when it becomes divided. The idea, far from being a paradox, is simple and profound in its dialectical realism. Any political movement (or any philosophical school of thought) as it grows and develops cannot help unfolding the contradictions inherent in itself and its environment; and the more it unfolds them the richer is its content and vitality. Stalin's conception of the monolithic party was one of his terroristic utopias, the pipe-dream of an autocrat, frightened to death of any dissension or 'deviation' and raising himself in his imagination above the realities of society and history. He managed to 'eliminate' contradictions from the communist movement only by suppressing the movement itself, by crushing the life out of it, and reducing it to an 'apparatus'. Even so, the contradictions continued to be reflected, as if in a distorting mirror, in his own policy, with its notorious 'right' and 'left' zigzags. Unreal though the monolith was in the deeper philosophical and historical sense, politically it dominated the Soviet Union and international communism for several decades; and the consequences of this fact are still with us.

The Soviet–Chinese conflict, coming after the struggle over de-Stalinization in the U.S.S.R. and the Hungarian and Polish upheavals of 1956, marks a new phase in the disintegration of the monolith. The international communist movement has once again become openly divided and to this extent real. Once again it struggles in its own way for its own identity and consciousness, instead of being, as it was in the Stalin era, a pseudo-movement or a para-movement with a merely derivative identity. If this change goes far enough, if the movement is allowed to unfold all its genuine contradictions and finds itself anew, the advantages which may

[1] Written for *Les Temps Modernes* and *New Left Review* in 1963.

accrue to it from split and disunity are bound to outweigh the
immediate disadvantages, on which communists and anti-communists alike have fixed their gaze, the former with apprehension, the
latter with gleeful hope.

I

The logic of the situation tends to recreate within communism
the essential divisions between Right, Centre, and Left. This is
still tendency rather than fact, potentiality rather than actuality.
The lines of demarcation are still blurred, intersected by diverse
cross-currents, overlaid by a fog of ambiguity. Only conditionally
therefore can one speak of these three currents in contemporary
communism: Maoism on the Left, Khrushchevism in the Centre,
and a rather shapeless but influential Right represented by Tito,
Togliatti, and their many quasi-anonymous co-thinkers within the
Soviet bloc. Willy-nilly, one recalls the three currents of the
1920s: the Bukharinist Right, the Stalinist Centre, and the Trotskyist Left. After the long interval, communism appears to come full
circle and resume a great ideological debate broken off some thirty
years ago. Not for nothing do the parties to the present controversy
fling at each other the labels of Trotskyism, Bukharinism, and
Stalinism. But how genuine is the continuity of the two debates?
In so far as the issues and dilemmas which underlay the divisions of
the 1920s have retained importance and topicality, the present divisions, if and when they crystallize, should broadly correspond to—
and should also develop—the divisions of the 1920s. The old controversies had centred on basic problems of the transition from
capitalism to socialism; and these have not yet been solved.
The 1920s were a formative period of great anticipatory ideas,
many of which, having been banned or confined to oblivion, are
re-emerging, and are likely to remain relevant for a long time to
come.

However, the continuity of the three trends manifests itself
through discontinuity; and for the time being the aspect of discontinuity stands out. So much has changed: the general historic
situation; the global balance of power; the social structure of post-
capitalist society; the colonial and semi-colonial world; the context
within which the Communist Parties are acting; and the framework

of their own tradition. The threads of the historic development cannot be merely picked up where they had been left in the 1920s because they were not truly left there. The old divisions are reproducing themselves in a new or partly new socio-political substance, against the background of the Soviet Union's new responsibilities as a nuclear power, of the victory and consolidation of the Chinese revolution, of the spread of revolution elsewhere, of the progressing industrialization of all communist ruled countries, of collectivization of farming in most of them, and so on. Some of the arguments of the 1920s would be meaningless now. Bukharin, if he were alive, would hardly advocate a policy favouring the growth of private or capitalist farming either in the U.S.S.R. or in China. (On the other hand, Gomulka's and Tito's policies towards their peasantries are in fact ultra-Bukharinist.) However, what weighs even more heavily on communism than do these changes in objective circumstances, is the decades of monolithic uniformity. They still determine the character and style of the present controversy.

In every one of its sectors, the Maoist, the Khrushchevite, and the 'Titoist', communism is at present reacting against Stalinism; but everywhere, it is reacting in a Stalinist manner; and in every sector it does this in a different way. In the 1920s official Bolshevism reacted against Leninism, while preserving the forms of Leninist orthodoxy. Now, as in the 1920s, we see the movement breaking with its past and tradition. In both cases the nature of the past and of the tradition has been reflected, positively and negatively, in the new phase.

The Leninist tradition had been woven of two main strands: revolutionary internationalism and proletarian democracy. Against Leninist internationalism, Stalin and Bukharin asserted the national self-sufficiency of the Russian revolution, i.e. socialism in a single country. They had to justify their new doctrine in terms of the old one—hence the casuistic manner in which they had to expound it. They superimposed their own brand of national communism upon the tradition of Bolshevik internationalism. Similarly, the Stalinist conception of the monolithic party, intolerant of any internal dissent, was incompatible with the Leninist 'democratic centralism', under which communist ranks were perpetually astir with debate, and with the early plebeian democracy of the Soviet Republic. All Bolshevik habits of thought and action had to be distorted or destroyed before the party could conform

to Stalin's ideal. Until this happened, the inertia of the old democratic habits was still there: up to the late 1920s the party remained
openly divided into Right, Centre, and Left; and the division was
still accepted as natural and legitimate. Stalin himself did not yet
dare to question the legitimacy of the great controversy. So large
and vital was even the residuum of inner party freedom and
proletarian democracy that it took Stalinism years to remove
it.

The present state of affairs is largely a reversal of the situation of
the 1920s. A new communist internationalism is making its appearance, but it has yet to break through the crusts of national egoism
that had grown up under Stalinism. Similarly, a new ferment of
ideas is under way, a new propensity to dissent and controversy,
a new thirst for inner party freedom and socialist democracy. But
all this is still contained within the Stalinist habits of totalitarian
discipline. Nearly forty years after the last great debate in communism, the renewal of debate has come as a terrifying shock to
communists and appears to them to be quite illegitimate. So heavy
is still the burden of Stalinism; and so difficult is it for the Communist Parties to free themselves from it! Even while they seem
to be becoming real once again, they find it extremely hard to
reconcile themselves with their own reality.

II

It is not easy to sift fact from fiction in the Sino-Soviet controversy, and to disentangle genuine motives from ideological pre-
tences and tactical tricks. It is one of the supreme ironies that
Khrushchev, one of Stalin's chief accomplices and one of the
conductors of the Great Purges, should voice the aspiration to
free communism from Stalinist petrifaction; while Mao Tse-tung,
whose commitment to Stalinism has been so much more superficial and remote, should have come forward as guardian of the
Stalinist orthodoxy.

We are told that the conflict between Peking and Moscow dates
back to the year 1958—ever since, for five long years, it was a
secret de polichinelle within the communist hierarchy. No one
who during those years followed the changing 'ideological' inflec-
tions in the voices of Moscow and Peking had any doubt about

it.[2] It is a measure of how deeply the fear and distaste of open debate is ingrained in leaders brought up in the Stalinist school that all this time they concealed their differences even from the communist rank and file. Only in a movement led by secretive oligarchies was this possible. But what is the result? When the differences were at last officially disclosed, the gulf between the Soviet and Chinese parties was already fixed and well-nigh unbridgeable. Both sides tried to maintain 'unity' and the fiction of the monolith; but the fiction could not conjure out of existence a fundamental conflict of interests and principles. The longer the conflict was allowed to simmer under the surface, the more violent was bound to be the eventual explosion. Now even the most gullible Khrushchevite or Maoist must realize that if the controversy had been conducted in the open from the outset, both sides would have had much more chance than they have now to argue in a rational manner and, if not to settle the issues, then at least to define them and clarify them in their own minds.

Even now Khrushchevites and Maoists alike shrink from facing and disclosing the full truth. Both indulge in the debate with something like a shudder, with the sense that they are committing a cardinal sin against their common party canon. Thus, it is only a half-truth that Moscow and Peking have been at odds since 1958. What had started in that year is the present phase of the conflict; but there were many earlier phases, open and latent. *The basic antagonism between the Chinese revolution and the Soviet bureaucracy is four decades old.* It began to manifest itself in the middle 1920s, when Stalin and Bukharin pressed the Chinese communists to stay within the Kuomintang, accept its discipline, submit to Chiang Kai-shek's orders, give up their own independent revolutionary aspirations, and so prepare the 1927 *hara-kiri*. It was then that Moscow, already committed to Socialism in a Single Country, sacrificed the Chinese revolution to its own dubious *raison d'état*, national egoism, and diplomatic convenience. Now, nearly forty years later, after the triumph of another Chinese revolution and after much de-Stalinization in Moscow, the core of the

---

[2] Only Western diplomacies, notably the State Department, and Western Sovietologists and Sinologists suspected that the idea of any Sino-Soviet conflict was a 'canard of Khrushchevite propaganda' designed to mislead them and to 'lull the vigilance of the West'. This is how a State Department spokesman described not so long ago one of my many accounts of the Sino-Soviet dispute which appeared in the American press.

conflict remains the same: Moscow still seeks to extort from the Chinese an ideological and political tribute to its own *raison d'état*.

III

This is not the place to relate the story of the ambiguous relationship between the post-Leninist U.S.S.R. and Chinese communism. Suffice it to recall that throughout the 1930s Stalin viewed Mao Tse-tung with ill-concealed embarrassment, never being quite sure whether to treat him as a glorious ally or as a damnable heretic; that throughout the Yenan period the Chinese Partisans obtained hardly any Soviet assistance; and that even in 1948 it was against Stalin's explicit advice that Mao decided to carry the civil war in China to a victorious conclusion. Just after the Second World War the Chinese were made to feel the full weight of Stalinist national egoism when Soviet occupation troops in Manchuria seized most of that country's industrial plant as 'war reparations' for the U.S.S.R. At that time, after the Japanese had de-industrialized China proper, Manchuria was China's greatest single industrial base. Then, after Mao's rise to power, Stalin sought to control and penetrate the Chinese economy by means of Soviet-Chinese Joint Stock Companies. Every one of these measures was a heavy blow to the interests of the Chinese revolution and to Chinese dignity. Mao and his comrades took these blows in resentful silence: they were too weak to protest. Engaged in civil war, faced with American intervention, anxious to secure whatever Soviet support they could obtain, they assiduously kept up the appearances of Stalinist orthodoxy. In practice, Mao consistently disregarded Stalinist dogma and Stalin's instructions and pursued his own strategy and tactics. But to avoid excommunication and preserve freedom of movement at home, he and his comrades yielded to Stalin's constant 'ideological' blackmail and paid due obeisance to the Father of the Peoples.

However, Mao's pretence of orthodoxy, opportunistic though it was, had far reaching consequences. The make-believe became part of the Maoist canon and ritual, and thus ceased to be mere make-believe. This showed itself when Moscow embarked upon de-Stalinization. In his message to the Twentieth Congress of the Soviet

F

Communist Party Mao invoked the apostolic succession of 'Marx–Engels–Lenin–Stalin', when everyone in Moscow, even Molotov and Kaganovich, was conveniently forgetting the time-honoured formula. Khrushchev's 'secret speech', we are now told, came to Mao as a complete surprise and shock. Yet soon thereafter he and his comrades appeared to make peace with de-Stalinization. They could not fail to realize that the 'new course' in Moscow met their own needs and aspirations: it put an end to Moscow's rigid supremacy over the 'socialist camp'; it foreshadowed equality for all members of the camp and promised respectful treatment to the U.S.S.R.'s major ally.

Mao raised therefore no objection when, in 1955, Khrushchev went to Belgrade to make amends to Tito; and he threw Chinese influence behind Gomulka when the latter defied Moscow in October 1956. Moreover, having lived down the shock of the Twentieth Congress, Mao himself made a bold attempt to carry de-Stalinization into his own party: he proclaimed that henceforth 'A Hundred Flowers were free to blossom' in communist China. In many respects this remains to this day by far the most radical essay in de-Stalinization attempted anywhere in the communist world. Less startling and melodramatic than Khrushchev's iconoclastic gestures, Mao's implicit critique of Stalinism went far deeper; and for the moment he ventured much further in disavowing the Stalinist conception of the monolithic party. He outlined a thoroughgoing reform which, if carried out, would have brought China far greater freedom than the Soviet Union had ever known, at least since the end of the civil war. He proclaimed, as Lenin once did, that the workers were justified in resisting their bureaucracy and entitled to back up their demands by any form of industrial action, including strikes. He put a large question mark over the entire single party system. At that stage Maoism had indeed reached the limit of 'revisionism'.

We know that soon thereafter the Hundred Flowers wilted, the campaign of 'rectification' was launched, and Maoism lapsed back into the posture of Stalinist orthodoxy. What accounted for this change of front? The view, expressed by Western commentators, that the Hundred Flowers Proclamation was a trick designed to deceive the elements of opposition and provoke them to expose themselves so that they might be crushed more easily, is too shallow to deserve serious consideration. The trend of thought reflected in the Hundred Flowers Proclamation was too weighty, too consistent with itself, and consistent also with Mao's encouragement of Polish anti-Stalinism to be dismissed as mere fraud.[3] Unfortunately, the Chinese themselves have failed to give a frank and convincing explanation of their behaviour. But it is clear that the Hundred Flowers incident had a traumatic impact upon their subsequent policy. Mao took fright at the consequences of his own pledge. He had solemnly invited the party and the nation to avail themselves of the new liberty in the hope that eight years after the revolution the régime was sufficiently consolidated to be able to stand open criticism from below, and even to benefit from it. This hope, which permeated almost every line in the Hundred Flowers Proclamation, may not have been groundless: China had in those eight years, achieved economic progress unprecedented in her history; the conditions of life had greatly improved for millions of workers and hundreds of millions of peasants; and the government had done its best to 'buy off' even the bourgeoisie and to mitigate their hostility. For a variety of reasons, Mao's government was in its first few years more fortunate than Lenin's had been; and it could afford to manage the nation's economic resources, and to cope with its social classes, more rationally. In Russia at the end of the civil war a wide gulf had already opened between rulers and ruled; and even N.E.P. did not bridge it. No such gulf had appeared in China.

Yet the manner in which the intelligentsia, the peasants, and the workers, even party members, reacted to the Hundred Flowers Proclamation (a spate of sharp and often bitterly hostile criticism of the régime came from all sides) led Mao and his colleagues to conclude that the nation was not 'ripe' for the freedom just promulgated. Historians may argue whether they did not take fright too soon; whether the spate of criticism really constituted a grave danger to the government; and whether they should not have relied on wide popular support persisting beneath the outward hostility and criticism. In every revolution there occur those critical and tragic moments—in Russia the analogous turns came in the spring

---

[3] It was also consistent with Mao's deeper mental reservations towards Stalinism. The Chinese Politbureau has now revealed that in 1949 or 1950 they forbade the calling of any place or institution by the name of any living communist leader. This was, and had to be, a highly secret decision: its anti-Stalinist edge was all too keen at a time when almost every other place or institution in the U.S.S.R. bore the name of Stalin, Molotov, Kaganovich or Voroshilov.

of 1921 and the autumn of 1923—when revolutionary governments become terrified of their real or apparent isolation, decide that they cannot afford to rule democratically, and seek to consolidate their power in an authoritarian fashion. This is what Mao and his comrades decided to do in the summer of 1957; and from then on they set their face against de-Stalinization.

They have since sought to justify the change of mind by claiming that bourgeois and reactionary elements, not socialist ones, were taking advantage of the new freedom, and that even within the party the Right wing, not the Left, was benefiting. This amounted to saying that the political balance in the nation was, despite all the achievements, heavily weighted against the *socialist* purpose of the revolution; and in view of the character of Chinese society—the predominance of the peasantry, the weakness of the working class, the conservatism of the old intelligentsia—this may have been, and may still be, true.

The Maoists then concluded that the effect of de-Stalinization was the same on the international scene as well, and even in the U.S.S.R. The civil war in Hungary confirmed them in this attitude. They drew from it the lesson that it was de-Stalinization that had brought Hungary to the brink of counter-revolution and had played into the hands of Communist opportunists and Right-wingers who, like Nagy, were prepared to abdicate to the Social Democratic and the peasant parties and take Hungary out of the 'socialist camp'. Simultaneously, in Moscow, Molotov and Kaganovich conducted their attack on Khrushchev along similar lines: de-Stalinization, they pointed out, was threatening to disrupt the whole Soviet bloc; and it was time to stop it. A coalition between the Chinese and the Russian opponents of de-Stalinization, old and new, was, or might have been, in the making; and Khrushchev managed to forestall it by calling a halt to 'liberalization', cultivating Mao's friendship, increasing economic aid to China, promising to develop her atomic power and even to equip her with nuclear weapons. Only after he had defeated his opponents at home did he risk the conflict with Mao, though he did not yet dare to bring it into the open.

Both Mao and Khrushchev have been acting under different and even contradictory domestic pressures, which up to a point compelled each of them to act against his own character. In the U.S.S.R. the modernization of society, industrialization on the basis of public ownership and planning, and progress of mass education had turned the Stalinist method of government into an unbearable anachronism. As totalitarian terror and purges had left no centres of opposition in existence capable of doing away with Stalinism, Stalin's acolytes had to discredit and renounce his legacy in their own, half-spurious and half-real, manner. It was something of an accident that Khrushchev should have become the mouthpiece of the revulsion against Stalinism; but through that accident an historic 'necessity', an overwhelming social and political need, manifested itself.

China, on the other hand, has remained industrially backward. Four-fifths of her population still consist of primitive, illiterate peasants, working with antediluvian tools (as against only forty per cent. of the Soviet population occupied in agriculture). The Chinese industrial workers are at present probably on the level at which the Soviet working class was in the early 1930s, when the bulk of it, just recruited from the peasantry, lacked all urban industrial outlook and socialist consciousness. If Stalinism was the combined product of revolution and barbarous backwardness, so is Maoism, with its methods of 'primitive socialist accumulation', paternalistic rule, and magic-ritualistic 'Marxism–Leninism'. There is no need to equate Maoism with Stalinism. The differences are obvious: Maoism has not been riddled with all the frightful inner tensions characteristic of Stalinism; it has not been nurtured in the same irrational fears; it has not resorted to the same savage terror and to Great Purges; it has not met popular egalitarian longings with the same hostility; it has not shamelessly falsified its revolutionary origin. Of course, China has not been the first country to overthrow capitalism; and the background of her national civilization and tradition is different from Russia. If Stalin was the inheritor of Lenin and Ivan the Terrible, Mao has amalgamated Leninism with Confucianism and with habits of thought of the old Mandarin ruling classes.

Yet for all these differences there exist also undeniable affinities between Maoism in power and Stalinism, affinities rooted in the contradiction between the socialist strivings of the revolution and the primitive pre-industrial structure of society. And so, despite all his deviations from Stalinism and a momentary determination to transcend it, Mao has not been able to go beyond Stalinism; and when he attempted to do so, he retraced his steps in a panic, and then came to the fore as the defender of Stalinist orthodoxy.[4]

IV

The present cleavages run between various national parties, between Russians, Chinese, Yugoslavs, Poles, Rumanians, and others. Each party, however, is keeping up its own national monolithic façade. Each has its own infallible leader—the Yugoslav party no less than the others. Each is riddled with dissent; but nowhere is open expression of dissent tolerated. None has so far been allowed the privilege of a single open debate on any major issue of policy. Their boasts about the 'restitution of the Leninist norms of inner party life' are hollow—they may be believed only from ignorance of the facts: Lenin was, at almost every party assembly, openly challenged—and sometimes, on major issues, outvoted—by colleagues and the rank and file. So many years after Stalin, the bureaucratic hierarchies remain the only policy-making bodies—the only centres of decision—within the Communist Parties. They jealously guard their monopoly, and protect it tenaciously against the rank and file; the infallible leader, their supreme arbiter, is there to safeguard it. Yet at the same time the quarrels and rows between the parties, as they grow in scope and vehemence, stimulate ferment and dissent within each party. The whole question is whether or for how long this dissent can be patched up, subdued, or suppressed. And when and how is the international differentiation—the three currents—going to be reflected within each national organization?

What then are the hallmarks of Left, Right, and Centre? The Maoists claim that it is they who represent the Left. We shall see later in what respect their claim is justified. But surely their insistence on Stalinist orthodoxy and discipline is a mark of bureaucratic conservatism rather than of anything else. (It was no matter of chance that the Left groupings in pre-Stalinist communism were anti-bureaucratic and cried out for 'proletarian democracy'.) From this point of view, the Khrushchevite de-Stalinization goes at least some way to meet the needs of any Left elements in present-day

---

[4] Yet the ambiguity of the Maoist attitude towards Stalin is by no means dispelled. 'The question of Stalin . . . is still a subject of much discussion. . . .', says *Peking Review*, '*it is likely that no final verdict can be reached on this question in the present century.*' And this is said in an article devoted to the glorification of Stalin!

communism. Despite its ambiguity and demagogic tricks, it stirs the rank and file to independent political thinking, arouses their self-confidence, poses new issues, and provokes new questions. Another criterion in the present division bears on the communist attitude towards economic privilege in post-revolutionary society. Here, too, the lines of division are blurred. Since Stalin's death the Soviet party has had to take some cognizance of the egalitarianism of the masses; it has reduced the discrepancies between high and low salaries and wages. The Maoist régime, on the other hand, does not seem to have ever allowed privilege to assume dimensions as shocking as those it assumed in the U.S.S.R. under Stalin, or to allow even such wage differentials as are still common in the Soviet Union today. About other countries in the Soviet bloc it is difficult to generalize: the Polish economy, for instance, appears to suffer from indiscriminate levelling of wages and salaries as much as from economic privilege. Everywhere, the ruling groups refuse to disclose the social stratification and even to reveal the national wage structures; and no one is as secretive in this respect as are the Chinese. Everywhere the contrasts between the upper and the lower strata of society are evidently too sharp to be exposed to daylight.

Only in one important field, that of the international political strategy of communism, has the division assumed definite shape: there indeed the Chinese have taken up the position of the Left, while Khrushchev is heading the Centre, and Tito, Togliatti, and their co-thinkers in the Soviet bloc stand on the Right.[5] The Mao-

[5] Within the countries of the Soviet bloc the Right is very influential, if only because it is up to a point a 'transmission belt' for powerful anti-communist pressures coming from the peasantry, the remnants of the bourgeoisie, and the intelligentsia. But the Right is also unorganized, ill-defined, shapeless; its adherents avoid identifying themselves with it. Of the party leaders Gomulka and Kadar place themselves vaguely between Right and Centre. In the Soviet Union the Right is even more amorphous than elsewhere: its elements obviously prefer to remain hidden, as it were, behind the Centre on which they exercise a constant pressure. (Such approximately was also the relationship between the Bukharinists and the Stalinists in the middle 1920s.) The Right stands for uninhibited, consistent application of the genuinely revisionist conceptions, which the Khrushchev-ite Centre advances only half-heartedly; it favours a line of 'peaceful coexistence' more straightforward than Khrushchev's diplomatic zigzags; a more determined dissociation of the U.S.S.R. and of the Soviet bloc from revolutionary movements in the outside world; a 'bolder' renunciation of Lenin's theory of imperialism and of other 'obsolete' parts of the Leninist heritage; a frank acknowledgment of the 'stabilization' of Western capitalism in the post-war era; and, consequently, of the need to transform the Communist Parties of the West into something like Left-reformist parties. Undiluted national communism is more congenial to the Right

ists attack the conduct of Soviet diplomacy and the Khrushchevite conception of 'peaceful coexistence'. Their argument has abounded in ultra-radical (or, as the Russians say, 'adventurist') overtones: early in the debate they appeared to deny the very possibility of peaceful coexistence, to deny Moscow even the right to pursue it; and they spoke as if they intended to make light of the danger of a nuclear holocaust. More recently, however, they have pruned their pronouncements of such overtones; but they go on slogan-mongering when they decry the Moscow Test Ban Treaty, and, *instead* of it, demand nuclear disarmament as the sole guarantee against world war. It should be clear that even complete nuclear disarmament cannot provide any such guarantee—world war could still be started with conventional weapons and each of the major nuclear powers could then replenish its nuclear arsenal quite rapidly. The Chinese are therefore inconsistent when they blame Khrushchev for 'spreading pacifist illusions' by signing the Test Ban Treaty, while they themselves are fostering an even larger illusion. But just as one may struggle for disarmament, without giving oneself to wishful thoughts about it, so one may welcome the Test Ban, without exaggerating its significance.[6]

The Maoists' 'wild talk', however, is not really essential to their main argument, which is that Khrushchev, in seeking a detente with the West, has been sacrificing the interests of the revolutionary movement in Asia, Africa, and Latin America, and that the Communist Parties of the West have been guided by Moscow's diplomatic convenience rather than by principles of class struggle. This, Peking says, is the real sense of Khrushchev's talk about a 'peaceful transition from capitalism to socialism' and of Togliatti's and Thorez' 'parliamentary road to socialism'. This is also why Moscow tells the colonial and semi-colonial peoples that they can achieve

than to the Centre; and this makes it hard and even impossible for the Right to acknowledge itself as an *international* current in communism. It is in this context that Togliatti's 'polycentrism' acquires its true meaning, as does also Tito's refusal to accept the world's division into blocs and to propagate Titoism internationally. (National-Communist Parties cannot form any International.) In so far as the Right elements are implicitly opposed to 'Soviet hegemony', they also defy the new Khrushchevite conformism to some extent, and although they make common cause with Khrushchev against Mao, they do it with a mental reservation, for they do not wish to see any international discipline reimposed upon the movement.

[6] Khrushchev's propagandists of course did exaggerate it grossly and ridiculously. They hailed the Test Ban as the dawn of a new era with all the appropriate drum beating. But then the drum is the only instrument on which they have ever learned to play.

full, economic as well as political, independence peacefully, without violent revolution and under the leadership of their 'national bourgeoisie'. Mao has opposed Khrushchev's summit diplomacy, suspecting that at the summit meetings Khrushchev was out to 'appease' the United States at the expense of the Soviet bloc and of other, mainly the underdeveloped, countries, (Iraq, Congo, Algeria, Cuba). Khrushchev—so the Chinese argue—has made needless concessions to Eisenhower and Kennedy, sometimes, as in Cuba, after having offered needless provocation. Has he not told the French people that General de Gaulle is the national leader in whom they should place their trust? Has he not contributed thereby to the demoralizing of the French communists who have done nothing to assist Algeria's struggle for independence? Has the Italian Communist Party, under Khrushchevite inspiration, not sought to ingratiate itself with the bourgeoisie, the Vatican, and even with N.A.T.O.? Did Togliatti not order his party to turn out *en masse* in the streets of Rome to welcome President Eisenhower during the latter's visit in Italy? And has Khrushchev not sought to impose a standstill on revolution in the Middle East, in Africa, and in Latin America, backing Nasser, Kassem, and, of course, Nehru, and confounding the Communist Parties on the spot?

This is a formidable list of charges. The Khrushchevite answer is that only moderation can secure peace, and that if the U.S.S.R. were, on Chinese promptings, to encourage 'imprudently' every revolutionary ferment and movement abroad, it would heighten international tension and provoke world war. The Chinese point out that the more audaciously communism acts and the wider revolution spreads, the more will the U.S.A. and N.A.T.O. be weakened, hamstrung, unable to counteract; and the less likelihood will there be of world war erupting. (The obvious counterpart to this argument is the perpetual debate in the West between the advocates of a 'tough' policy *vis-à-vis* communist governments and the adherents of negotiation and limited agreements.) It is this, say the Chinese, not the desirability or undesirability of peaceful coexistence that is at issue. Even Khrushchev does not rule out the use of nuclear weapons as a retort to aggression; and there is no reason to assume that Mao (who has no nuclear weapons) is more willing to use them than Khrushchev is. The controversy is rather over the question: which policy is more likely to prevent world war: the self-containment of communism, as Khrushchev

says or implies, or the spread of revolution, as Mao maintains?
Here the controversy does indeed link up with the great debate
of the 1920s; the echoes of that debate are constantly mingling with
the exchanges between Peking and Moscow. Unwittingly and perhaps even unknowingly, Mao resumes here Trotsky's argument
against Stalin and against the implications of Socialism in One
Country for international communism, while Khrushchev speaks
and acts in the Stalinist tradition. Yet each of them stubbornly
refuses to acknowledge himself as the echo of the voice he repeats.
Khrushchev pretends that he, not Stalin, has originated the policy
of peaceful coexistence (which Lenin in his wisdom had barely
foreshadowed); and Mao alleges that what he advocates is a straight
continuation of Stalin's line. Both falsify the past; Khrushchev in
order to make it fit his de-Stalinization, Mao in order to suit it to
his reaffirmed Stalinist orthodoxy.

The truth is that Stalin initiated and pursued the policy of peaceful coexistence, exactly as Khrushchev understands it, subordinat-
ing international communism to his *raison d'état*. Stalin's 'friendship' with Chiang Kai-shek; his 1935 pact with Laval, followed by
the Popular Front; his determination to keep, through the Spanish
communists and the G.P.U., the Spanish revolution within 'bourgeois democratic' limits; his 1939 pact with Hitler; his Teheran
and Yalta pacts with Churchill and Roosevelt; and the moderate
(pro-Gaullist and pro-Badoglio) policies of the French and Italian
Communist Parties—these were Stalin's main applications of the
doctrine of peaceful coexistence. Despite all the changed circumstances, Khrushchev's variations on the theme are not so different
in kind. Even his zigzags, alternating between 'adventurism' and
'opportunism', follow the Stalinist pattern. (In Cuba he first provoked the United States and then climbed down, as Stalin had
done over the blockade of Berlin in 1948.) On the other hand, one
needs only to compare the Maoist indictment of Khrushchev with
Trotsky's, Zinoviev's, Kamenev's, and Radek's, criticisms of Stalin's
conduct of Comintern affairs to find the same *motifs* here and
there—only that Mao is much cruder in argument, has far less
knowledge and understanding of the West, and his heavily oriental idiom and accent jar even on those not too numerous pro-
Chinese ears that are to be found in the West.[7]

[7] One example of the crude ignorance is Peking's bizarre insistence that Tito
has restored capitalism in Yugoslavia. Or is it sheer malice?

V

But is this controversy, one is asked, 'truly ideological' in character? Does it reflect genuine differences of approach to revolution and international communism? Or are the Maoists using the cloak of revolutionary internationalism merely for promoting their national ambitions? Is not Khrushchev's refusal to equip China with atomic weapons the real cause of Maoist hostility? And if so, is it not all an ordinary game of national power politics?

This stark contrast between 'ideology' and 'national ambition' is rather artificial, to say the least. Of course, all bureaucratic hierarchies are inclined to be nationally arrogant and play power politics. This may be as much true of the Maoists as of their adversaries. Stalinism not merely represented its own brand of national communism—and it did so twenty-five years before Titoism; it was a school of national communism for all Communist Parties. Even now, every Communist Party from the Elbe to the China Sea dreams of its 'own' socialism in its own 'single country'.[8] True, Stalin had harnessed all parties to serve solely his *raison d'état*. But no sooner had his hand dropped and had the harness loosened, than every party began to show its nationalist proclivities and bents. All were supposed to be part of one international monolith; and all were committed to resist any centrifugal forces in their midst; yet all have carried over into their 'socialism' the nationalist feuds inherited from the *ancien régime*. This again may be just as true of the Maoists as of their opponents—hence their latest hints about China's inveterate territorial grievances against Russia and possible frontier disputes.

But this is only one part of the truth. What is not less important

---

[8] This is a formidable obstacle in the way of the integration of Soviet and Eastern European economic planning within the *Comecon*. Now the Chinese too speak of their economic autarchy. That the Soviet blockade forces them to rely on their own resources is, of course, true. But they seem to make, in truly Stalinist fashion, a virtue out of the bitter necessity, and to discover in China's old Great Wall the predestined framework of socialism. Against this, Khrushchev dwells on the progressive merits of 'international division of labour' within the socialist camp. This idea was anathema under Stalin—it was a Trotskyist heresy then. Khrushchev's conversion to it would be more convincing, if he did not so often use economic reprisals against recalcitrant members of the socialist camp. Great Russian chauvinism, the bureaucratic whip, and international division of labour do not go well together.

is that the international position of the Chinese People's Republic has so far given its leaders very little scope for playing at national power politics, and that the spread of revolution still holds out to them the sole prospect of genuine national security. Ostracized, subjected to blockade, or at best half boycotted by the West, and now hectored and again boycotted by the U.S.S.R., they can only look forward to those upheavals in countries near and distant that may sap the imperialist strength of the West, bring new members to the 'socialist camp', enlarge the camp, and weaken the Soviet supremacy over it. If nothing else—yet there is much else besides— then national interest alone impels the Maoists some way towards revolutionary internationalism. And their 'ideology', even if it cloaks national ambitions, still has its own substance, weight, and appeal. How many national ambitions, how many narrow interests of principalities, cities, and ecclesiastical hierarchies were once involved in the Reformation and Counter-Reformation and in the interminable Protestant splits, all filling the air of Europe with the din of ecclesiastical doctrines and theological canons? Yet, only the crudest *Schustermarxist* would dismiss as meaningless the ideological terms in which Luther, Calvin, Zwingli, the Popes, and the Jesuits conducted their disputes. Ideas, when they get hold of the minds of millions, are a power in themselves. And the Maoists, whatever their ulterior motives and limitations, are impressing ideas of revolutionary internationalism on the minds of millions, as no one has done since Lenin's days. Therein lies the world historical significance of their stand against Khrushchev.

Having said this, we must still ponder the 'motives and limitations'. Peking is now censuring the record of the most important Communist Parties, ranging back over the whole post-Stalinist decade, and touching even the last years of the Stalin era. The gravamen of all their accusations is that Khrushchevism has been working to deprave the communist movement, that it has imposed a standstill on revolution in the underdeveloped countries, and has encouraged Western communists, especially the French and the Italians, to make their truce with the bourgeois–imperialist Establishment.

But where, one may ask, have the Maoists been all this time? Why did they keep silence till the summer of 1963? Obviously they could not give attention to these matters while they were fighting their own civil war, seizing power and consolidating it; and perhaps they could not have their say before the end of the Stalin era. But how can they justify their silence in the next ten years? If what they say about the corruption of international communism by Moscow is true—and much of it undoubtedly is—then their discretion does not seem to have been the better part of their valour. If Khrushchevism has been demoralizing the Communist Parties all over the world, then the Maoists have through their silence connived at the demoralization. If Moscow has, for diplomatic reasons, obstructed the revolutionary movements, say, in the Middle East, then they have given it a free hand. Or do they think that they have saved their souls by venting displeasure at occasional conventicles of the eighty Parties and in confidential dispatches to the Soviet Presidium?[9]

Peking has come out with the exposure of Khrushchevite opportunism rather late in the day. Much of the revolutionary wave in the Far and Middle East and in Africa rolled over in the first post-Stalin decade, when the Communist Parties were banking on Nasser, Kassem, Soekarno, and their like. Since then most of the ex-colonial and semi-colonial countries have found relative stability; and nothing foreshadows the imminent rise of a new wave of revolution comparable to that of the past decade. The leaders of the 'national bourgeoisie' are in the saddle almost everywhere; and the local communists who may have had a chance in the struggle for power in the 1950s, are not likely to get another such chance very soon. It is indeed on the ebb of the Afro-Asian revolution that the Chinese have come out with their bold prescriptions for a political offensive of communism. Like some of the ultra-radicals of the old Comintern, they do not seem quite able to tell ebb from flow.

VI

For the time being the various factions are absorbed in their tactical games, in wire pulling, and jockeying for positions. Half a

[9] One wonders what advice the Maoists offer their Indonesian comrades, the leaders of the largest Communist Party outside the Soviet bloc, a party reputed to be under Maoist influence. Does Peking urge them to go on backing Soekarno (as Stalin once urged the Chinese to support Chiang Kai-shek)? Or does it encourage them to work for the overthrow of Soekarno's pseudo-Bonapartist dictatorship and for revolution?

year after the open break between Peking and Moscow they have reached a stalemate. The Communist Parties of Asia are in varying degrees backing Maoism (except for the Indian party, which is led by Khrushchevites, though the Maoists have their solid strongholds in the rank and file). In the Communist Parties of the West the tide runs against Maoism, although a leftish undercurrent makes itself felt. Non-communist radicals in the underdeveloped countries reserve their attitude. (Castro, who at one time seemed pro-Chinese but after a visit to Moscow came out with rapturous eulogies for Khrushchev, has placed himself uneasily on the fence.)

That the main line of division should run so straight between East and West (and the 'West' includes here the U.S.S.R.) is in itself a reflection on the nature of the controversy: on one side of the divide are the parties tied to the U.S.S.R. and those 'adjusted' to the Western 'welfare state' and its capitalist prosperity; on the other, are those confronted by the unresolved and unmitigated problems of the 'underdeveloped' world. One of the dangers of this alignment is that it may develop into undisguised racial antagonism between white and coloured communists. Neither Peking nor Moscow dares to perpetuate this line of division; and neither has been able to shift it. If Khrushchev hoped to convene an international conference with the purpose of excommunicating Maoism, he has had to give up or shelve the plan. The communists of Asia have made it clear that they would not endorse the excommunication. What is more, even such staunch pro-Khrushchevites as Togliatti and Gomulka have shown their reluctance. The communist Right, both within and without the Soviet bloc, fears that excommunications and expulsions may cause the whole movement to slide back into Stalinism; and that a witch-hunt started against the Left might turn against the Right as well. In this unexpected way the division between Right and Centre, the latent division running parallel to the open gulf which separates both these groupings from the Maoists, makes itself felt.

Thus, what was once the supra-national monolith is now split across its middle and along national lines. The Communist Parties are no longer bound together by any genuine international ties. The enormous bureaucratic structure, which had its origin in the old Comintern, has dissolved into national fragments. But each fragment outwardly remains a monolith in itself. This state of affairs can hardly last—it may be merely a transitory stage between the ossification of communism in the Stalinist mould and its re-formation on a new basis. The decisive question is whether the movement can re-form—whether the ferment of ideas is strong enough to break through the national monoliths. The old mechanically disciplined and mute C.P.s fitted naturally within the framework of the Stalinized Comintern and Cominform; they are utterly at variance with the present discordant aspect of international communism. Will the rank and file, seeing their infallible chiefs at loggerheads with one another, become aware of the deep sickness of the movement and realize that only free criticism and free debate—free within each party—can cure it? To pose this question is to ask how much regenerative power is still left in the communist movement after decades of bureaucratic corruption. Can the communist Jekyll still come back into his own after he has for so long been eclipsed by the Stalinist Hyde?

If any party is in a sense real only in so far as it is divided and as it gives free play to—and makes constructive use of—its inner contradictions, then the communist movement of today is still only half real. But it cannot remain so. It will either attain full reality through further divisions, and recover unity in genuine inner democracy—through uninhibited debate over all its crucial problems, over its past and future. Or else the movement will not be able to break through the moulds inherited from Stalinism; and then it will disintegrate through the work of its own centrifugal forces.

MAOISM—ITS ORIGINS AND OUTLOOK[1]

I

WHAT does Maoism stand for? What does it represent as a political idea and as a current in contemporary communism? The need to clarify these questions has become all the more urgent because Maoism is now openly competing with other communist schools of thought for international recognition. Yet before entering this competition Maoism had existed as a current, and then as the dominant trend of Chinese communism for thirty to thirty-five years. It is under its banner that the main forces of the Chinese revolution waged the most protracted civil war in modern history, and won their victory in 1949, making the greatest single breach in world capitalism since the October Revolution, and freeing the Soviet Union from isolation. It is hardly surprising that Maoism should at last advance politically beyond its national boundaries and claim world-wide attention to its ideas. What is surprising is that it has not done so earlier and that it has for so long remained closed within the confines of its national experience.

Maoism presents in this respect a striking contrast with Leninism. The latter also existed at first as a purely Russian school of thought; but not for long. In 1915, after the collapse of the Second International, Lenin was already the central figure in the movement for the Third International, its initiator and inspirer—Bolshevism, as a faction in the Russian Social Democratic Party, was not much older then than a decade. Before that the Bolsheviks, like other Russian socialists, had lived intensely with all the problems of international Marxism, absorbed all its experience, participated in all its controversies, and felt bound to it with unbreakable ties of intellectual, moral, and political solidarity. Maoism was from the outset Bolshevism's equal in revolutionary vitality and dynamism, but differed from it in a relative narrowness of horizon and a lack

[1] Written for *Socialist Register* and *Les Temps Modernes* in 1964.

of any direct contact with critical developments in contemporary Marxism. One hesitates to say it, yet it is true that the Chinese revolution, which in its scope is the greatest of all revolutions in history, was led by the most provincial-minded and 'insular' of revolutionary parties. This paradox throws into all the sharper relief the inherent power of the revolution itself.

What accounts for the paradox? An historian notes first of all the total absence of any Socialist-Marxist influence in China prior to 1917.[2] Ever since the middle of the nineteenth century, from the Opium Wars and the Taiping Rebellion, through the Boxer Rising and till the overthrow of the Manchu dynasty in 1911, China had been seething with anti-imperialism and agrarian revolt; but the movements and secret societies involved in the risings and revolts were all traditional in character and based on ancient religious cults. Even bourgeois Liberalism and radicalism had not penetrated beyond the Great Wall till the beginning of this century : Sun Yat-sen formulated his republican programme only in 1905. By that time the Japanese Labour movement, of which Sen Katayama was the famous spokesman in the Socialist International, had officially embraced Marxism. In Russia the invasion of Western socialist ideas had begun by the middle of the nineteenth century; and ever since Marxism had gripped the minds of all revolutionaries, Populists and Social Democrats. As Lenin put it, Bolshevism stood on the shoulders of many generations of Russian revolutionaries who had breathed the air of European philosophy and socialism. Chinese communism has had no such ancestry. The archaic structure of Chinese society and the deeply ingrained self-sufficiency of its cultural tradition were impermeable to European ideological ferments. Western imperialism managed to sap that structure and tradition, but was unable to fructify the mind of China with any vital liberating idea. Only the revolutionary explosion in neighbouring, yet remote, Russia shook the immense nation from its inertia. Marxism found a way to China via Russia. The lightning speed with which it did so after 1917, and the firmness with which it then struck roots in China's soil are the most stupendous illustration of the 'law of combined development' : here we see the most archaic

[2] The first Chinese translation of the *Communist Manifesto* appeared only in 1920; it was then that Mao, at the age of twenty-seven, read the *Manifesto* for the first time. The year before he still went on a pilgrimage to the grave of Confucius, although he was not a believer.

G

of nations avidly absorbing the most modern of revolutionary doctrines, the last word in revolution, and translating it into action. Lacking any native Marxist ancestry, Chinese communism descends straight from Bolshevism. Mao stands on Lenin's shoulders.[3]

That Marxism should have reached China so late and in the form of Bolshevism was the result of two factors: the First World War, exposing and aggravating to the utmost the inner contradictions of Western imperialism, discredited it in the eyes of the East, intensified socio-political ferments in China, made China 'mature' for revolution and extraordinarily receptive to revolutionary ideas; while Leninism, with its original, vigorous emphasis on anti-imperialism and the agrarian problem, rendered Marxism, for the first time in history, directly and urgently relevant to the needs and strivings of the colonial and semi-colonial peoples. In a sense, China had to 'jump over' the pre-Bolshevik phase of Marxism in order to be able to respond to Marxism at all.

Yet the impact of undiluted Leninism on China was very brief. It lasted only through the early 1920s till the opening of the 'national' revolution in 1925. Only a very small *élite* of the radical intelligentsia acquainted itself with the programme of Leninism and adopted it. At the foundation Congress of the Chinese Communist Party in 1921 only twelve delegates were present—Mao Tse-tung was one of them—representing a total membership of fifty-seven! At the second Congress, in the following year, the same apostolic number of delegates spoke for a membership of 123. There were still no more than 900 party members in the whole of China at the beginning of 1925, shortly before the communists were to find themselves at the head of insurgent millions.[4] On these first communist propaganda circles the basic ideas of Leninism left a deep impression. No matter how much the Stalinized Comintern did later to confound the mind of Chinese communism, the germ of Leninism survived, grew, and became transformed into Maoism.

---

[3] A parallel may be drawn here between the fortunes of Marxism and revolution in Europe and Asia. Just as in Europe Marxism first exercised a wide influence in industrial Germany so in Asia it found its first important following in industrial Japan, the 'Prussia of the Far East'. But in neither of these two 'advanced' countries did Marxism go beyond propaganda and agitation. On both continents it fell to the great 'backward' nations to accomplish the revolution.

[4] Ho Kan-chih, *A History of the Modern Chinese Revolution* (Peking, 1959), pp. 40, 45, 63, 84.

Leninism offered its Chinese adepts a few great and simple truths rather than any clear-cut strategy or precise tactical prescriptions. It taught them that China could achieve emancipation only through revolution from below, for which they must work as tirelessly, indomitably, and hopefully as the Bolsheviks had worked for their revolution; that they ought to distrust any bourgeois reformism and hope for no accommodation with any of the Powers that held China in subjection; that against those Powers they ought to join hands with patriotic elements of the Chinese bourgeoisie, but that they must distrust any temporary bourgeois allies and be ever ready for their treachery; that Chinese communism must look for support to the destitute masses of the peasantry and unfailingly be on their side in their struggles against war-lords, landlords and money lenders; that China's small urban working class was the sole consistently revolutionary and potentially the most dynamic force in society, the only force capable of exercising leadership ('hegemony') in the nation's struggle for emancipation; that China's 'bourgeois-democratic' revolution was part of an 'uninterrupted', or 'permanent', revolution, part of a global upheaval in which socialism was bound to overcome imperialism, capitalism, feudalism, and every form of archaic Asian society; that the oppressed peoples of the East should rely on the solidarity with them of the Soviet Union and the Western working classes; that the Communist Party, acting as the vanguard of the movement, must never lose touch with the mass of workers and peasants, but should always be ahead of them; and, finally, that they must guard jealously the party's total independence in policy and organization *vis-à-vis* all other parties.[5] This was the quintessence of Leninism which the few pioneers of Chinese communism had absorbed before the revolution of 1925-27.

As far as Maoism is concerned, these were still the years of its 'pre-history'. It was only during the revolution that Maoism began to announce itself; and only in consequence of the revolution's defeat did it form a special trend in communism. The 'pre-historical' period is nevertheless of obvious importance, because some of the lessons Maoism had learned in the school of Leninism, although

---

[5] The Second Congress of the Communist International occupied itself, in 1920, especially with the problems of the colonial and semi-colonial countries; and Lenin was the prime mover of the theses and resolutions on this subject. See Lenin, *Sochineniya* (Moscow, 1963), vol. 41.

they were to be overlaid by other ideological elements, entered firmly into its political make-up.

II

The next formative influences were the revolution itself and the traumatic shock of its defeat. The years 1925-27 brought to eruption all the national and international contradictions by which China had been torn; and the eruption was astounding in suddenness, scale and force. All social classes—and all the Powers involved —behaved as Leninism had predicted they would. But the most outstanding feature of the events—a feature that was not to be found in the next Chinese revolution and is therefore easily forgotten or ignored—was the revelation of the extraordinary political dynamism of China's small working class.[6] The main centres of the revolution were in the industrial and commercial cities of coastal China, especially Canton and Shanghai. The most active organizations were the trade unions (which had almost overnight become a great mass movement). General strikes, huge street demonstrations and workers' insurrections were the main events and turning points of the revolution, as long as the revolution was on the ascendant. The agrarian upheaval in the background, widespread and deep, was far slower in the take-off, scattered over immense areas, and uneven in tempo and intensity. It gave a nation-wide resonance to the action of the urban proletariat but could not affect the events as directly and dramatically as that action did. It cannot be emphasized too strongly that in 1925-27 China's working class displayed quite the same energy, political initiative, and capacity for leadership that Russia's workers had shown in the revolution of 1905. For China these years were what the years 1905-06 had been for Russia—a general rehearsal for revolution, with this difference, however, that in China the party of the revolution drew from the rehearsal conclusions very different from those that had been drawn in Russia.

[6] Mao gives the number of Chinese industrial workers, employed in large-scale enterprises as two million. There were about ten million coolies, rikshas, etc. Mao Tse-tung, *Izbrannye proizvedeniya* (Moscow, 1952), vol. I, pp. 24-5.

Mao explains the decisive role of the workers in the revolution by the high degree of their concentration in big factories, their extraordinarily oppressive conditions, and exceptional militancy. Russia had no more than three million workers employed in modern industry about the time of the revolution; and Trotsky explains their decisive role in much the same way.

This fact, in combination with other, objective factors, discussed later, was to be reflected in the differences between the socio-political alignments in the China of 1949 and the Russia of 1917.

At the time of the Chinese 'rehearsal', official Moscow was already reacting against its own high hopes and international-revolutionary aspirations of the Lenin era—it had just proclaimed Socialism in One Country as its doctrine. The Stalinist and Bukharinist factions, which still jointly exercised power, were sceptical of the chances of Chinese communism, afraid of international 'complications', and resolved to play for safety. To avoid challenging the Western Powers and antagonizing the Chinese bourgeoisie, Stalin and Bukharin acknowledged the Kuomintang as the legitimate leader of the revolution, cultivated 'friendship' with Chiang Kai-shek, proclaimed the necessity of a 'bloc of four classes' in China, and instructed the Communist Party to enter the Kuomintang and submit to its guidance and discipline. Ideologically, this policy was being justified on the ground that the Chinese revolution was bourgeois in character, and must be kept within the limits of a bourgeois revolution. No proletarian dictatorship was therefore on the order of the day—only 'a democratic dictatorship of the workers and peasants', a vague and self-contradictory slogan which Lenin had advanced in 1905, when he still held that the Russian revolution would be only 'bourgeois democratic'.

To follow this course, the Chinese communists had to give up almost every principle Moscow had inculcated in them quite recently. They had, as a party, to resign their independence and freedom of movement. They had to give up, in deeds if not words, the aspiration of proletarian leadership and accept bourgeois leadership instead. They had to trust their bourgeois allies. In order to bring about and keep in being the 'bloc of the four classes', they had to curb the militancy of the urban workers and the rebelliousness of the peasantry, which constantly threatened to explode that bloc. They had to abandon the idea of continuous (or permanent) revolution, for they had to 'interrupt' the revolution whenever it tended to overlap the safety margins of a bourgeois order, which it constantly tended to do. They had to break the proletarian-socialist momentum of the movement—or else Moscow would denounce them as adherents of Trotskyism. Socialism in One Country, in the U.S.S.R., meant no socialism in China.[7]

[7] See my account of these events in *The Prophet Unarmed*, pp. 316-38.

At this point Chinese communism fell a prey to its own weaknesses as well as Moscow's opportunism and national egoism. Having no Marxist tradition of their own to fall back upon, being dependent on Moscow for inspiration, ideas, and the sinews of their activity, finding themselves raised by events of dizzy suddenness from the obscurity of a tiny propaganda circle to the leadership of millions in revolt, lacking political experience and self-confidence, bombarded by an endless stream of categorical orders, instructions and remonstrances from Moscow, subjected to persuasion, threats and political blackmail by Stalin's and the Comintern's envoys on the spot, bewildered and confounded, the pioneers of Chinese communism gave in. Having learned all their Leninism from Moscow, they could not bring themselves to say, or even think, that Moscow was wrong in urging them to unlearn it. In the best circumstances they would have found it very hard to rise to their task and would have needed firm, clear, absolutely unequivocal advice. The advice they got from Moscow was unequivocal only in prompting them to equivocate, to shirk their responsibilities, and to abdicate. They did not know that the Trotskyist Opposition was defying Stalin's and Bukharin's 'General Line'; and that Trotsky himself opposed the idea that the Chinese party must enter the Kuomintang and accept its dictates. (They had no contact with the Opposition and Trotsky was criticizing Stalin's and Bukharin's 'friendship' with Chiang Kai-shek in the privacy of the Politbureau.) To the Chinese therefore Stalin and Bukharin spoke with the voice of Bolshevism at large.

It was at that moment, the moment of the surrender to the Kuomintang, that Mao first registered his dissent. His expression of dissent was only oblique; but within its terms it was firm and categorical. In the second half of 1925 and at the beginning of 1926 Mao spent much time in his native Province of Hunan, organizing peasant revolts, and participated in communist activity in Canton and Shanghai, representing the party within some of the leading bodies of the Kuomintang. His experience led him to assess the social alignments, especially the class struggle in the countryside, in two essays (*The Classes of Chinese Society*, written in March 1926, and *A Study of the Peasant Movement in the Hunan Province*, March 1927). He did not attempt to analyse China's social structure in depth or to criticize the party line in general; but he made his assessment in terms that conflicted implicitly and irreconcilably with every premiss of the party's and the Comintern's policy.

'. . . There has not been a single revolution in history', he wrote in March 1926, 'that has not suffered defeat when its party guided it along the wrong road. To gain confidence that we shall not lead the revolution along the wrong road . . . we must take care to rally our genuine friends and strike at our genuine enemies . . . [we must be able] to tell our genuine friends from our genuine enemies. . . .' The 'genuine friends' of the revolutionary proletariat were the poor peasants and the semi-proletarian elements in the villages; the 'genuine enemies'—the landlords, the wealthy peasants, the bourgeoisie, the Right wing of the Kuomintang. He characterized the behaviour of all these classes and groups with such total lack of illusion and such clarity and determination that, in the light of what he said, the 'bloc of the four classes', the party's submission to the Kuomintang, and the idea of a containment of the revolution within bourgeois limits appeared as so many absurdities, suicidal for the party and the revolution. He was not yet turning his eyes from the town to the country, as he was to do presently, although he already responded far more sensitively and fully to what the peasants were feeling and doing than to the workers' movement. But he still insisted, in good Leninist style, on the workers' primacy in the revolution; and his emphasis on this reflected the actual relationship of workers and peasants in the events of that period.

By this time in the Soviet Union only the Trotskyists and Zinovievists still spoke such language;[8] Mao was something of a 'Trotskyist' Jourdain unaware of what kind of prose he was using. His role in the party was not prominent enough for the Comintern to notice his heresy; but already in 1926 he was at loggerheads with

[8] A comparison of the documents contained in Trotsky's *Problems of the Chinese Revolution* with Mao's writings of 1926-27 shows the complete identity of their views on these points. Ho Kan-chih in op. cit. (which is the official Maoist account of the Chinese revolution) unwittingly gives many other illustrations of that identity. Thus, he relates that early in 1926 Mao protested against the Chinese party's decision to vote for the election of Chiang Kai-shek to the Executive Committee of the . . . Kuomintang and to back his candidature to the post of Commander-in-Chief of the Armed Forces. About the same time Trotsky protested in Moscow against Chiang's election as an Honorary Member of the Executive of the Comintern. The Maoist historian blames only Chen Tu-hsiu for the 'opportunist' policy, pretending not to know that Chen behaved as he did on Moscow's orders and that Chiang was Stalin's candidate to the post of the Commander-in-Chief. The fact that Chiang was Honorary Member of the Comintern's Executive is not even mentioned in the Maoist *History*.

the Chinese Central Committee and Chen Tu-hsiu, the party's undisputed leader and his own erstwhile intellectual and political guide. In the *Study of the Hunan Peasant Movement*, written shortly before Chiang Kai-shek's *coup d'état*, Mao vented his indignation at those Kuomintang leaders and those 'comrades within the Communist Party', who sought to tame the peasantry and halt the agrarian revolution. 'Quite obviously'. he castigated them,

this is a reasoning worthy of the landlord class . . . a counter-revolutionary reasoning. Not a single comrade should repeat this nonsense. If you are holding definite revolutionary views and happen to be in the country even for a while, you can only rejoice at seeing how the many millions of enslaved peasants are settling accounts with their worst enemies . . . All comrades should understand that our national revolution requires a great upheaval in the country . . . and all should support that upheaval—otherwise they will find themselves in the camp of counter-revolution.

This attitude cost Mao his seat on the Central Committee. He was to regain it a year later; but the streak of radicalism or of 'pristine Leninism' was to survive in him, even underneath many later accretions, and was to bring upon him the charge of Trotskyism . . . thirty-six years later.

III

It was, however, from the defeat of the revolution that Maoism took its proper origin, and that it acquired those features that distinguished it from all other currents in communism and from—Leninism.

The defeat caused much heart-searching among the Chinese communists, especially after they had learned the truth about the struggle over China that had gone on in the Russian Politbureau. There were several conflicting reactions to what had happened. Chen Tu-hsiu ruefully acknowledged that he had misguided his party but pleaded that he himself (and the Central Committee) had been misguided by Moscow. Exposing dramatically the inner story of the revolution, relating the many acts of pressure and blackmail to which Moscow had subjected him, he acknowledged that Trotsky had all along been right over China. He was for this expelled from the party, slandered and persecuted by both the Kuomintang and the Comintern.[9] Chen Tu-hsiu and his few friends, arguing from an analogy with the Russian revolution (and accepting Trotsky's guidance), saw ahead of them a period of political stagnation, an interval between two revolutions; and they proposed to act as the Bolsheviks had acted during the interval between 1907 and 1917: retreat, dig in, and hold out primarily among the industrial workers; regain and build up strongholds in the cities which would be the main centres of the next revolution; combine clandestine work with open propaganda and agitation; struggle for 'partial demands', wage claims and democratic freedoms; press for the unification of China and call for a National Constituent Assembly; support the peasantry's struggles; use all discontents against Chiang Kai-shek's dictatorship and so gather strength for the next revolution, which would at last be the uninterrupted revolution Lenin and Trotsky had preached.

This was, theoretically at least, a comprehensive prospect and a coherent programme of action. What the Comintern, through its nominees, Li Li-san and Wang Ming, offered was an utterly incoherent combination of basic opportunism and ultra-left tactics, designed to justify the policy of 1925-27 and to save Stalin's face. The canon was upheld that the next revolution would also be only 'bourgeois democratic'—the canon could be used in future to justify a renewal of a pro-Kuomintang policy and a new 'bloc of the four classes'. (Stalin always held that policy in reserve, even during his wildest ultra-left zigzags.) Meanwhile the Comintern, denying that the Chinese revolution had suffered any defeat, encouraged the Chinese party to stage hopeless coups and armed risings. These tactics, initiated with the armed Canton insurrection in December 1927, fitted in well with the Comintern's new 'General Line', which consisted in a forecast of imminent revolution in East and West alike, a call for 'direct struggle for power', rejection of any socialist-communist united front in Europe, refusal to defend democratic

---

[9] Chen Tu-hsiu's fate—denounced as 'traitor' by the Comintern, he was imprisoned and tortured by the Kuomintang police—was a terrible warning to Mao who henceforth avoided any *open* breach with Stalinist orthodoxy, even while he was at loggerheads with its successive Chinese guardians. Mao was never to risk a conflict with both Stalin and Chiang Kai-shek. His cautious, ambiguous attitude towards Stalinism reflected something of the sense of weakness and ultimate dependence on Soviet backing which had caused Chen Tu-hsiu to accept Stalin's and Bukharin's dictates in 1925-27. But unlike Chen, Mao, for all his outward deference to Stalin, was never to give up his own judgment on Chinese affairs and swerve from his own course of action.

freedoms, slogans about social-fascism, etc. In Germany this policy led to the disaster of 1933. In China the hopeless risings, coups, and other mad adventures demoralized and disorganized what had been left of the Chinese labour movement after the 1927 defeat.

It was against this background that Maoism made its entry. Although its official historians (and Mao himself) never admit it, Mao shared Chen Tu-hsiu's view that the revolution was in decline and that a political lull was ahead. He rejected the Comintern's ultra-left tactics, beginning with the Canton rising and ending with the various versions of 'Li-Li-sanism'. He held, however, that communism would for a long time to come have no chance at all of re-entrenching itself in the cities and regaining footholds in the working class—so deep, as he saw it, was the moral débâcle that followed the surrenders of 1925-27. He did not as yet give up the hope that eventually the urban proletariat would rise again; but he turned his eyes wholly to the peasantry, which had not ceased to struggle and rise up in revolts. What was supposed to be merely the agrarian 'accompaniment' of the revolution in the cities could still be heard, loud and stormy, after the cities had been reduced to silence. Was it possible, Mao wondered, that this was no mere 'accompaniment'? Were perhaps the revolts of the peasants not just the backwash of a receding wave of revolution, but the beginning of another revolution of which rural China would be the main theatre?

A historian of Maoism may follow the subtle gradations by which Mao arrived at the affirmative answer to this question. Here it will be enough to recall that late in 1927, after his quarrel with the Central Committee, he retired to his native Hunan; then after the defeat of the Autumn Harvest Rising he withdrew at the head of small armed bands into the mountains on the Hunan-Kiangsi border; and from there he urged the Central Committee to 'remove the party as a whole', its headquarters and cadres, 'from the cities to the countryside'. Official Chinese textbooks now credit Mao with having conceived already then, in 1927-28, the far-sighted strategy that was to bring victory twenty years later. Mao's contemporary writings suggest that at first he thought of the 'withdrawal into the countryside' as a temporary expedient and possibly a gamble, but not as desperate a gamble as were the party's attempts to stir the urban workers back into insurrectionist action. Again and again he argued that the 'Red Base' he and Chu Teh had formed in the Hunan-Kiangsi mountains was only a 'temporary refuge' for the

forces of the revolution.[10] Yet this temporary and provisional expedient did already point to the later Maoist strategy. The party
leaders, 'opportunists' and 'ultra-radicals' alike, rejected Mao's advice, holding that it amounted to a break with Leninism. And,
indeed, who could imagine Lenin, after the 1905 defeat, 'withdrawing the party' from Petersburg and Moscow and going at the
head of small armed bands into the wilderness of the Caucasus, the
Urals, or Siberia? The Marxist tradition, in which the idea of the
supremacy of the town in modern revolution held a central place,
was too deeply ingrained in Russian socialism for any Russian socialist group to embark upon such a venture. Nothing like it occurred
even to the Social Revolutionaries, the descendants of the Narodniks, Populists and agrarian socialists.

IV

Mao gradually became aware of the implications of his move and
in justifying the 'withdrawal from the cities', he recognized more
and more explicitly the peasantry as the sole *active* force of the
revolution, until, to all intents and purposes, he turned his back
upon the urban working class. He treated his new 'road to socialism'
as a 'uniquely Chinese phenomenon', possible only in a country
which was neither independent nor ruled by a single imperialist
Power, which was the object of an intense rivalry between several
Powers, each with its own zone of influence, and its own war-lords,
compradores, and puppets. That rivalry, he argued, made it impossible for China to achieve national integration; the Kuomintang
would no more be able to achieve it, and to set up a cohesive
national administration, than previous governments had been.
Chiang Kai-shek could smash with a few military blows the concentrated strength of the urban workers, but would not be able to
deal likewise with the peasantry, which, being dispersed, was less
vulnerable to the white terror and could fight on for many years.
There should therefore always exist 'pockets' in rural China where
forces of the revolution could survive, grow, and gather strength.
Renouncing the prospects of a revolutionary revival in the
towns, Maoism banked on the permanence of the agrarian revolution.

[10] Mao, *op. cit.*, vol. I, pp. 99-110 and 117 ff and *passim*.

Mao assumed in effect a prolonged stalemate between the defeated urban revolution and a paralytic counter-revolution, a prolonged and unstable equilibrium between the divided imperialisms, the impotent Kuomintang bourgeoisie, and the apathetic working class. The stalemate would allow the peasantry to display its revolutionary energies, and to support the communists and their Red Bases as scattered islands of a new régime. From this assumption he drew (in 1930) this broad generalization about the international prospects of communism:

If . . . the subjective forces of the Chinese revolution are weak at present, so are also the reactionary ruling classes and their organization . . . based on a backward and unstable socio-economic system . . . In Western Europe . . . the subjective forces of the revolution may at present be stronger than they are in China; but the revolution cannot immediately assert itself there, because in Europe the forces of the reactionary ruling classes are many times stronger than they are in China . . . *The revolution will undoubtedly rise in China earlier than in Western Europe* (my italics).[11]

This assumption, so characteristic of Maoism, was not altogether original—it had appeared fleetingly in some of Lenin's, Trotsky's, Zinoviev's, and Stalin's reasonings a decade earlier.[12] But Mao made of it the cornerstone of his strategy, at a time when no other communist school of thought was prepared to do so. In retrospect, the events have amply justified him. Yet if the Maoist orientation and action are judged not retrospectively, but against the background of the late 1920s, and early 1930s, they may not appear as faultless as they seem now. It may be argued that the superiority of the 'reactionary ruling classes' in Western Europe would not have been so overwhelming, and that it might even have crumbled, if the Stalinist and Social-Democratic self-defeating policies (passivity *vis-à-vis* rising Nazism, and the shams of the Popular Fronts) had not worked to preserve and enhance it. One may further argue that the Maoist road of the Chinese revolution was not necessarily predetermined by the objective alignment of social forces, that the Chinese working class might have reasserted itself politically, if the Comintern had not recklessly wasted its strength and if the Chinese party had not 'withdrawn from the cities', and so deserted the workers, at a time when they needed its guidance more than ever.

---

[11] Mao, *ibid.*, p. 196.
[12] See *The Prophet Armed*, pp. 456-7 and *The Prophet Outcast*, p. 61.

As so often in history so here, the objective and subjective factors are so enmeshed and intertwined after the events that it is impossible to disentangle them and determine their relative importance.

It should further be noted that the period of the middle 1930s was extremely critical for Maoism; its major premisses were brought under question and nearly refuted by the events. In the south of China, the area to which Mao's action had been confined till 1935, the peasantry was utterly exhausted by its many revolts and was crushed by Chiang Kai-shek's punitive expeditions. The Red Bases of Hunan and Kiangsi, having held out against Chiang's 'extermination drives' for seven years, were succumbing to blockade and attrition. Mao and Chu Teh just managed to lead the Partisans out of the trap and start on the Long March. They thereby acknowledged their defeat in that part of China which had been the main theatre of their operations. It looked as if the counter-revolution, far from being impotent in the countryside, had demonstrated its superior strength there and gained a decisive advantage. In the meantime, the workers of Shanghai and other coastal cities had shown a new defiance and staged turbulent strikes and demonstrations. But, lacking competent leadership and organization, they were defeated again and again. Maoist historians cast a veil of obscurity over this chapter of the movement in the cities, precisely because it raises the question whether under effective guidance those struggles of the urban workers might not have opened up a new revolutionary situation much earlier than it could be opened up from the country. Was it inevitable that the interval between the two revolutions should last not ten years, as it lasted in Russia, but more than twice as long? Or had the Maoist withdrawal from the cities something to do with it? Whatever the truth of the matter—the historian can pose the question but not answer it— around 1935 the Maoist strategy was on the point of collapse and nearly bankrupt. These facts are recalled here not for any polemical purpose, but because they lead to a conclusion of some topical relevance, namely, that Maoism as a strategy of revolution owes its ultimate vindication to an extraordinarily complex and largely unpredictable set of circumstances.

In 1935 Mao fought his way out of the impasse by means of the Long March, which has since become the heroic legend of Chinese communism. Yet at the end of the Long March Mao had under his orders only one-tenth of the force he had before the March—30,000 out of 300,000 Partisans.[13] What saved Maoism and decisively contributed to its further evolution were, apart from its own heroic determination to survive, two major events or series of events: the Japanese invasion, and the deliberate de-industrialization of coastal China by the invader. The Japanese conquest deepened the contradictions between the imperialist Powers and interrupted the unification of China under the Kuomintang. It thus reproduced that impotence of the reactionary ruling class on which Mao had based his calculations. Northern China was in turmoil; the Kuomintang was unable to assert its military control there and to prevent the emergence and consolidation of the Northern 'Soviets'. Maoism derived fresh strength from the Kuomintang's inability to secure the nation's independence and from its own revolutionary–patriotic, 'Jacobin', stand against Japan. On the other hand, with the systematic de-industrialization of coastal China, the small working class was removed from the scene. As the Japanese dismantled industrial plant in Shanghai and other cities, the workers dispersed, became *declassés*, or vanished in the country.[14] From this fact Maoism obtains a kind of retroactive vindication. Henceforth no one could hope for the rise of a new 'proletarian wave' in the cities. The class alignments of 1925-27 could not be expected to reappear in the next revolution. The Marxist–Leninist scheme of class struggle became inapplicable to China. The peasants were the sole force struggling to subvert the old order; and Mao's party focused and armed all their rebellious energies. It was now, in the late 1930s, that Mao finally formulated the main and most original principle of his strategy: The Chinese revolution, unlike other revolutions, will have to be carried from country to town.[15]

[13] Ho Kan-chih, *op. cit.*, p. 270. The author blames the recklessness of the 'ultra-lefts' in the party and army for these disastrous losses.

[14] A most instructive description of this process and of its political effects is to be found in Chen Tu-hsiu's correspondence with Trotsky (The Trotsky Archives), quoted in *The Prophet Outcast*, pp. 423-4.

[15] From what has been said it is clear that the validity of the Maoist method of revolution is of necessity limited. Mao himself, in the early days of Partisan warfare, used to underline this—he spoke of the 'unique Chinese character' of the conditions in which his method could be applied. Only in primitive countries, where the body politic has not achieved national integration (or where it has disintegrated) and where there does not exist any bourgeoisie capable of exercising national leadership, can Partisans enjoying the peasantry's support carry revolution from the country to the towns; and then it depends on the revolutionaries' 'ideology' and international connections whether they can impart a socialist impulse to their revolution. An analysis of the social alignments in the Cuban

V

The relationship between Maoism and Stalinism was ambiguous from the beginning. The motives which had led Maoism to take on the protective colour of Stalinist orthodoxy are obvious enough. In the late 1930s, Mao and his colleagues were aware of the weight of the influence on Chinese affairs that Stalin's government would exercise in consequence of the Second World War; and they feared that it might exercise it in a narrowly self-interested manner, and as opportunistically as in 1925-27. They knew their dependence on Moscow's goodwill; but they were determined *not* to allow Moscow to use them as it had used Chen Tu-hsiu, Li Li-san, and Wang Ming. They were determined to prevent another abortion of the Chinese revolution. They played, therefore, a most intricate game, pursuing their independent strategy without arousing Stalin's suspicion and wrath. Stalin could not have been quite unaware of this. Yet the Comintern neither sanctioned nor condemned Mao's 'un-Marxist' and 'un-Leninist' strategy. Stalin would not have tolerated anything like the Maoist heresy in any Communist Party situated in a sphere of world politics which he considered more vital to his interests. But Maoism had started upon its career on what looked to Stalin like a remote periphery; and Mao behaved as some heretics had once behaved in the Catholic Church who, defying their local bishop or cardinal, strenuously avoided any collision with the Pope himself. Later, when Maoism moved closer to the centre of Chinese politics, it was already too strongly entrenched—yet was outwardly

and Algerian revolutions, and in other Afro-Asian upheavals, may show to what extent, and with what variations, the 'Chinese' conditions have or have not been reproduced in those countries. Victorious leaders of a Partisan movement are, of course, inclined to claim for their experience wider validity than it inherently possesses. Thus Che Guevara, in his essay on guerilla warfare, recommends the Castroist strategy to revolutionaries all over Latin America. In those Latin American countries, however, where the bourgeois régime is more broadly based, integrated, and centralized than it was in Cuba under Batista, Che Guevara's recommendation, if acted upon, may lead to abortive coups.

We may mention here as a grotesque curiosity that the leaders of the French counter-revolution in Algeria, the O.A.S. colonels, also tried to 'apply some lessons of Maoism.' Mao is undoubtedly a great authority on the military aspects of Partisan warfare. But the main secret of the success of his strategy lies in its close combination with agrarian revolution. It is impossible to apply his military prescriptions without his social strategy, as the leaders of the O.A.S. have learned to their detriment.

still submissive enough—for Stalin to conclude that to excommuni-
cate Mao was both risky and unnecessary. He did not himself
believe, not even as late as 1948, that Mao's Partisans would ever be
able to conquer the whole of China and carry out a revolution; he
was willing to use them as bargaining counter or instruments of
pressure on Chiang Kai-shek, whom he again considered his chief
ally in Asia.

   In the Comintern the years after 1935 were again a period of
'moderation', the period of Popular Fronts. Translated into Chinese
terms, the policy of the Popular Fronts meant the re-establishment of the 'bloc of the four classes' and of the 'friendship' between
the Kuomintang and the communists, this time in a united front
against the Japanese invader. The old, never abandoned and now
emphatically reasserted canon about the exclusively bourgeois–
democratic character of the Chinese revolution served as the
'ideological' justification of this turn of policy. For Maoism, engaged as it was in civil war against the Kuomintang, the Comintern's new demands were a severe trial. Only the show of an
unreserved acceptance of the Comintern's line could prove that
Mao and his comrades remained loyal to Stalinism. And so Mao
'moderated' his Yenan régime and his propaganda and agitation;
he appealed to the Kuomintang for patriotic solidarity and joint
action against Japan; and he even used his influence to save Chiang
Kai-shek's position and probably even his life during the Sian incident. Yet the Partisans never yielded to the Kuomintang even as
much as an inch of their territory and power.

   Mao's Stalinism was in some respects, however, more than sheer
mimicry. The persistence with which Mao asserted and reasserted
the purely bourgeois character of the Chinese revolution accorded
well with the complete identification of his Partisans with the
peasantry. To the great mass of the peasantry the perspective of an
'uninterrupted revolution', that is of a revolution solving the land
problem, unifying China and also *opening up a socialist upheaval,*
was either meaningless or unacceptable. In the primitive pre-
industrial society of Shensi and Ninghsia—where Mao's writ ran
during the Yenan period—there was no room for the application
of any measures of socialism. It was only after its conquest of the
cities in 1949 that Maoism was to run up against the inevitability
of the uninterrupted (permanent) revolution and obey its dictates.

VI

From the theoretical Marxist viewpoint the central question posed by all these events is how a party, which had for so long based itself only on the peasantry and acted without any industrial working class behind it, was after all able to go beyond the 'bourgeois'–agrarian upheaval and initiate the socialist phase of the revolution. Communist writers have so far avoided discussing this embarrassing question frankly and have allowed anti-communist 'Marxologists' to monopolize it. Has not the course of events in China, the latter argue, refuted once and for all the Marxist and the Leninist conceptions of revolution and socialism? Surely, the idea of proletarian revolution in China belongs to the sphere of mythology—and, surely, the Chinese experience shows up the Russian revolution too to have been the work of a ('power hungry', 'totalitarian') intelligentsia which used the workers and their allegedly socialist aspirations only as the ideological cover for its own ambitions. All that both these revolutions have achieved, M. Raymond Aron, for instance, is quick to point out, is merely to change the ruling élites, which is nothing surprising to anyone who has learned his lessons from Pareto and Max Weber. (Even a writer like the late C. Wright Mills, convinced of the relevance of Marxism to the problems of our age, concluded that not the working class but the revolutionary intelligentsia is the real historic 'agency' of socialism.) Ex-Marxists, who have found out that socialism has been 'the illusion of our age', and that the reality behind it is state capitalism or bureaucratic collectivism, invoke the old Marxist dictum that 'socialism will be the work of the workers or it will not be at all'. How then, they ask, is it possible to speak of a revolution in which the workers have played no part as being socialist in any degree whatsoever? In a different context and on a different level of argument, the question arises whether the famous Russian controversy between Narodniks and Marxists over the relative roles of workers and peasants in modern revolution has in fact been as irrevocably resolved as it seemed to have been until recently. Even if the Marxists were right in Russia, are the Narodniks not vindicated in China? Has not the peasantry there turned out to be the sole revolutionary class, the decisive agent of socialism?

There is no question that the record of Maoism compels a critical

H

review of some habitual Marxist assumptions and reasonings. How this is necessary is illustrated *inter alia* by the assessment of Maoism which Trotsky gave in the 1930s. Grasping all the intensity of the agrarian upheaval in China, but apprehensive about the Maoist withdrawal from the cities, Trotsky bluntly ruled out the possibility of the consummation of the Chinese revolution without a previous revival of the revolutionary movement among the urban workers. He feared that Maoism, despite its communist origin, *might* become so completely assimilated with the peasantry as to become nothing but its mouthpiece, that is the champion of the small rural proprietors. If this were to happen, Trotsky went on, Mao's Partisans, on entering the cities, might clash in hostility with the urban proletariat and become a factor of counter-revolution, especially at that critical turn when the revolution would tend to pass from the bourgeois into the socialist phase. Trotsky's analysis, reverberating unmistakably with decades of the Russian Marxist–Narodnik controversy and the experience of the Russian revolution, was reduced *ad absurdum* by some of his Chinese disciples who denounced the victory of Maoism in 1949 as a 'bourgeois and Stalinist counter-revolution'.[16]

The phenomenon of a modern, socialist (or be it even 'bureaucratic collectivist') revolution of which the working class had not been the chief driving force stood indeed without precedent in history. What drove the Chinese revolution beyond the bourgeois phase? The peasantry was interested in the redistribution of land, the abolition or reduction of rents and debts, the overthrow of the power of the landlords and money-lenders, in a word in the 'bourgeois'–agrarian upheaval. It could not give the revolution a socialist impulse; and Maoism, as long as it operated only within the peasantry, could not have been more reticent than it was about the prospects of socialism in China. This changed with the conquest of the cities and the consolidation of Maoist control over them. Yet the cities were almost dead politically, even if a galvanized remnant of the old labour movement stirred here and there.

We are confronted here, on a gigantic scale, with the phenomenon of 'substitutism', i.e. the action of a party or a group of leaders

---

[16] See the controversy over this among the Chinese Trotskyists, reproduced in several issues of the *International Information Bulletin* of the Socialist Workers' Party (New York), for the year 1952. Trotsky's articles on the Chinese Partisans had appeared in the *Byulleten Oppozitsii*.

which represents, or stands in the stead of, an absent, or inactive, social class. The problem is familiar from the history of the Russian revolution, but it presents itself there in quite a different form. In Russia the working class could not have been more conspicuous as the driving force of the revolution than it was in 1917. Yet, after the civil war, amid utter economic ruin and industrial collapse, the working class shrank, disintegrated, and dispersed. The Bolshevik party set itself up as its *locum tenens*, and as trustee and guardian of the revolution. If the Bolshevik party assumed this role only some years *after* the revolution, Maoism assumed it long *before* the revolution and during it. (And Mao and his followers did this without any of the scruples, compunction, and *crises de conscience* that had troubled Lenin's party.)

Liberal or 'radical' Paretists, who see in this yet another proof that all that revolutions achieve is a change of ruling *élites*, have still to explain why the Maoist *élite* was determined to give the revolution a socialist (or collectivist) turn, instead of keeping it within bourgeois limits. Why has the Chinese communist *élite* behaved so differently from the Kuomintang *élite*? This was not even the case of a 'young' *élite* replacing an old and 'exhausted' one, for both *élites* were contemporaries and had entered the political stage almost simultaneously. Why then have Mao and his comrades given China a new social structure, while Chiang Kai-shek and his friends floundered hopelessly in the wreckage of the old? And what accounts for the stern puritanical morale of Maoism and for the notorious corruption of the Kuomintang? The answer surely is that Chiang Kai-shek and his men identified themselves with the classes that had been privileged under the old order, while Mao and his followers embraced the cause of those that had been oppressed under it. Behind the change of the *élites* there was a profound transformation in the basic social relationships of China, the decline of one social class and the rise of another. No one doubts the extent to which the peasantry backed the Partisans during the twenty-two years of their armed struggle—without that support they would not have been able to hold out, to make the Long March, to shift their bases from one end of China to the other, to keep the Kuomintang's greatly superior military strength engaged all the time, to repulse so many 'annihilation drives', etc. So strong and intimate were the ties between the Partisans and the peasantry that at one time Mao appeared to many, to friend and foe alike, as the commander of a gigantic jacquerie rather than as the leader of a Communist Party—as a kind of Chinese Pugachev.

Yet this Chinese Pugachev, or super-Pugachev, had gone through the school of Leninism; and no matter how far he deviated from it in his methods of action, some general ideas of Leninism continued to govern his thought and action. He did not abandon his commitment to socialism (or collectivism) in favour of the peasants' individualism and attachment to private property, even while he was doing his best to satisfy that individualism and unfold its bourgeois-revolutionary potentialities. Nor should it be forgotten that revolutionary agrarian movements have always produced their Utopian communists, their Münzers and Anabaptists. Of the peasants' 'two souls'—the expression is Lenin's—one is craving property, while the other dreams of equality and has visions of a rural community, the members of which own and till their land in common. It might be said that Maoism expressed both 'souls' of the peasantry, had it not been for the fact that it never was just the peasantry's mouthpiece. It always looked upon itself as the legatee of the defeated revolution of 1925-27, of which the industrial workers had been the driving force. Identifying itself ideally with those workers, Maoism continued to echo their socialist aspirations. Was this arrogance or usurpation? But what else could a party, committed to the communist programme, do after the dispersal of the urban working class and the political decline of the cities?

In carrying the revolution beyond the bourgeois phase Maoism was actuated not merely by ideological commitments but also by a vital national interest. It was determined to turn China into an integrated and modern nation. All the experience of the Kuomintang was there to prove that this could not be achieved on the basis of a belated, and largely imported, capitalism, superimposed upon patriarchal landlordism. National ownership of industry, transport, and banking, and a planned economy were the essential preconditions for any even half-way rational deployment of China's resources and for any social advance. To secure these pre-conditions meant to initiate a socialist revolution. Maoism did precisely that. This is not to say that it has turned China into a socialist society. But it has used every ounce of the nation's energy to set up the socio-economic framework indispensable for socialism and to bring into being, develop, and educate the working class, which alone can make of socialism a reality eventually.

International factors, in the first instance the relationship between China and the U.S.S.R., co-determined the course and outcome of the revolution. That relationship has been much wider and more positive than the ambiguous connection between Maoism and Stalinism. Whatever the mutations of the political régime of the U.S.S.R., the Chinese revolution could not—and cannot—be dissociated from the Russian. Although the Partisan armies had received little or no Soviet support and had overthrown the rule of the Kuomintang in the teeth of Stalin's obstruction, Red China, born into a world split into two Power blocs, and herself confronted by American hostility and intervention, could not but align herself with the U.S.S.R. In this alignment, Maoism found another potent motive for carrying the revolution beyond the bourgeois phase. The ultimate guarantee of the solidity of that alignment lay in the collectivist structure of the Chinese economy. As I have pointed out elsewhere,

the revolutionary hegemony of the Soviet Union achieved [despite Stalin's initial obstruction] what otherwise only Chinese workers could have achieved—it impelled the Chinese revolution into an anti-bourgeois and socialist direction. With the Chinese proletariat almost dispersed or absent from the political stage, the gravitational pull of the Soviet Union turned Mao's peasant armies into agents of collectivism.[17]

No Marxist textbook has or could have foreseen so original a concatenation of national and international factors in a revolution: Maoism does not fit into any preconceived theoretical scheme. Does this refute the Marxist analysis of society and conception of socialism? When Marx and Engels spoke of the working class as *the* agency of socialism, they obviously presupposed the presence of that class. Their idea had no relevance to a pre-industrial society in which such a class did not exist. It should be recalled that they themselves pointed this out more than once; and that they even made allowance for the possibility of a revolution like the Chinese. They did this in the exchanges of views they had with the Russian Narodniks in the 1870s and 1880s. The Narodniks, we know, saw Russia's basic revolutionary force in the peasantry—no industrial working class existed as yet in their country. They hoped that by preserving the *obshchina*, the rural commune, the Russia of the *muzhiks* could find her own way to socialism and avoid capitalist

---

[17] *The Prophet Outcast*, p. 520.

development. Marx and Engels did not dismiss these hopes as groundless. On the contrary, in a well known letter addressed, in 1877, to *Otechestvennye Zapiski* Marx declared that Russia had 'the finest chance [to escape capitalism] ever offered by history to any nation'; and that even as a pre-industrial agrarian society she could start moving towards socialism. For this, as he saw it, one condition was necessary, namely that Western Europe should make its socialist revolution before Russia had succumbed to capitalism. Russia would then be carried forward by the gravitational pull of Europe's advanced, socialist economy. Marx repeated this view some years later in an argument with Vera Zasulich, pointing out that his scheme of social development and revolution, as he had expounded it in *Das Kapital* and elsewhere, applied to Western Europe; and that Russia might well evolve in a different manner. Engels expressed himself in the same sense even after Marx's death.[18]

All this has been well known and many times discussed. What have been less clear are the implications of this argument. How did Marx view the social alignments in that hypothetical Russian revolution which he anticipated? Evidently he did not see the industrial working class as its chief driving force. The revolution could find its broad base only in the peasantry. Its leaders had to be men like the Narodniks, members of the intelligentsia, who had learned something in the Marxist school of thought, had embraced the socialist ideal, and considered themselves to be the trustees of all the oppressed classes of Russian society. The Narodniks were, of course, the classical *zamestiteli,* the arch-substitutists, who acted as the *locum tenentes* for an absent working class and a passive peasantry (the *muzhiks* did not even support them) and who championed what they considered to be the progressive interest of society at large. Yet Marx and Engels encouraged them to act as they did and trusted that their action would be fruitful for socialism, if revolution in more advanced countries transformed the whole international outlook early enough.

True, Marx's prospect failed to materialize in Russia because, as Engels pointed out much later, the Western European working classes had been 'far too slow' in making their revolution and in the meantime Russia had succumbed to capitalism. But on an incom-

[18] *Perepiska K. Marksa i F. Engelsa s russkimi politicheskimi deyatelyami,* pp. 177-9, 241-2 and *passim.*

parably larger scale, and against a changed international background, that prospect has materialized in China. It should be noted
that the Maoists were far more broadly based on the peasantry
than the Narodniks had ever been, that their socialist consciousness was far more mature—they engaged in mass action not in
individual terrorism; and that, on assuming power, they could
lean on the advanced collectivist structure of the U.S.S.R., which
even as an economic Power was rising to the second place in the
world. In proclaiming that socialism can be the work only of the
workers, Marxism did not preclude the inception of socialist revolution in backward pre-industrial nations. But even in such nations
the working class remains the chief 'agency' of socialism in the
sense that fully fledged socialism cannot be attained without industrialization, without the growth of the working class and its self-
assertion against any post-revolutionary bureaucracy, in a word,
without the real, social and political ascendancy of the 'proletariat'
in post-capitalist society.

VII

The present outlook of Maoism has crystallized in the post-revolutionary period, which has now lasted nearly fifteen years. Yet the
seizure of power was not for the Chinese communists the sharp and
decisive turn in their fortunes it had been for the Bolsheviks: even
as Partisans they had controlled considerable areas of their country;
their leaders and cadres had been half-rulers and half-outlaws before they became full rulers. On gaining national victory, the party
had to 'urbanize' itself and to cope with a wide range of new tasks.
But it was less dependent on the old bureaucracy for the business
of government than the Bolsheviks had been and therefore probably less exposed to infiltration by socially and ideologically alien
elements.

It is unfortunately impossible to be categorical or precise about
these questions, because the Maoists do not provide us with enough
information. Such is their secretiveness that we know incomparably
less of the 'inner story' of the fifteen years of their rule than we
know from official Bolshevik sources about the early periods of the
Bolshevik régime. However, a comparison between Maoism and
Bolshevism, viewed at approximately the same remove from the

moment of the revolution, a comparison between the China of 1963-64 and the Soviet Union of the early 1930s, based only on the generally established facts, brings out certain crucial similarities, differences, and contrasts which may help to illumine the picture of Maoism in the post-revolutionary era.

It is a truism that the Chinese revolution has occurred in a socio-economic environment far more backward than that in which the Russian revolution had taken place. China's industrial output had never been more than a fraction of the Russian, an infinitesimal fraction in relation to the needs of a far larger population. The predominance of the archaic rural structure of society was almost absolute. The Chinese peasantry was even more primitive than the Russian (although, unlike the latter, it had not been subjected to centuries of serfdom, a fact which may show to some advantage in its character—in the greater independence, sobriety, and industriousness of the Chinese peasants). Age-old economic, technological, and social immobility, rigid survivals of tribalism, despotic ancestral cults, immutable millenary religious practices—all these have made the task of the Chinese revolution even more difficult and have affected Maoism itself, its methods of government and ideological outlook. Bent on industrializing China, Maoism has had to initiate primitive socialist accumulation on a level far lower than that on which accumulation had proceeded in Russia. The extraordinary scarcity of all material and cultural resources has necessitated an unequal distribution of goods, the formation of privileged groups, and the rise of a new bureaucracy. National history, custom, and tradition (including the deep philosophical influences of Confucianism and Taoism) have been reflected in the patriarchal character of the Maoist government, the hieratic style of its work and propaganda among the masses, and the magic aura surrounding the leader. Like Stalinism (and partly under its influence), Maoism allows no open discussion or criticism of its high priest and hierarchy. And the fact that for two decades before its rise to power the party had existed as a military organization has favoured the perpetuation of unquestioning discipline and blind obedience in its ranks.

Yet encumbered as it is by the greater backwardness of its environment, the Chinese revolution has in some respects been more advanced than the Russian, if only because it has come after it. It has never experienced the fearful isolation that has cramped and crippled the mind and the character of Bolshevism. It has come into the world as a member of the 'socialist camp', with the U.S.S.R. as its powerful, though difficult, ally and protector; even the exposed flanks of Red China have to some extent been protected by the high tide of anti-imperialist revolt that has swept Asia. Despite American hostility, Mao's China did not have to beat off anything like the 'Crusade of fourteen nations' that the Russia of Lenin and Trotsky had to repulse. In embarking upon primitive socialist accumulation China was not wholly reduced to her own meagre resources: Russian assistance, limited though it was, helped her in priming the pump of industrialization. More important than the material aid was the Russian experience from which the Maoists could learn: China did not have to pay the terrible price for pioneering in socialization and economic planning Russia had had to pay. Her industrialization, despite the partial failure of the Great Leap, has proceeded more smoothly than Russia's did in the early stages. And, despite a long sequence of natural calamities and bad harvests, Red China has not known any of the terrible famines that the Soviet Union suffered in 1922 and 1930-32, when millions of people starved to death.

Altogether, the social tensions have not been even remotely as acute and dangerous in China as they had been in the Soviet Union. Nor has the post-revolutionary conflict between the rulers and the ruled been as severe and tragic. Maoism in power has enjoyed the peasants' confidence to a degree which Bolshevism has never attained. The Chinese have been far less reckless and brutal in collectivizing farming; and for a long time far more successful. Even the rural communes do not seem to have antagonized the peasants as disastrously as Stalin's collectivization did.

The fact that the Chinese peasantry has not been driven into a mortal enmity towards the régime has influenced the behaviour of all other social classes, of the workers who, recruited from the peasantry, are bound to reflect its moods; and of that section of the intelligentsia which has its roots in the country. Nor has the Chinese bourgeoisie been as hostile and aggressive towards the new régime as the Russian bourgeoisie, feeling the peasantry's backing, was in its time; and Mao's government has treated the bourgeoisie more prudently than Lenin's government did; wherever possible it has preferred to buy off the entrepreneurs and merchants rather than expropriate them.

Yet another vital difference in the starting points of the two revolutions has decisively contributed to making the social climate in China milder than in the Soviet Union. In Russia the civil war was waged *after* the revolution, whereas in China it had been fought *before* the revolution. The question whether communists enter the civil war as a ruling party or as a party of opposition is of the greatest consequence for their subsequent relationship with all classes of society. If, like the Bolsheviks, they have to fight as a ruling party, they bear in the eyes of the people the odium of the devastation, suffering, and misery caused by civil war—as a rule the people's despair and fury at the conditions of their existence turn against those in office. In 1921-22 the Bolsheviks had wielded power for four or five years, during which they could do nothing to improve the lot of the workers and peasants, or rather to prevent its disastrous worsening. 'Is this what we have made the revolution for? Is this how the Bolsheviks keep their promises?'—these were the angry questions the Russian workers and peasants asked. A gulf was already fixed between the rulers and the ruled; a gulf, which it was impossible to bridge; a gulf to which the Bolsheviks reacted with a self-defensive, panicky distrust of society and which they perpetuated and deepened thereby until there was no escape from it; a gulf which yawns ominously through the whole record of Stalinism.

In China, by contrast, the people blamed Chiang Kai-shek's government for all the devastation and misery of the civil war. The revolution came as the conclusion, not the opening of hostilities. The communists, having seized power, could at once give their undivided attention to their economic problems and use at once all available resources constructively, so that very soon the lot of the people began to improve and went on improving steadily. And so the first years of the new régime, far from producing disillusionment, were characterized by rising popular confidence. If the Bolsheviks set out to industrialize Russia after they had nearly exhausted their political credit with the masses, the Maoists were able to draw on an immense and growing credit. They had far less need to use coercion in the realization of their ambitious programme. They did not have to resort to the inhuman labour discipline Stalin had imposed on the workers; or to send punitive expeditions to the villages in order to extract grain, to deport huge masses of peasants, etc. Lenin once said that it had been easy to make the revolution in Russia, but far more difficult to build socialism; and that in other countries it would be far more difficult to overthrow the bourgeoisie, but much easier to cope with the constructive tasks of the revolution. Lenin made this prediction with an eye to Western Europe, but to some extent it has come true even in China. Although the material resources of the Chinese revolution were so much poorer than those of the Russian, its moral resources were larger; and in revolution as in war the Napoleonic rule holds good that the moral factors are to the material ones as three to one.

Maoism has therefore been far less hag-ridden with fear than Stalinism had been. As in the nation at large so within the ruling party the tensions have been less explosive and destructive. Here, paradoxically, Maoism benefits from certain advantages of backwardness, whereas Bolshevism suffered from progressiveness. The establishment of the single party system in China was not the painful and dramatic crisis it had been in Russia, for the Chinese had never had the taste of any genuine multiparty system. No Social Democratic reformism had struck roots in Chinese soil. Maoism has never had to contend with opponents as influential as those that had defied Bolshevism: there were no Chinese Mensheviks or Social Revolutionaries. And, lacking Marxist tradition, and the habits of inner party freedom, the habits of open debate and criticism, Maoism was never in the throes of a deep conflict with its own past, such as troubled the Bolshevik mind when it was being forced into the monolithic mould. Maoism had so much less to suppress both within itself and in society that it did not have to give to suppression (and self-suppression) the prodigious mental and physical energy the Soviet Communist Party had to waste on that job.

Nor has the Chinese party become the ruthless promoter of inequality and the champion of the new privileged strata that the Soviet party had become. While in China too, amid all the prevailing want and poverty, the recrudescence of inequality has been inevitable, this has *not* so far been accompanied by anything like Stalin's frantic and shameless drives against egalitarianism. This circumstance throws fresh light on the problem of inequality in post-revolutionary society. Although the 'general want and poverty' are, according to Marx, the objective causes for the recrudescence of inequality, the intensity of the process depends on subjective human factors such as the character of the ruling group, the degree

of its identification with the new privileged strata, and the vicious-
ness (or the lack of it) with which it is prepared to foster inequality.
The fact that Mao and his colleagues have spent the best part of
their lives in the midst of the poorest peasants, hiding with their
Partisans in the mountains, sleeping in the caves, fighting, marching and starving together, allowing no estrangement between officers and men, and no differences in food rations and uniforms—
this extraordinary experience of the Maoists, an experience of over
two decades, no other ruling group has gone through, may have
left its imprint on their character and in some measure shielded
them from the worst corruption of power. Characteristically, the
Chinese party insists that its brain workers and dignitaries should
periodically descend from their high offices to the factories and
farms and, for about a month every year, perform manual labour,
so as not to lose touch with the workers and peasants. Such practices, sometimes bizarre in form, cannot overcome the contradictions
between the rulers and the ruled and between brain workers and
manual labourers; but they may help to keep these contradictions
within certain limits, and they indicate that the egalitarian conscience is not dead even in the ruling group. (On the other hand,
Chinese officialdom, like the Russian, refuses to disclose just how
wide are the discrepancies between high and low wages and salaries,
which suggests that it is afraid of disclosing the real scope of the
existing inequality.)

Against these features which distinguish so favourably Maoism
from Stalinism must again and again be set the marks of its backwardness, which make for its affinity with Stalinism. The Chinese
party is strictly monolithic, far more so than the Soviet party is
now, in the post-Stalin era. Having had no proletarian background
and no Marxist, socialist-democratic traditions of its own—having
formed itself at a time when the whole Communist International
was already Stalinized—Maoism was born into the monolithic
mould and has lived, grown, and moved within it, as the snail
moves within its shell. Except for one pregnant moment (when the
Hundred Flowers were to blossom all over China), Maoism has
taken its monolithic outlook for granted. The Leader's infallibility
is at least as firmly established as it had ever been in Russia, with
this difference that for about twenty-five years no one has seriously
challenged it. The Chinese party has not so far been involved in
any convulsions as terrible as those that once shook the Russian

party. It has had its important and obscure purges, one of which resulted in the 'liquidation' of Kao Kang in 1955; but the composition of the ruling group has not significantly changed since the days of the revolution or even of the Partisan struggle. Mao has not had to contend against a Trotsky, a Bukharin, or a Zinoviev. But neither do the assemblies and conferences of the Chinese party resound with the abject recantations of defeated Opposition leaders that had poisoned Soviet political life by 1932, and were to end in the Moscow trials.

VIII

The Maoist challenge to Moscow's 'leadership' of the Communist movement is partly a result of the consolidation of the Chinese revolution—the Maoists would not have risked such a conflict with Moscow earlier; and consolidation and growth of strength and confidence are expressed in a 'shift to the left' and in the Maoist ambition to speak for all the militant elements of world communism.

Here again, a comparison with the Soviet Union of the early 1930s lights up a signal contrast. The prevalent mood in the Soviet Union at that time was one of moral-political weariness and of a reaction against the high revolutionary internationalism of the Lenin era. In the name of Socialism in One Country, the ruling group had initiated ideological 'retrenchment', and was seeking to disengage the Soviet Union from its commitment to world revolution—Stalin was already then practising the revisionism of which Mao is now accusing Khrushchev. The fact that at a comparable remove from the revolution, opportunism and national egoism ruled supreme in the Soviet party, while the Chinese party proclaims its radicalism and proletarian internationalism is of immense historic and political consequence.

We have seen how the radical Leninist streak, now submerged and now coming into the open, has run through every phase of Maoism, and in decisive moments did not allow it to yield or surrender, under Stalinist pressure, to the Kuomintang and abandon the road of revolution. It is this, the Leninist element in Maoism that is at present asserting itself more strongly than ever and that seems to be transforming the outlook of Chinese communism.

If Bolshevism after some years in power was morally declining, its enthusiasm withering and its ideas shrinking, Maoism is on the ascendant, discovers new horizons, and enlarges its ideas. The debacle of official Bolshevism was epitomized in its vehement and venomous repudiations of permanent (continuous) revolution, which was not merely Trotskyist doctrine but the principle Lenin's party had deeply and passionately held in the heroic years of the Russian revolution. Maoism, on the contrary, had long and stubbornly dwelt on the limited bourgeois character of the Chinese revolution; yet now it is solemnly proclaiming that permanent revolution is the principle by which it lives, the *raison d'être* of international communism. At the close of his career, Mao appears once again as the Trotskyist Jourdain he was at its beginning. Like Trotsky, though without the latter's deep roots in classical Marxism yet with all the resources of power at his command, Mao is calling communism to return to its source, to the irreconcilable class struggle Marx and Lenin had preached.[19]

Part of the explanation for this shift to the left lies certainly in the West's attitude towards Red China, in the continuing American blockade, in the fact that so many Western Powers have not yet recognized the Peking government and have barred it from the United Nations. It should not be forgotten that the first great wave of opportunism came over the Soviet Union in the years 1923-25, after Clemenceau's and Churchill's *cordon sanitaire* had broken down, when most Western governments established diplomatic relations with Moscow. Beneficial in so many respects, this change in the international position of the Soviet Union had its adverse side: it encouraged the ruling group to practice *Realpolitik*, to take distance from the oppressed classes and peoples of the world, and to make far-reaching concessions of principle to the 'class enemy'. China's ruling group has not so far been exposed to such temptations. On the contrary, events constantly remind it that to capitalism's unabated hostility it has one reply only—its own unflagging defiance. Moreover, the ideological retreat of the Russian party was also a reaction to the many defeats the revolution had suffered in Germany and in the rest of Europe between 1918 and

---

[19] Mao's view of class antagonisms in post-revolutionary society is also far closer to Trotsky's than to Stalin's. Recently Maoist theorists have written about what Trotsky called the Thermidorian spirit of the Soviet bureaucracy very much along the lines of his argumentation. And several decades after Trotsky, they hint at the 'danger of capitalist restoration' in the . . . U.S.S.R,

1923; whereas Maoist militancy has drawn nourishment from the upsurge of anti-imperialism in Asia, Africa, and Latin America. Here too, China is benefiting from the fact that she has not been the first country to embark upon the road of socialism. It is proving much more difficult for the capitalist world to tame or intimidate the second major revolution of the century than it was to contain, if not to 'roll back', the first.

Of course, grave dangers may be lurking behind the breach between the U.S.S.R. and China. How will Maoism react to isolation from the Soviet Union, if the isolation deepens and hardens? How will it be affected by a relative stabilization of the 'national bourgeois' régimes in most of the formerly colonial or semi-colonial countries? And if some Western Powers were to try to play China against the Soviet Union, instead of playing the latter against the former—might Peking not succumb to the temptation? The prospect would be clearer than it is if one could be sure that Maoist professions of revolutionary internationalism are not merely a response to Western provocation but that they genuinely reflect the frame of mind of the Chinese masses. But we know far too little, next to nothing, about that aspect of the problem.

The credibility and effectiveness of the Chinese call for a restoration of Leninist principles would be far greater if Maoism did not seek to rescue the myths of Stalinism from the discredit into which they have deservedly fallen. In this Maoism is acting from motives of self-defence: it has to vindicate its own record, its past commitments, and its rigidly ritualistic party canon which, like every such canon, requires that its formalistic continuity be unalterably upheld. The infallible leader could not have been in error on any of those past occasions on which he extolled the Stalinist orthodoxy. The obeisance Mao paid to the living Stalin compels him to pay obeisance to the dead as well. Maoism's affinity with Stalinism lies precisely in this need to uphold established cults and magic rituals designed to impress primitive and illiterate minds. No doubt, one day China will grow out of these crude forms of ritualistic ideology, as the U.S.S.R. is growing out of them; but that day has not yet come. Meanwhile, the conservative element in Maoism, its backwardness, is at loggerheads with its dynamic element, especially with its revolutionary internationalism. In a similar way, elements of backwardness and advance, differently assorted, have been in constant collision within the Soviet party after Stalin. The prospects would be infinitely more hopeful if it were possible for the diverse progressive urges in the two great Communist parties to release themselves from the grip of retrograde factors, and to coalesce—if the Chinese fervour for Leninist internationalism went hand-in-hand with a zeal for a genuine and consistent de-Stalinization of the Communist movement. The impossibility of disentangling progress from backwardness is the price that not only Russia and China but mankind as a whole is paying for the confinement of the revolution to the underdeveloped countries. But this is the way history has turned; and now nothing can force its pace.

THE FAILURE OF
KHRUSHCHEVISM[1]

I

THE decade in the course of which N. S. Khrushchev stood at the head of the Soviet Communist Party and of the U.S.S.R. was an interregnum and a provisorium.[2] One cannot speak of a 'Khrushchev era' as one speaks of the Stalin era, not merely because Khrushchev was in office only one-third of the time Stalin had been, and exercised not even one-third of the power.[3] Khrushchevism has not represented any great positive idea (or even policy) of its own. It did not even stand for a new canon or myth which might meaningfully express, as 'Socialism in One Country' did, the 'false consciousness' of a real historic situation. Khrushchevism was devoid of any creative aspiration; whenever Khrushchev himself voiced any of the familiar and elementary purposes of socialism, he invariably produced a vulgar parody (a 'goulash communism'). In many respects he continued along lines long set by Stalin, but pretended that he was putting forward his own, breathtaking innovations. 'Peaceful coexistence' is a case in point. So is the slogan of a 'peaceful transition from capitalism to socialism'. So are the 'national roads to socialism'. These are all refurbished Stalinist concepts dating back to the Popular Fronts of the middle 'thirties and the National Coalitions of the middle 'forties. And Khrushchev

[1] Written for *Socialist Register* and *Les Temps Modernes* in 1965.

[2] Khrushchev was First Secretary of the Central Committee of the C.P.S.U. from September 1953 and Prime Minister of the U.S.S.R. from March 1958. He 'resigned' from both posts in October 1964.

[3] This difference alone might not matter. Lenin's 'term of office' was only half of Khrushchev's; yet the five or six years during which Lenin led the Bolshevik Revolution were one of history's greatest formative epochs, far more important in its impact on mankind than had been the previous five decades or even five centuries of Russia's existence.

I

was an epigone of Stalin above all in his emphasis on the 'mono-lithic character' of the Soviet party and state. His determination to tolerate no opposition, no open criticism, no free debate, inevitably led to the 'cult' of his own 'personality', that is, to attempts at establishing his own autocratic rule.

Yet Khrushchev, the epigone of Stalinism, was almost completely overshadowed by the popular image of the champion and hero of de-Stalinization. Such was the paradox of his career that, despite his stake in Stalinism and his large share in its misdeeds, he had to assume an even larger share in its destruction. He was torn between his attachment to Stalinism and his revulsion against it, and, on personal grounds, between his adoration for Stalin and his burning memories of unbearable humiliation suffered at Stalin's hands. In this he was representative of a whole generation of party leaders on whose backs Stalin had risen to power and who then had to endure the master's kicks and cruel whims. Helpless in Stalin's lifetime, they revenged themselves on the ghost. However, they were in a position to satisfy their emotional urge for revenge only because broader political interests—the needs of the nation at large —called for de-Stalinization.

But was Khrushchev really the initiator and champion of the progressive reforms of the post-Stalin decade? Historians who will one day relate the 'inner story' of the campaign of de-Stalinization will probably represent other members of the Presidium, especially Mikoyan and Malenkov, as the moving spirits. In any case, up to the time of the 20th Party Congress, i.e. till February 1956, Khrushchev either sided with Molotov and Kaganovich, the Stalin-ist 'die-hards', or hesitated and sat on the fence. In the meantime de-Stalinization, necessitated by economic and social needs, had gone so far that it was impossible to halt it; indeed, it was necessary to carry it much further. The slave labour camps had been dis-banded even before the 20th Congress. The surviving victims of the terror and the Great Purges had been released and were claiming full rehabilitation for themselves and their dead comrades and relatives. Their cry broke into the debates of the 20th Con-gress. For any Soviet leader it was suicidal folly to ignore it or resist it, as Molotov and Kaganovich were presently to find out; the Stalinist terror had already been exposed and had been con-demned by a new national consciousness. Fairly late in the day Khrushchev yielded to the prevalent mood and let himself be swayed by it. His 'secret speech' was the surprise of his life, even to himself. Through it he became the medium of a tremendous popular emotion, the mouthpiece of a national sense of grief and shame; and so he surpassed himself and the scope of his own personality. The more reluctantly and belatedly he had assumed his new role, the more abrupt and explosive was his performance. He concealed his embarrassment and inner misgivings behind his over-emphatic gestures and his strident denunciation of Stalin. And ever since the 20th Congress his activity was marked by this contrast between the melodrama of his anti-Stalinism and his anxiety to keep progressive reform within narrow limits.

A large section of Soviet opinion was well aware of the ambiguity of Khrushchev's political character, and of the motives that had induced him to give his blessing to the party's break with Stalinism. This blessing, largely platonic, was becoming a curse in disguise, for it was concealing a stubborn and cunning obstruction to any genuine socialist democratization of the U.S.S.R. (Incidentally, the image of Khrushchev the champion of de-Stalinization was in recent years far more widely accepted in the West and in some East European countries, especially Poland, than it was in the U.S.S.R.) Consequently, at the moment of Khrushchev's fall Soviet opinion was quite confident that this event far from impeding further progress would facilitate it.

The 1964 'crisis of leadership' was an event unprecedented in Russian history. Never before had a Russian ruler been stripped of power in this way, while holding all supreme offices in the State. For this to be possible, the old inertia of autocratic rule had to be broken. The crisis was resolved by a combination of a palace revolt and a quasi-democratic vote at the Central Committee. Neither the revolt nor the vote would have gone as smoothly as they did if only a few 'power-hungry men' had joined hands to oust Khrushchev. For the action to succeed the main body of the ruling group had to turn against the Leader. The several hundred members of the Central Committee would not have agreed to the deposition of the man who had for eleven years been their First Secretary unless they, their friends, and their associates had become convinced that this was justified and necessary on grounds of policy. True, Khrushchev had antagonized the Central Committee by posturing as the single leader; and so he provoked it to assert its claim to collective leadership. All the same, his quasi-autocratic ambition was, by Moscow's standards, rather mild; and the fact that it should have aroused so determined a reaction is itself remarkable. Any bureaucratic oligarchy or caste, so the 'political scientists' have told us, prefers one-man-rule to government by committee and invariably replaces any collective leadership by the single leader. This, we have been told, is the 'iron law' governing every struggle for succession at the top of the Soviet hierarchy. What then has, in this case, undone the 'law'? Why did the Soviet ruling group unequivocally refuse to reconcile itself to Khrushchev's one-man-rule?

II

Looking back upon the post-Stalin era, one can see that it falls into two distinct chapters; the first, covering the period from 1953 till 1959, was crowded with intense reformist activity and was alive with de-Stalinization; the second, extending over the remaining years of Khrushchev's government, was on the whole characterized by stagnation and even retrogression. The two chapters may overlap; yet their contrast is real and sharp.

It was during the first period that the terror and the arbitrary power of the political police was broken and the mammoth concentration camps were disbanded; that the old draconic labour code was abolished in industry and the extreme inequalities prevailing hitherto were mitigated; that the *kolkhoz* peasantry were offered a New Deal; that the overcentralization of the economy was relaxed; and that official control of intellectual and artistic life relented. Soviet citizens began to breathe more freely than they had been allowed to in a quarter of a century; and the effect was seen in rising curves of economic, social and cultural activity and achievement. Most of the many-sided progress the Soviet Union accomplished in the post-Stalin era was accomplished in those first years. It was then, between 1953 and 1958, that Soviet agriculture, overcoming a depression lasting several decades, raised its output by over fifty per cent. Although the gain was insecure—much of it had been obtained through extensive farming on virgin lands— it nevertheless provided the basis for an appreciable rise in the national standard of living.[4] For the first time the Soviet Union appeared to cope successfully with the perilous disproportion between its huge and ever-expanding industry and its narrow and shaky agricultural base. The *élan* of the industrial expansion was extremely powerful; it provided the impulse for the triumphant flights of the first Sputniks.[5] There was a new spirit abroad among workers, managers, and administrators, and a new confidence in the future.

This forward trend was reversed or slowed down in the latter part of Khrushchev's term of office. The decisive setback occurred in agriculture, the weakest sector of the economy. This was by no means only a matter of the natural calamities and the disastrous harvest of 1963. The slump had occurred much earlier and was followed by a protracted depression: of the five harvests reaped in the years 1959-63, four were bad or mediocre, only one was average. What the natural calamities of 1963 did was to reveal with exceptional force the weakness of the agricultural structure. Exposed also was the incompetence of the administration, which was unable to distribute meagre food resources adequately. The cities and towns experienced a scarcity of food such as they had not known since the grim aftermath of the Second World War; and some sections of the population appear to have been hit worse than the Chinese people were by three years of floods, droughts, and poor crops. The rise in the popular standard of living came to a halt, even though production of industrial consumer goods continued to expand.

In the last six years of the Khrushchev régime the average wages of Soviet workers rose only by 2·4 per cent. per annum, according to what A. N. Kosygin told the Supreme Soviet in December 1964.

[4] The following table shows the physical volume of all retail trade, which is a good index of the volume of consumption (1940 = 100):

Year	All goods	Foodstuffs	Other goods
1940	100	100	100
1950	110	94	140
1955	208	177	263
1956	226	190	289
1957	258	214	336
1958	274	225	359
1959	296	241	390

The index of retail trade per head of population rose from 100 in 1950 to 208 in 1957.

[5] These technological feats had, of course, been partly prepared by the intensive research and investment of the Stalin era.

Because of a partial inflation—official prices of meat and milk had been increased by 25 to 30 per cent.—real wages were reduced or remained unchanged. An undeclared wage freeze had actually been in force since 1959 or 1960 (and the world was to learn about it only by the end of 1964 from a brief aside in an exposé of the new Soviet Prime Minister). The realization of legislative measures providing for a further shortening of working hours in industry and for the rise of low incomes and old-age pensions was postponed. Even the housing programme, never yet planned to match the people's real needs, was curtailed. The general rhythm of economic activity slackened. Net national income rose in 1964 only by 5 per cent. compared with a 7 or 8 per cent. rate of growth in previous years (and an 8 per cent. rate planned again for the year 1965). The rate of growth in the construction and equipment of factories amounted to only 3.3 per cent. in 1964—it was planned at 8.2 for 1965. The scale of industrial development was still impressive: the steel industry, for instance, with its 85 million tons of annual output, almost caught up with the American level of the early 1960s. But the growth was once again, as it had been in the Stalin era, uneven and lopsided, relatively smooth in old-type heavy industry and armament, but slow and jerky in new industries (e.g. in synthetic fibres and electronics). Quantity of production was not matched by quality; and so State trading organizations reported huge unsaleable surpluses of durable consumer goods of inferior make. These surpluses were valued at 2 billion roubles, a sum amounting to about one-third of annual capital investment in light industry. Behind this mass of unsold goods there looms the reality of an immense consumer strike, a development which, though unthinkable in the years of acute scarcity of consumer goods, indicates how rigidly backward and inadaptable Soviet light industries have been. The social disproportions that were characteristic of Stalinism have reappeared on a higher level of development, together with new elements of disequilibrium.

Why did the reformist impulse, so powerful in the first half of the Khrushchev decade, exhaust itself in the second half? In part the predicament was (and is) inherent in objective circumstances, especially in the burden of the unending, nuclear and conventional, arms race. It is not known just how large is the actual Soviet armament expenditure, as distinct from the nominal defence budget.

But it seems that of the sum total of the net national income (which amounted to 175 billion roubles in 1964 and was planned to reach 189 billion in 1965) only 55 per cent. or so is allocated to private consumption, social services and education.[6] The rest is distributed, in unknown proportions, between the national accumulation fund and armament expenditure. Of all new, strictly industrial investment, about 15 per cent., at the most, is allocated to consumer industries; new investment in farming is approximately of the same order. It is enough to state these proportions to realize the magnitude of the problem. A nation spending continuously nearly half its income on new investment and defence is bound to suffer from severe strains and stresses in its economy and its social organism. True enough, the national income has more than doubled in the post-Stalin era; and the volume of civilian consumption, even if it represents an unchanging proportion of the income, has grown accordingly. But, as we have seen, the major part of that growth occurred before the year 1960. The subsequent slowdown has had its moral-political consequences. As long as the poverty and destitution of the Stalin era were fresh memories, even a slight rationalization of economic policy and modest concessions to consumer interests were enough to evoke contentment and boost morale. But with the rise in the general level of the national economy the level of social needs and expectations has risen accordingly; and, as many needs and expectations remained unsatisfied, there was bound to be much frustration and discontent.

These difficulties were (and are) dangerously aggravated by the arbitrariness, the muddle, and the corruption of officialdom. Of this the Soviet Press brings countless grotesque and shocking illustrations, reminiscent of pages of Gogol's Dead Souls. The stupidity and wastefulness of its own administration cost the Soviet Union no less than do some of the most expensive armament drives—they 'freeze' immense resources and energies. Genuine social control over the bureaucratic Establishment is therefore the precondition of any thorough-going rationalization of the economy. Yet the bureaucracy has stubbornly resisted control; and in his last year Khrushchev personified that resistance. His arbitrary decisions—his 'pro-

---

[6] I have made this calculation on the basis of official statistics, using the Soviet definitions of the national income and its components. In view of the vagueness of some of the official data, a margin of error in the calculation cannot be ruled out; but this is not likely to affect significantly the broad proportions between consumption, investment and armament expenditure.

jectomania' denounced by his successors—had much to do with the disarray in agriculture. He wilfully promoted extensive farming on immense areas of virgin land in preference to intensive cultivation; and in doing so he disregarded opposition within the party, expert advice, and warnings about the danger of soil erosion and of crop failures on the virgin lands. He was so confident that he had *the* answer to the chronic shortage of meat—maize—that he forced cultivation of maize all over the country, regardless of soil and climate. He prescribed the modes of grass cultivation to be adopted throughout the length and breadth of the Soviet Union. By his decision the small plots of land the collective farmers owned and cultivated privately were reduced or confiscated in recent years. (This decision affected many millions of farmers; yet it remained a 'secret' while Khrushchev was in office and only his successors disclosed it.) He feverishly manipulated the machinery of the administration, overhauling it time and again. These reorganizations were his substitute for genuine reform: he was like the orchestra conductor of the Russian proverb who continually re-seats his musicians in order to improve the music. As a rule the reorganizations changed the modes in which control over the bureaucracy was to be exercised from above; they hardly ever created any opening for control from below. Without satisfying the mass of the people, they irritated the bureaucracy which became weary of the all too frequent shake-ups, and turned against Khrushchev.

III

In the first years after Stalin the conflict between state and society, or between bureaucracy and people, was greatly mitigated; now it is again becoming acute. The old tension between the progressive dynamics of the U.S.S.R. and the conservatism of its ruling groups is mounting again. This was the conflict and the tension which had undermined Stalinism in the early 1950s. The new structure of Soviet society had by then become incompatible with the backward political superstructure. A method of government designed to keep in subjection a semi-barbarous and pre-industrial nation could not be imposed on a nation transformed by a quarter century of mass education, urbanization and industrialization. Nor could an ideology and a party canon, which reflected the Soviet Union's post-revolutionary isolation and moral depression, suit the Soviet Union which a generation later stood at the head of 'one-third of mankind'. Stalin's successors and ex-disciples alleviated the conflict; but they could not resolve it. They could offer only half solutions and palliatives. They lifted from the state they had inherited the insanity of the Terror and the Purges; but they failed to bring sanity into its workings. They freed the Soviet people from fear, but they were unable to inspire them with hope. They relieved them from harsh oppression, but denied them genuine freedom. They encouraged them to think for themselves, but did not allow them to express critical thought. As to Khrushchev, he began with trimming the bureaucratic Establishment and cutting its privileges. But, although he did this in order to consolidate its dominance and immunity, the Establishment clung to its privileges and pretensions, and showed little zeal for subduing even rank corruption in its midst.

The popular mood differs, of course, from what it was in 1953-54. Stalin's rule had left the mass of the people resentful yet awe-struck, despairing yet numb with helplessness, unable to endure their lot, yet unable also to change it. At the end of Khrushchev's rule there was hardly any sense of awe, and there was only little of the old numb resentment. Instead there was open discontent over the disarray in the economy, and over the suppression of criticism and opposition; and there was much irritated impatience with incompetent and incorrigible officialdom.

It is true that the bureaucracy has, since Stalin's days, greatly changed to the better. But Soviet society has changed even more. Its intrinsic progressive dynamics have been working within it and transforming it. Urbanization and industrialization have been ceaselessly altering its entire structure. The table on p. 130 shows the scope of this transformation which stands unique in history.

Within the lifetime of one generation the urban population of the U.S.S.R. has grown by nearly 100 million souls; and nearly half of this growth has occurred since the end of the Stalin era! In the early 'fifties the rural population still formed the great majority; in the early 'sixties the majority consisted already of town dwellers; at present the latter constitute about 55 per cent. of the population.

Simultaneously, the mass of industrial workers and office employees has grown from 44 million in 1953 to over 75 million in 1965, that is by over 70 per cent. (55 million or so are workers).

The Progress of Urbanization in the U.S.S.R.

Year	Total population in millions (round figures)	Urban population	Rural
1920	137	21	116
1926	147	26	121
1939	171	56	115
1950*	178	69	109
1959	209	100	109
1962	220	112	108
1964	226	118	108
1965	230	122	108

* The statistics for the years beginning with 1950 include the population of the lands incorporated by the U.S.S.R. since 1939. The figures for 1959 are those of the official census; for the following years we have only official estimates.

People employed by the state constitute about three-quarters of the entire working population. The *kolkhoz* peasantry form the remaining 25 per cent. In little over a decade the entire balance between the social classes has changed. For the first time the working class forms the majority of the nation. The peasantry is not much more numerous than is the intelligentsia, the mass of doctors, teachers, office workers, managers, scientists, officials, etc.[7] The Russia of the *muzhiks* has receded far away into the past, much further than she had moved by the early 'fifties. Not only has the peasantry shrunk in size; its moral-cultural weight has also greatly diminished. The ties which used to bind the working class and intelligentsia with the *muzhik's* way of life and way of thinking have been dissolving. With every few years passing now, that section of the urban population whose mentality is not marked by rural origin

[7] The brain workers constitute at present 22 per cent. of all gainfully employed people, only 3 or 4 per cent. fewer than the kolkhoz peasants. The growth of the 'intelligentsia' (in the broadest sense of the word) is indicated by the following data: the number of technicians and other specialists employed in the Soviet economy has risen from about 2 million people in 1940 to about 11 million in 1964-65 (40 per cent. of these have higher education and 60 per cent. have secondary schooling). There were 2.5 million teachers and educational workers before the Second World War; there are 6 million of them at present. Scientists, research workers, and employees of research institutes amount to 2.5 million, compared with less than half a million in 1940. Doctors and employees of the health services make up over 4 million, compared with 1.5 million before the war. The size of the state administration (including central economic managements) has decreased from 1.8 million in 1940 to 1.3 million in 1962.

and a culturally primitive background is growing. Ever more people are town dwellers in the second and third generation. The outlook of the cities and towns has been changing; there has been less and less of the old Slavonic sloth and listlessness; and the urban crowds have become more 'westernized', i.e. they have been acquiring individuality and modernity. Continuous educational advance has given breadth and depth to the change. In the last ten to twelve years the number of pupils in secondary schools has approximately doubled; so has the number of university students.

Khrushchevism represented quite faithfully the social balance and cultural climate of the early and middle 'fifties, when the weight of rural primitivism was much greater than it is now. Khrushchev himself belonged to the borderline between the old and the new Russia; he stood with one foot in the modern town, with the other in the archaic village. 'Despite all the progress achieved hitherto,' I argued in 1959,

there still exist vast areas of backwardness and primitivism in the Soviet Union today; and it is the strength of Khrushchevism that it is the authentic product of this mixture of progress and backwardness. There is still much of the old *muzhik* in Khrushchev himself—he is the *muzhik* who has reached the threshold of the atomic age, the last *muzhik* to speak in the name of Russia. . . . In another few years there will be hardly a trace left of the Russia of the *muzhiks*. A new working class is growing up. Already in the 1950s most of the young workers who came to the factory bench had received secondary education. They have played their part in changing the atmosphere in industry. They have behaved towards managers and party bosses with the self-assurance that comes with education. With every year the weight of these educated 'factory hands' is growing; and demands for workers' control of industry will acquire new meaning with the workers' growing ability to exercise such control . . . mass education is narrowing the gulf between manual labour and brain work. It was in the abysmal depth of that gulf that the Russian bureaucratic absolutism—and Stalinism—had been rooted; and one can foresee that the narrowing and bridging of the gulf will render obsolete and impossible even the milder, the Khrushchevite form of bureaucratic dictatorship.

Despite his great self-confidence, untameable vigour, and slapdash drive [so I concluded], Khrushchev presides over what can be only a relatively unstable and short interregnum. What lies ahead is not a Khrushchev era comparable to the Stalin era. Not only are Khrushchev's days as grass—he has risen to power in his sixties, whereas Stalin did so in his forties. Far more important is the tremendous flux in which Soviet society finds itself, and by which it is being transformed so rapidly that the passage of only a few years renders obsolete and makes untenable relations, institutions, laws and political practices, which have long seemed to be deep-rooted and almost indestructible. This flux has broken through the heavy crust of Stalinism; it will break through the much thinner and flimsier crust of Khrushchevism.[8]

Yet, despite the manifestly changed outlook of the Soviet working class and intelligentsia, despite their new cultural capacities, and despite also their evident restiveness, they have not formed so far any articulate political movement from below, any nation-wide opposition to the bureaucratic régime. There has been no lack of industrial strikes, local street demonstrations, even food riots. Clandestine opposition groups have existed in Russian universities— various 'Leninist study and propaganda circles', membership of which has been punished as high treason. An impressive number of tracts, essays, poems, and short stories, which could not pass the censorship—a whole semi-clandestine literature—is circulating from from hand to hand in Moscow, Leningrad and other cities. Yet all these reflexes of social discontent have been sporadic and scattered; they have not merged into any national expression of protest. In this one respect the situation has not decisively changed in all the years since Stalin. And even if a few poets and novelists have managed to raise dissenting voices and to find wide response, society at large is still inarticulate. The working class remains politically mute.

What accounts for this state of affairs? And what are the prospects? In the 1950s the 'crust' of Stalinism had to be broken from above, by the Stalinists themselves precisely because no movement was rising from below to change or reform the system of government. After a further decade, for the same reason, the 'crust' of Khrushchevism is being broken by the Khrushchevists themselves. No one else was able and ready to break it. The ruling groups seek once again to readjust structure and superstructure by means of Reform from Above. Yet the limits of such reform are rather narrow, much narrower than they were in the 1950s. Then Stalin's successors could shed a huge ballast of terrorism, and still leave the basis of the bureaucratic régime intact. Khrushchev's successors cannot achieve any comparable feat; they cannot once again

[8] Isaac Deutscher, *The Great Contest*, London, 1960, pp. 20-1.

appease popular discontent by concessions as startling as those of the 'fifties. The new concessions must cut deeply into the bureaucratic structure itself, which now stands exposed and stripped of safety margins. What is at stake is no longer the 'right' of a Leader and a ruling group to terrorize the nation, but the very essence of their political monopoly, their right to speak for a people which is not allowed to speak for itself. The predicaments with which the Soviet Union is contending at present call not for a new dose of patriarchal-bureaucratic 'liberalism', but for genuine liberty and a genuine advance to socialism.

The continuing disparity between the need for control from below and the apparent inability of those below to exercise control is puzzling and even alarming. At the end of the Stalin era that inability was not surprising: thirty years of totalitarian pressure had atomized the working class and the intelligentsia and reduced their political thinking to utter formlessness. During the post-Stalin decade the masses have been re-learning the habits of independent opinion-formation; but they have been re-learning much too slowly, and the ruling oligarchy has been all too successful in obstructing the process. It is not so much police persecution that has prevented any progressive Soviet opposition from crystallizing and acting on a national scale. In recent years there has probably been less persecution than there was in Tsarist Russia, when, generation after generation, rebels and revolutionaries put forward their programmes and fought for their aims openly and clandestinely. Evidently the antagonism between rulers and ruled is now different in kind, and less fundamental, for it is not a class antagonism; and it is hard for people to overcome the hiatus that decades of monolithic conformism have left in their political thinking and social initiative. Yet, in their own interest, and for the sake of socialism, they have to overcome it.

IV

The international record of Khrushchevism runs parallel to the domestic one. There too the marked progress of the early years came to a halt or was reversed later until foreign policy and the conduct of international communist affairs were left in an impasse. Since the early 'fifties significant shifts have occurred in the world's balance of power. The growing economic and military potential of the U.S.S.R., Soviet triumphs in the outer space, Sputniks, missiles, and multi-megaton-bombs contributed powerfully to the 'balance of deterrents' that now forms the basis of 'peaceful co-existence'. At the same time, however, the extreme polarization of power, which had resulted from the Second World War, has been weakened. The two super-powers no longer confront each other across the economic-military vacuum that Western Europe was in the early 1950s. The exceptionally prolonged and vigorous expansion of the capitalist economy has more than counter-balanced the growth of Soviet power. It has given the bourgeoisie a new confidence in the soundness of 'neo-capitalism'. It has immensely impressed the Western working classes, subdued their socialist aspirations, and fostered in the labour movement an ultra-opportunism compared with which the old social-democratic reformism looks almost like revolutionary extremism. Amid the recuperation of the old social system all over the West, German capitalism has achieved its second resurrection and placed itself, by sheer economic weight, at the head of Western Europe. German militarism too has risen from the ashes to reach out for nuclear weapons, to become America's potentially most powerful ally in Europe, and to become once again the terror of Europe, especially of the peoples of the U.S.S.R., Poland, and Czechoslovakia.

To prevent such a development was the declared purpose of Stalin's successors, the purpose of their new version of 'peaceful co-existence'. Yet once capitalism was preserved to the west of the Elbe, and given the circumstances of the cold war, nothing could avert this resurgence of German power. The idea, which Stalin once entertained, that the members of the 'Grand Alliance' would jointly de-industrialize and de-militarize Germany, looks now like the reactionary illusion of a very remote past. In theory Stalin's successors could either appease the U.S.A. and Germany or unyieldingly oppose them. But Soviet diplomacy lacked the courage and the consistency it needed either to resist or even to appease its enemies. It has cashed in on a few more or less platonic gains, such as the partial nuclear test ban and a mild abatement of the cold war. It has not been able to render less explosive the world's political storm centres, Berlin or South Vietnam. Indeed, twenty years after the war the powder kegs are all there in the familiar spots, threatening to blow up the world.

Amid these dangers the Soviet Union had an overriding interest in consolidating the unity of the Soviet bloc and, quite especially, in cultivating its alliance with China. This was admittedly no easy task. Stalinism had left behind a heavy burden of tensions and resentments: it had wounded, offended, and humiliated all its communist allies. The first sound impulse of post-Stalinist diplomacy was to do away with that legacy. In the middle 'fifties Moscow was compensating many communist governments for the wrongs inflicted on them: it disbanded the Joint Stock Companies through which Stalin had controlled the Chinese and the Eastern European economies; it annulled the unequal trade treaties he had imposed upon them; and it gave up other forms of 'penetration'. The Stalinist 'empire' was being transformed into a 'socialist commonwealth'. The logic of de-Stalinization led Khrushchev, Malenkov, and Bulganin to pronounce the rehabilitation of Tito, Rajk, Gomulka, and other 'traitors' and 'spies'. The Soviet government could not impose abroad the rigid despotism it could not or would not maintain at home. True, the desecration of Stalin brought in its wake the Berlin rising of 1953, the Hungarian insurrection of 1956, and moral sickness among communists everywhere. All the same, the advantages of de-Stalinization outweighed the disadvantages. The hopes and expectations to which the new course gave rise were stronger than the disillusionment.

And (strange though this may seem in the light of the new-fangled legend about Mao's unswerving fidelity to Stalinism) the heyday of de-Stalinization in the U.S.S.R. was also the heyday of Sino-Soviet solidarity and co-operation. It was between the years 1954 and 1958 that Soviet economic and cultural aid to China reached its culmination, enabling China to make a much more powerful start in industrialization than she would have been able to make had she relied only on her own resources; it enabled China to tackle primitive socialist accumulation in a far less painful manner than the U.S.S.R. had to tackle it in the 1930s. Even if the U.S.S.R. had to make certain 'sacrifices' in order to assist China, these were amply compensated by the strength accrued to the entire Soviet bloc. An inspiring long-term prospect was opening up before the Soviet Union, China, and all their allies: the prospect that they would be moving towards socialism not in isolation from one another, not while each of them would be developing its own autarchical socialism in its own 'single country', but in close co-operation

on the basis of a broad and planned international division of labour.
A fresh wind of internationalism was dispelling the stifling air of
distrust, fear and national egoism that had hung over Stalin's
'empire'.

These hopes were nipped by the aftermath of the Hungarian civil
war and the Russo-Chinese conflict. The trend towards international
integration was reversed. This is not the place to survey in detail the
vicissitudes and 'ideological' accompaniments of this development.
Overshadowing them all there is one act of Khrushchev's policy, the
full import of which was not clear until recently: his recall from
China, in July 1960, of all Soviet engineers and technicians engaged
in developing China's industry.[9] This was the most outrageous and
bizarre excess of Great Russian arrogance and brutality that Moscow had ever allowed itself. It is quite immaterial whether the
Chinese, as Khrushchev claims, had provoked the recall by disre-
garding the advice of the specialists and insulting their superiors in
Moscow. No such provocation could justify the indiscriminate,
wholesale and savage retaliation. At a stroke a vast number of industrial constructions was brought to a standstill, because the Soviet
technicians had been ordered to deprive the Chinese of all Soviet
construction plans, blueprints and patents. The Chinese had heavily
invested in the factories and plants under construction; the invest-
ments were frozen; masses of half-installed machinery and un-
finished buildings were left to rust and rot. For a poverty-stricken
nation, only beginning to equip itself industrially, this was a crip-
pling blow. Its effects were as cruel as might have been the impact
of full-scale armed intervention. For about five years China's industrialization was interrupted; it was slowed down for a much longer
period. Millions of workers were suddenly condemned to idleness
and privation and had to trek back to the villages. The blow was
even more devastating because it coincided with widespread floods,
droughts and bad harvest.

Such a shock is bound to have traumatic consequences. The
Chinese felt that they had been betrayed. Mao told them that they
must never again rely on any foreign assistance; that as far as the
Russians and their 'revisionist' friends were concerned, proletarian
internationalism was an empty phrase. This reaction has in some
ways been comparable to the sense of betrayal and isolation to

[9] I must admit that when I wrote my essay on Maoism for *The Social Register*
1964 I was not fully aware of the scope and consequences of this event.

which the Bolsheviks had succumbed in the formative years of Stalinism. The Maoists too have sometimes seemed to respond to their isolation with an ideology of isolationism, with their own version of 'Socialism in a Single Country'. However, they contradict themselves and also speak emphatically as internationalists. They know that against Moscow's Great Russian arrogance they must appeal to the international conscience of communism; and that they can strengthen their positions in the world only through their solidarity with the rising peoples of Asia, Africa and Latin America. But there is no denying the painful tug-of-war between the conflicting ideological elements in Maoism, a tug-of-war of which it is still impossible to predict the outcome. Even if the record of Khrushchev's foreign policy consisted of the most striking successes (which is by no means the case), this one Herostratus-like deed of his would be enough to ruin it for ever.

The Russo-Chinese conflict has imparted fresh impetus to all the centrifugal forces, open and latent, that had been at work in the Soviet bloc and in international communism. The Maoists blame for this Khrushchev's de-Stalinization, saying that it robbed the socialist camp of the moral authority that was its unifying element. In truth, de-Stalinization could only help to release the centrifugal forces; it did not bring them into existence. Stalinism had taken care of that. It cannot be repeated too often that by its bureaucratic effrontery, which offended every nation, great and small, within the Soviet orbit, Stalinism was preparing a terrible explosion of nationalist emotions. And just as, after 1953, the tensions pent up within the Soviet Union could not be contained any longer, so the strains and stresses within the 'socialist camp' could not be repressed any further. They had to find an outlet. It was necessary that the accumulated national grievances and resentments should be openly voiced in order that they should be remedied or removed. And it was even more necessary that whoever now ruled Moscow should be free, and should be seen to be free, from any taint of Great Russian chauvinism and brutality. Only then could the U.S.S.R. gain, or re-gain, the confidence of other peoples; and only then could the released centrifugal forces, instead of acting disruptively, contribute to a new balance and cohesion of the Soviet bloc. Not less but more de-Stalinization, i.e. another kind of de-Stalinization, was needed in order that the U.S.S.R. and its allies should be able to cope with so difficult a historic transition. Khrushchevism allowed the griev-

K

ances to come into the open, but then it incensed them instead of calming them. It released powerful centrifugal forces, but then it stirred them to the highest pitch of disruptiveness. That is why the stroke against China was followed by the new crop of nationalist discords in Eastern Europe and the disintegration of 'international communism'.

V

The key to most problems, foreign and domestic, which confront the U.S.S.R. lies in the relationship between the ruling group and the working masses. With Khrushchev's overthrow the system under which the single leader tyrannized the bureaucracy while the latter terrorized the working classes has been shattered for a second time. The ruling group did not allow Khrushchev to establish himself on its back—it shook him off before he managed to saddle and bridle it. This was for the bureaucracy something like an act of political self-determination, through which it proclaimed that henceforth its collective interest and ambition must prevail. Under Stalin the bureaucracy was only a pretorian guard, devoid of a political identity of its own. Now the pretorian guard has become a ruling stratum, jealous of its prerogatives and conscious of its rôle, ready to delegate power to its leaders but unwilling to abdicate to them.

The Soviet ruling group has established its 'internal democracy' for its own exclusive use. It is careful not to extend democratic rights to workers and peasants, to the lower ranks of the bureaucracy and to the intelligentsia. The contradictoriness of such an attitude is obvious. The ruling group has owed its own 'emancipation' from the despotism of a single leader to the nation's new cultural level and self-confidence and to its need for a more modern and rational system of government. But these factors, having rendered well-nigh impossible the re-establishment of any personal rule, militate also against the rule of an oligarchy. Having outgrown the despotic paternalism of the Dictator, the working masses cannot reconcile themselves to any 'collective' form of a bureaucratic tutelage either. Even if they are unable to struggle against it openly and on a national scale, they are obstructing it silently and are finding innumerable ways to render it less and less effective.

The scattered and inarticulate yet pervasive pressure from below is the determining factor in Soviet politics. The hierarchy has, willy-nilly, to share its newly won freedom with others and to demonstrate that it no longer treats the state and the national economy as if these were its own private domains. Khrushchev in the new party programme proclaimed that the U.S.S.R. was no longer ruled by a proletarian dictatorship, because the Soviet state now 'belonged to the entire people'. The Maoist retorted that by 'liquidating' the proletarian dictatorship, Khrushchevism had abandoned the Marxist teaching on the state and brought to light the 'bourgeois degeneration' of the Soviet ruling group and even the danger of a capitalist restoration in the U.S.S.R. But here the Maoists have confused appearances with realities. From a theoretical Marxist viewpoint the idea of the Soviet state 'belonging to the entire people' is, of course, as incongruous as was the Lassallean concept of the *Volkstaat,* which Marx had demolished in his *Critique of the Gotha Programme.* In Marx's scheme of things the proletarian dictatorship was to 'wither away' and usher in a classless and stateless society. But the Khrushchevite 'thesis' (just as some of the canons of Maoism) has little to do with Marxist theory. It was (and is) important for what it was meant to convey and to suggest, rather than for its so-called theoretical content. It was addressed to a people in whose minds proletarian dictatorship and Stalinism had become one; and to them the slogan about the end of proletarian dictatorship was a pledge and a promissory note—a pledge that there would be no return to Stalinist methods of government and a promise of an extension of civil liberties for which the people had been yearning.

We have said that uncontrolled government (apart from the burden of armament) is the greatest single obstacle to the balanced growth of the Soviet economy and to a healthier development of society. No new overhauls of the administration and no new devices and artifices of planning can serve as substitutes for free criticism and social control. Civil liberties are for the U.S.S.R. today less than ever a matter of pure politics—they are indispensable elements of the rational planning and management of a modern and publicly owned economy. As long as the workers are not free to make and express their own choices, either as producers or as consumers, the economy is estranged from its own human elements, a prey to bureaucratic fantasies and corruption. Khrushchev dodged this problem; but the various projects, advertised since his downfall, like the so-called Lieberman scheme, also fail to come to grips with the issue. They propose novel methods of accountancy, changed amortization rates on fixed capital, the adjustment of the supply of consumer goods to demand, and other administrative rearrangements. Whatever the merits and de-merits of those proposals, they cannot add to overall national efficiency even a fraction of what would be contributed to it by the producers' feeling that the bureaucracy has ceased to be the sole master of the economy. Such a feeling would release immense creative energies. It would amount to something like a second nationalization of industry, the genuine nationalization as distinct from the formal one prevailing hitherto. Only when the state which controls the economy is itself controlled by the society does socialism begin to function. The incapacity of the Khrushchev régime to remedy the faults and disproportions of the economic structure reflected the continuing deep cleavage between state and society.

Irresponsible government has also been the greatest single source of the disarray in Soviet foreign affairs and of the disastrous exacerbation of the conflict with China. Clearly, it is not the political differentiation and the division of the Communist Parties into Right, Left, and Centre that should be blamed for this state of affairs. On the contrary, this division, resulting from the dissolution of the ideological monolith, is potentially a most progressive development. The emergence of various schools of thought reflects real contradictions inherent in a living historical process and real dilemmas confronting a living movement. The tragedy consists in what the various 'communist' bureaucracies—the Soviet one in the first instance, but the Chinese also—have done and are doing first to suppress the divisions, then to magnify them beyond all measure, and to distort them. As the interests of the bureaucracies are national by definition, and as their thinking moves always within the confines of their 'own' nation-state, they have perverted and falsified the clash of opposed viewpoints, and its essentially international dialectics, into a collision of nationalist ambitions and emotions. Thus a controversy, which at the outset centred on the validity or obsolescence of Lenin's view of imperialism and on the strategy and tactics of communism under the menace of nuclear war, has degenerated into a feud over territorial claims and frontiers and into vulgar displays of nationalist pride and prejudice worthy of old-fashioned racialists and imperialists. Even if Moscow and Peking recover soberness and stop these excesses (as Moscow and Belgrade have stopped their mud-slinging), the release of so much stupid and downright reactionary propaganda is bound to leave behind a huge trail of demoralization.

But would the Russo-Chinese controversy have ever assumed such grotesque forms if in Moscow and Peking the leaders had to account for what they were doing to a Congress of Soviets or to another representative body? If Russian communists could say publicly, without fear or favour, that they were in sympathy with Mao's, or anyone else's, views rather than with Khrushchev's? And if, similarly, the Chinese were free to reject as false the revelations of their Divine Oracle?

To pose the question is almost to answer it. There is no need to idealize the state of mind of the masses. Nearly half a century after the October revolution some Soviet workers, peasants and intellectuals are still infected with virulent chauvinism, even with racialism; and the same is no doubt true in other countries of the Soviet bloc. Whether under Stalin or under Khrushchev, the ruling groups have, for their own purposes, all too readily condoned or fanned nationalist prejudices and emotions; and then, having warped the minds of the masses, they have felt that they have to pander to their hatreds and suspicions. Such is the interplay, familiar also from western social-democratic experience, between the reactionary inclinations of the leaders and the reactionary emotions of the led. Yet, as Lenin often underlined, there is a difference between the ignorant and bewildered chauvinism of ordinary workers and peasants, and the sly, calculating and incurable national arrogance of the rulers (just as there is an even deeper difference between the nationalist feelings of the oppressed and those of the oppressors). Deep down in the people, and in the intelligentsia, there are at least two large currents of thought, one tending towards internationalism, the other towards nationalism. Indeed, at every level of Soviet society these two trends have been struggling with one another. An open confrontation between them would almost certainly weaken the reactionary elements and enhance the progressive ones. Social control over bureaucracy would at the very least make it much more difficult for the latter to pursue its nationalist intrigues and power political games directed against other 'workers' states'. It is difficult to imagine that a duly informed Soviet public opinion would ever have approved as unscrupulous an attack on China's vital interests as the recall of the Soviet specialists. Not for nothing did Khrushchev—Stalin's true disciple in this—conceal this move from the Soviet people and the world in the course of nearly four years, until the Chinese themselves began to expose the immensity of the outrage.

An end to secrecy, open debate, and public criticism of those in office are essential for the U.S.S.R. and for all its allies, if they are to get out of the slough in which Khrushchevism has left them.

Unfortunately, Khrushchev's successors still belong, as he did, to the breed of leaders that had been formed under Stalinism, even though they have been reformed in the post-Stalin era. Leaders of a different kind can come only from a younger and more civilized generation; but they have not yet had the time and the opportunity to step forward. Meanwhile, Khrushchev's successors have committed themselves explicitly to continue the work of de-Stalinization and implicitly to do away with the 'Khrushchev cult'. It is in their own interests that they should honour this pledge; but as they also have their stakes in both Stalinism and Khrushchevism, their behaviour is likely to be compounded of ambiguities.

How these ambiguities have been piling up! Stalin employed barbarous means to drive barbarism out of Russia; Khrushchev was destroying Stalinism in a Stalinist manner; and now Brezhnev, Kosygin, and their associates are trying to deal with the confused balance of Khrushchevism in a more or less Khrushchevite fashion. Each of the successive régimes has thrown out of Russian life much of the evil it fought against; yet because of the nature of the means employed much of the evil has kept creeping back. Huge elements of the primordial Russian barbarism were still there in the U.S.S.R. at the end of the Stalin epoch; a large residuum of Stalinism remained embedded in Khrushchevism even after Stalin's mummy had been ejected from the Mausoleum; and now, after Khrushchev's exit, the Soviet scene remains cluttered up with the debris of Khrushchevism. However, history has not been moving in a vicious circle. What has remained of the old barbarism and of Stalinism has been gradually diluted to suit the needs of national and international progress. Now the retrograde elements of Khrushchevism are perhaps being similarly reduced. And as the ambiguities follow one after another, they also parody each other: if Khrushchevism filled only an interval between two epochs, the régime of Brezhnev and Kosygin may be no more than its insipid tail-end. The opening, the unequivocal opening, of a truly new phase of the Russian—and not only Russian—revolution is long overdue.

PART TWO

TWENTY YEARS OF COLD WAR

VIETNAM IN PERSPECTIVE[1]

I

'WAS this war necessary?' is a question often asked by historians of every major armed conflict. Historians and critics of the cold war are also beginning to ask it. I am not proposing to do this. As an historian I am always conscious that it is far more difficult to understand what has actually happened and what is happening in human history, than to speculate on what might have happened; and as a Marxist I am not at all inclined to think that the cold war, global in scope and now nearly two decades old, has been merely a regrettable misunderstanding or an incident which could be deleted from our affairs, an incident caused only by someone's ill-will or imbecility.

I accept the fact that from whichever angle you look at it, the cold war has to some extent been unavoidable. It developed directly from the tensions which underlay the Grand Alliance in which the United States, Great Britain and the Soviet Union were united in the second world war. These tensions had been deeper and graver than those that can be found in any wartime coalition. But even if this had not been so, it was not to be expected that the Grand Alliance should survive its victory over Nazi Germany. The victory was too huge for the victors to digest it. The spoils were too vast; the unsettlement too frightening; and the disequilibrium of social and political power in the world too acute. Often in history, wars far milder than the world wars of our age were followed by reversals of alliances, when one power or group of powers was frightened by the new strength which their former ally or allies drew from the ruin of a common enemy. In the traditional terms of power politics and diplomacy nothing, therefore, was more natural than

[1] Notes for a speech at the National 'Teach-in' in Washington, May 1965, in which I took part at the invitation of the Inter-University Committee. (*Tribune*, May 1965)

the reversal of alliances which our generation witnessed between 1945 and 1950.

We cannot account for the origins and the course of the cold war merely in the conventional terms of power politics and diplomacy. Both technologically and ideologically history has transcended those terms. Mankind has reached the brink of the nuclear abyss and it has been torn internally as never before, divided over all the great issues of its social and moral existence. Who knows, if the dangers and risks confronting us had been less frightful, we might not have been able to celebrate the twentieth anniversary of the cease-fire in the relative peace in which we have celebrated it.

Not daring to wage a war and unable to make peace, governments and peoples of the world seemed to have resigned themselves to the prospect of an interminable cold war. Yet the danger is only too obvious that this cold war may terminate in total nuclear war, and even if it does not, it has already inflicted and it is still inflicting on mankind devastation and wounds which are all the more terrifying because they are, for the most part, hidden from our eyes.

For what is the cold war; what are its targets and what are its weapons? While still holding the threat of the physical holocaust over our heads, it delivers us immediately to the moral holocaust; it aims immediately at the destruction and mutilation not of our bodies but of our minds; its weapons are the myths and the legends of propaganda. It has often been said that in war truth is the first victim. In cold war, the truth without which men cannot lead any purposeful and fruitful existence is the main and the total victim as it has never been before. And the weapons designed to crush and reduce to ashes the human mind are as potent as any of the weapons designed for physical destruction. And in yet another decisive respect the cold war has already given us the foretaste of the fully-fledged nuclear war: its fall-out cannot be confined to enemy territory; it hits our own lands, it even hits *primarily* our own lands and our own people, it contaminates the moral texture, it destroys and warps the thinking processes of the popular masses in our countries, in all the countries engaged in waging the cold war.

How did this tragedy begin? It is a commonplace of contemporary historians that from the second world war the United States and the Soviet Union emerged as the two victorious colossi, staring at each other across a power vacuum. This suggestive image, though partly true, seems to me to offer an erroneous *a priori* interpretation of the origins of the cold war and of its course. It puts the two colossi on a plane of equality, as it were, investing each of them with the same power, the same ability to harm the other, and the same threatening looks and gestures. I propose to show briefly what each of these two colossi looked like just before their clash and during it.

There could be no doubt about the power, the vigour, the health, and the self-confidence of one of the colossi, the American. The United States had during the second world war more than doubled its wealth, its productive apparatus and its annual income. And it held the monopoly of atomic energy. It is no reflection on the bravery and ingenuity of American soldiers, airmen, and sailors, to say that this nation, the wealthiest of the world, had also the good fortune of having bought its victory at the cheapest price. Not a single bomb had fallen on American soil, and the loss of life the American armed forces had suffered was very small indeed. The American colossus, it might be said, returned from the battlefield with barely a scratch on his skin. And yet there was weakness in him as well, but it lay where he least suspected it—in his own bewilderment with his size and power, and, unfortunately also, in his complacency, self-righteousness, and arrogance.

What a different picture the Russian colossus presented! After all his battles and triumphs, he was more than half prostrate, bleeding profusely from his many wounds. The most densely populated, the wealthiest, the most civilized parts of the Soviet Union had been laid waste. At the end of the war 25 million people in those provinces had been rendered homeless and lived in dug-outs and mud huts. The list of casualties amounted to at least 20 million dead! When the first post-war population census was carried out in the U.S.S.R. in the year 1959, it showed that in all age groups older than 32 years, there were only 31 million men compared with 52 million women. Think what these figures imply. Can you imagine the dreadful shadow they cast upon every aspect of Russian life and policy? For many, many years after the war only old men, cripples, women and children could be seen on the fields of Russia tilling the land. Elderly women had to clear with their bare hands thousands upon thousands of acres of rubble from their native cities. And do you visualize what this deficit of 21 million men, what this lost Russian generation, has meant to the sexual life of the nation, to its family relationships, to its nerves and to its morale? I am speaking about this not in order to enlist here any belated sympathy with Russia's ordeal, but to demonstrate to you how misleading are some of the images and assumptions which have become customary to popular thinking in the cold war.

Yes, at the beginning of the cold war the two colossi confronted each other, but one was full-blooded, vigorous and erect, and the other prostrate and bled white. This is the incontrovertible truth of the matter. And yet shortly after the end of the war the image of the Russian colossus, of a malignant colossus, bent on world conquest and world domination, haunted the popular mind of the West and not only the popular mind. In his famous Fulton Speech of March 1946, the speech that rallied the West for the cold war, Winston Churchill declared that nobody knew 'what Soviet Russia and its communist international organization intends to do in the future, or what are the limits, if any, to their expansive and prosely-tizing tendencies'. He spoke of the growing Soviet challenge and peril to civilization, of the dark ages that may return, and he exclaimed: 'Beware, I say, time may be short. Do not let us take the course of letting events drift along until it is too late.'

A year later President Truman's Message to Congress, the text of the so-called Truman Doctrine, resounded with the same urgency in proclaiming America's duty to resist communist subversion all over the world and in particular in Eastern Europe. A year later President Truman, already preparing the North Atlantic Alliance, spoke again of the Soviet Union's 'designs to subjugate the free community of Europe' and the text of the Atlantic Alliance, signed on 4 April, 1949, provided that 'an armed attack' against any member of the Alliance 'in Europe or North America shall be considered an attack against them all'.

Thus the leaders of the West in the most solemn and formal manner warned the whole world about the reality of the military threat from Russia. This threat served as the justification for the formal reversal of the alliances and the beginning of the rearma-ment of Western Germany. Yet, if one thing was or should have been clear, it was this: Russia, with 20 million of her people killed and uncounted millions crippled, for many years to come would not be able to wage any major war. She might perhaps fight for her survival if forced, but she was certainly in no physical or moral condition to undertake any large-scale invasion of foreign countries.

Any intelligent demographic expert might have calculated the number of years—fifteen or twenty—which it would take her to fill the gaps in her manpower. Let me also add that between 1945 and 1948, demobilization in Russia proceeded at such a pace that the Soviet armed forces were reduced from nearly 11½ million men to less than 3 million. Only a year after the proclamation of the Truman doctrine did Stalin decide to re-start mobilization; then, in the course of three or four years, after N.A.T.O. had been formed, after the rearmament of Germany had begun, he raised the number of his men under arms to 5 million. More than once in history had major powers formed alliances and even opened hostilities with the help of false scares. But never before had responsible statesmen raised a scare as gigantic and as unreal as was the alarm about Russia's design for world conquest and world domination, the alarm amid which the North Atlantic Alliance came into being.

But what about Russia's Fifth Columns? The various Communist Parties subservient to Stalin? I would be the last to deny or excuse that subservience for I have exposed and opposed it for nearly thirty-five years, first as a member of the Communist Party and then as a Marxist belonging to no party. But it is one of the shoddiest myths of our time that Stalin and his minions have used the Communist Parties to promote world revolution. It is true that anti-communists as well as communists of the Stalinist persuasion have purveyed that myth. But this does not make it more credible. In truth Stalin more often than not used the subservient Communist Parties to slow down, to hamper, and even sabotage the growth of world revolution. He had emasculated them as organs of revolutionary struggle and turned them into the auxiliaries of his diplomacy. He had trained them to extol his tyranny, to praise his 1939 pact with Hitler, to justify his Teheran and Yalta bargains with Churchill and Roosevelt, and to damp down the revolutionary spirit of the Western European working classes in the aftermath of the second world war.

In the first few years after the war the French Stalinists served gladly in General de Gaulle's Governments as its junior and meek members, disarming the fighters of the communist Resistance and urging moderation on the workers. The Italian Stalinists, led by Palmiro Togliatti, did the same. It is indeed doubtful whether the bourgeois order would have survived in Western Europe, or rather whether it would have been possible to restore it in the years 1944-45 if the Communist Parties had not, under Stalin's inspiration, so willingly and zealously assisted in this. It is possible to argue that in the post-war revolutionary turmoil, Stalin did more to save Western Europe from communism than the American Administration did or could do; that he had saved France and Italy from communism even before President Truman proclaimed his doctrine. We know now in the teeth of what obstruction from Stalin the Yugoslav communists, led by Tito, accomplished revolution in their country. And we know also how cynically Stalin abandoned the embattled Greek communists to their fate when they were crushed by British armed intervention.

The key to Soviet policy lay not in any design for world conquest, but in the so-called gentlemen's agreement which Stalin concluded with Churchill in October 1944, on the division of spheres of influence in Europe. Under that agreement, later shame-facedly endorsed by Roosevelt, Russia was to exercise 90 per cent. of influence in Eastern Europe and in the Balkans, while 10 per cent. was reserved for all other powers. Britain was to exercise 90 per cent. of influence in Greece, and in Yugoslavia the division was to be fifty-fifty. To this grotesque gentlemen's agreement Stalin adhered to the letter. Having granted the British a 90 per cent. predominance in Greece, he denied the Greek communists any help and he did not utter even a murmur of protest when they were being put down by force of British arms.

But, naturally enough, he felt entitled to exercise his own preponderance in his own zone of influence in a like manner. He began to impose the Stalinist régime on Eastern Europe. Yet more cunning than Churchill and working in a different social and political medium, he did not have to send out his armoured divisions to crush popular uprisings. He obtained control over his so-called sphere of influence by means of a method which was half-conquest and half-revolution. Yet, up to the moment when the Truman Doctrine was proclaimed, and even for some time later, he still acted slowly and prudently so as to avoid offending his war-time allies. In 1947 the leaders of the anti-communist parties still sat in the governments of Eastern Europe, just as the communists did in Western Europe, in more or less subordinate positions.

It was only after the communists had been ejected from the

French and Italian Governments—and it was an open secret in Paris and Rome how much the American Ambassadors in those capitals had exerted themselves to bring this about—it was only after this that Stalin began to eject the anti-communists from the Eastern European Governments and to establish the single party system. Then in June 1947 came the challenge of the Marshall Plan under which the United States offered on certain terms its economic assistance to all nations of Europe including the U.S.S.R. This was a dangerous challenge to Stalin's government and it would probably have been dangerous to any other Soviet Government. For American economic superiority to Russia was at that time so overwhelming, that from the Soviet viewpoint the Marshall Plan represented a threat of an irresistible penetration of American capital into Russia and Eastern Europe.

Stalin not only rejected and forced all Eastern European Governments to reject Marshall Aid but, with the communist *coup* in Czechoslovakia in February 1948, he carried the Stalinization of Eastern Europe to its logical conclusion. And he finally pulled down the iron curtain over the whole of his zone of influence so as to render impossible any penetration of American or other Western influences. It goes without saying that his actions and the ruthlessness and brutality with which he clamped down a régime of terror on the whole of Eastern Europe provided in Western eyes a justification, one might say a *post factum* justification, for the Truman Doctrine and for the other measures of cold war.

In examining any international conflict it is usually an arid intellectual exercise to ask the simple question: Who had started it all? And I do not propose to dwell on this issue or to apportion the blame for unleashing the cold war. As we look back upon the scene of the late 1940s it is, I think, quite clear that two of the major assumptions underlying the Western strategy in the cold war, were unreal: the assumption of a more or less imminent military threat from Russia, and the assumption that the motive of Stalin's policy was an international revolutionary aspiration, indeed, a boundless subversive ambition.

I urge you to consider this central paradox of Stalin's rule, a paradox which has had its effect upon the cold war up till now. In his dealings with his own people Stalin was a most ruthless, unscrupulous, and bloody tyrant; in his dealings especially with the members of his own party and with communists at large, he was a

L

fraudulent and treacherous manipulator; he had no compunction in extracting from the Russian workers and peasants their sweat and their blood. His great purges, his mammoth concentration camps, and his insane G.P.U., stand in history as black monuments to his infamy. Yet this treacherous tyrant was also in his way strangely strict and almost scrupulous in his dealings with bourgeois diplomatic partners. In these dealings he adhered always to the letter of his obligations with a certain Byzantine legalistic punctiliousness. From that letter he would snatch whatever advantage he could by processes of tortuous interpretation, but he rarely if ever permitted himself an open violation of the letter. Even in Stalinizing Eastern Europe he still acted within the letter of his war-time agreements with Churchill and Roosevelt as he interpreted them.

And it may be held that he acted even within the spirit of those agreements. Had not Churchill granted him 90 per cent. of control over Eastern Europe and the Balkans? And were Churchill and Roosevelt really so innocent as not to know or guess the manner in which Stalin would exercise that 90 per cent. control? And even if they were, was this Stalin's fault or the fault of his Government? He stuck to his bargain, got the most out of it in Eastern Europe and did not allow Western European communism to raise its head in the days of its strength and influence. It is now well established that in the years 1948 and 1949 Stalin was to the last opposed to Mao Tse-tung's plans for the seizure of power by the communist armies in the whole of China (although he was not even obliged under any of his wartime diplomatic agreements to exercise a moderating influence in China).

If the purpose of Western cold war strategy was to contain communism, then the historic irony of the situation consisted in this that no one contained communism more effectively and no one could contain it more effectively than Stalin himself did.

We are confronted here with one of the great puzzles in contemporary history. When the leaders of the West spoke in those early phases of the cold war about the threat from Russia, were they themselves seeing visions and nightmares, or were they conjuring up dangers in which they themselves did not believe?

It is difficult to give a clear-cut answer to this question. In all probability our leaders and cold war strategists themselves partly believed in the dangers they conjured up. Nightmare and reality have mingled and are still mingling in Western cold war thinking. The second world war, like the first, had produced a genuine revolutionary aftermath of which our possessing and ruling classes had every reason to be afraid. But they failed to understand the phenomenon which inspired them with fear. They saw the social turmoil in which much of Europe was engulfed after the collapse of the Third Reich; they saw the dissolution of the old empires in Asia and Africa; they saw the rising of countless colonial and semi-colonial peoples; yet they could not believe, or they preferred not to believe that this revolutionary turmoil had a dynamic force of its own, that it had sprung from all past history, that it was anchored in the aspirations of the peoples themselves, and that it was not and could not be anyone's puppet creation.

The conservative mind sees in revolution, as a rule, the malignant intrigue of instigators and agitators, and never the outcome of any legitimate struggle. And so Churchill and Truman, and their associates came to suspect or half suspect that the great instigator and agitator behind the revolutionary ferment of the post-war years was none other than Stalin himself, their war-time ally. True, during the war Churchill had more than once expressed his appreciation of the essentially conservative quality of Stalin's statesmanship. 'I know of no Government,' Churchill said in the last months of the war, 'which stands to its obligation, even in its own despite, more solidly than the Russian Soviet Government. I decline absolutely to embark here on a discussion about Russian good faith.' Yet, only a year later Churchill was already denouncing Stalin in terms in which he had denounced Hitler.

In truth, Stalin's policy was ambiguous. As leader of the new privileged groups in Soviet society, of the bureaucracy and of the managerial elements, he was primarily interested in preserving the social *status quo* within the U.S.S.R. and without. This accounts for the essentially conservative character of his international policy and diplomacy. He was almost as much afraid of the revolutionary turmoil in the world as were the leaders of the West. He viewed with distrust and even with outright hostility the aspirations of the exploited and oppressed peoples, and yet as the inheritor of the Russian revolution, as Lenin's successor and as the head of the communist movement which even in its degenerated condition still professed its Marxist orthodoxy, he had to present himself as the friend and promoter of every revolutionary interest in the world.

Wherever any revolutionary movement came to the top despite his obstruction, he had to assume the posture of its inspirer and protector. This was the posture he had first assumed towards the Yugoslav revolution, this was the posture he maintained throughout towards the Chinese revolution. Moreover, his kind of revolution, revolution from above, was indeed his answer in Eastern Europe to the Truman Doctrine and the Marshall Plan. Stalin confronted the leaders of the West as a Janus-like opponent: one face conservative, the other revolutionary. And the leaders of the West reacted bitterly and resentfully, because their own political consciences were troubled. They had allied themselves with communism against Nazism and the necessities of this alliance led them to yield up Eastern Europe to Stalin. From the viewpoint of their class interest and class psychology the leaders of the American and British bourgeoisie had acted a most paradoxical and self-contradictory rôle; they had yielded ground to their class enemy; they then sought to regain that ground.

Churchill and Truman tried to wrest from Russia the zone of influence that Churchill and Roosevelt had yielded to her at Teheran and Yalta. They sought to contain Stalin's power at the frontiers of the U.S.S.R. This was the first programme of the so-called containment policy, its maximum programme of the years 1946-48. It failed at once and it failed utterly. It speeded up the disaster it was designed to prevent. It provoked Soviet power to erupt all the more violently, to cover hermetically the whole of the Soviet zone of influence and to grip remorselessly the whole of Eastern Europe.

This first and almost instantaneous defeat of the containment policy was followed by another, by a defeat incomparably more vast and more momentous, the defeat in China in 1949. Here was a gigantic demonstration of the unreality of the major assumptions of Western cold war strategy. No Russian designs against the West and no Russian subversion had brought about or could bring about the explosion of the Chinese volcano. Both Stalin and Truman had worked, each in his own different way, to contain the Chinese revolution and the volcano had exploded over the heads of both. But while Stalin quickly came to himself and not only bowed to reality but assumed the posture of the friend and protector of the revolution that had won despite him, our Western cold war strategists refused and are still refusing to face reality.

Shutting their eyes to the inherent momentum, to the innate

dynamic force of the Chinese revolution, they treated it as a result of an ignoble intrigue and as a Russian puppet. The vital lesson of the Chinese revolution was that when any great nation struggles to re-cast the very foundations of its social and political existence nothing can stop it, and that the most clever containment policy is and will ever be impotent against the genuine element of revolution. If our statesmen believe that arms and diplomacy can stop mankind in its search for new forms and for a new content of its social existence they are only reactionary utopians; they can delay the process of world-wide change, they can make it more painful and spasmodic, but they cannot halt it.

II

Let me now consider another erroneous cold war assumption. While Western strategists overlooked Russia's real weakness in the early phases of the cold war, when Russia was exhausted and bled white, they also strikingly underrated her potential strength. In the early phases, the cold war was fought on the assumption that Russia would not be able to break the American monopoly of the atomic energy for a very long time to come. In those years we were told that Russia lacked the raw materials, the uranium ore, the engineering capacity, and the know-how needed for the production of nuclear energy and for the building up of a nuclear arsenal. Later we were told that even though the Russians had managed to split the atom, they would not be able to pile up a substantial stock of atomic bombs.

Later still we were assured that though she may have a large number of atomic bombs, she would certainly not be able to manufacture H-bombs. And when this proved wrong the experts maintained that although the Russians had the warheads they did not and would not have the means of delivery that would allow them to strike at the American continent. Intercontinental ballistic missiles were supposed to be beyond the reach of Russian technology. For over twelve years, until the first Russian Sputnik broke into outer space in 1957, the cold war was waged on the assumption of an absolute and unchallengeable American superiority in all fields of technology.

How could so much wishful thinking blind Western statesmen

and experts? They sincerely believed in the unchallengeable superiority of the social system which they administered, the capitalist system, and they looked down with genuine contempt on the new economic system with the help of which Russia, in the worst of circumstances, was trying to raise herself from her age-old poverty and backwardness. They did not believe that that system could work. They dismissed all data about Russia's difficult, uneven, and yet tremendous economic and social progress as so much bluff and Red propaganda. Only with the great shock of the Sputniks and Luniks came the reluctant realization of the fact that the cold war had reached a stalemate, and that peace rested on a shaky and explosive balance of deterrents.

Yet again and again the assumption of Western and more specifically of American technological and military superiority recurs in Western strategic thinking until it is disproved by some new facts; and then it gives place to panic and fear. In fact, arrogance and panic seem to drive the policy-makers around in a vicious circle.

But let us turn back to the more political presuppositions and notions of the cold war. We have seen how unreal was the notion of a Russian colossus bent on subversion and world domination. During the greater part of the cold war, indeed until quite recently, Western strategic thinking assumed also that the Soviet colossus was a monolith, that the Soviet Union and China and all their allies and satellites formed a single bloc. We were told that Soviet power derived its malignant and threatening character precisely from this, its monolithic quality. Again, this notion had some limited basis in reality. Stalinism had pressed all its subjects into a single totalitarian mould and had imposed an absolute dogmatic, though unprincipled, uniformity upon the entire Communist movement.

As a historian I remain convinced that Stalinism would have never succeeded in that, as it did, if the Soviet Union had not been exposed to constant hostile and war-like pressures from outside. Those pressures enabled Stalin to blackmail the Soviet people (and foreign communists too) into total obedience. Without the very real threat from Hitler, without the need to counter that threat with a desperate arms race, the people of the Soviet Union would not have submitted to Stalinist terroristic exactions as meekly as they did submit in the 1930s and in the years of the war. They might have refused to accept his dictates after the war if Russia had not had to rebuild her ruins amid new and dangerous pressures from the outside.

Our cold war strategists thus helped to cement the Stalinist monolith. Yet the idea that the Stalinist monolith needed to expand, because expansion fortified and consolidated it, was completely wrong. On the contrary, as it expanded, the Stalinist monolith began to crack and to break up. Tito's 1948 revolt against Stalin foreshadowed this development. By the time of Stalin's death social changes and discontents inside Russia and dissensions between Russia and the other communist countries worked against the Stalinist monolith. An epoch of change was opening in the communist camp. A few of us here in the West, and we were very, very few indeed, saw the coming change and analysed its first symptoms. We were decried as wishful thinkers and false prophets; our cold war propagandists and our Congresses for Cultural Freedom assumed that the Stalinist monolith was immutable and that it was going to survive Stalin for a long, long time to come.

Among Western statesmen only Winston Churchill, who was again Britain's Prime Minister, kept his eyes and ears open. Shortly after Stalin's death he sought to turn the attention of the Western Governments and peoples to the 'wind of change and the new movement of feeling in Russia' and he urged his colleagues in N.A.T.O. to see whether they could not come to some terms with Stalin's successors. But Churchill, the proud prompter and inspirer of the cold war, was now disavowed by the White House and by his own Foreign Office and his insight was ridiculed. We shall never know what opportunities to halt or abate the cold war and the arms race were missed then. Suffice it to say that these were years when the Soviet Presidium was deeply divided between the faction that was determined to hold on to Berlin, and another faction favouring a Soviet withdrawal from Germany.

Those determined to hold on won the day, not without some assistance, one may assume, from Western irreconcilability. The notion of a Soviet monolith, the notion in which Stalinism itself had gloried, continued to dominate Western strategic thinking. And it did so even when the deep breach between Khrushchev's Russia and Mao's China became quite apparent to those who could read the signs. The first accounts of this breach—I myself was publishing them in the American press as early as in 1958—were dismissed by official American spokesmen as utterly groundless.

As late as 1961 official Washington was still declaring that those who talked about a Russo-China controversy were dupes of Soviet propaganda. Until the early 1960s the cold war strategy still rested on the assumption of the Russo-Chinese monolith.

When this assumption, too, at last collapsed, the cold war strategists swung abruptly to the opposite extreme and began grossly to exaggerate the extent of the Russo-Chinese controversy, and to exploit it. A new image of Russia began to make its appearance in the West, the image of an emerging bourgeois Russia which must be terrified of the growing power of China, the new dangerous colossus rising across her frontiers. All the malignant character that the cold war ideologists had for so long attributed to the Soviet Union was now transferred to China.

Peking rather than Moscow was now seen as the fount of world-wide subversion, as the threat to world peace. Of course, the Mao-ists spoke to the West in an idiom more militant and defiant than that used by the Khrushchevites. Of course, their resentment against the West, especially against the United States, was and is very sharp. And the ostracism under which the United States has kept communist China makes the resentment more and more acute. But all this does not add up to a Chinese menace to the West; and those who speak of that menace do so in order to justify the obsessive hostility towards communist China shown by all successive American Administrations. And so in the last few years Chinese communism became the chief villain; and to drive a wedge between Russia and China was gradually becoming the declared new purpose of Western strategy. There is, of course, nothing reprehensible in the attempt of any power to benefit from the internecine quarrels of its opponents: it has been the loudly proclaimed purpose of communist policy to benefit from the internal contradictions in the capitalist imperialist camp. There would be nothing inherently wicked in the American attempt to drive a wedge between Russia and China, if the wedge were not recklessly driven through the living body of the people of Vietnam and if it did not threaten the peace of Asia and, indeed, of the world. The American Administration, I suggest, is dangerously overplaying its hand in Vietnam because it underrates the necessity for Russia to maintain some solidarity with China in the face of armed American pressure on South East Asia.

Underlying the Russo-Chinese controversy over strategy, tactics, and ideology there is still the basic solidarity between the anti-capitalist régimes of the two countries. They can afford to quarrel only when the full blast of Western hostility towards the one and the other has abated somewhat. When that hostility mounts again and hits one of them, they must draw together. Last summer's American armed forays in the Bay of Tonkin caused the gravest alarm in Moscow. Two months later Khrushchev, the advocate of a Russian *rapprochement* with America, and Mao Tse-tung's chief antagonist, was overthrown. Whatever may have been the domestic reasons for that *coup*, the White House, the Pentagon, and the State Department contributed to Khrushchev's fall. Khrushchev's successors set out to mend Russia's disturbed relations with China; and although they have not healed the breach, they have stopped its continuous aggravation.

Whereas Khrushchev spoke of a Russian withdrawal from South East Asia, his successors insist on Russia's presence there. They are sending arms to Vietnam and talk of sending volunteers. Against the American intervention Peking and Moscow are speaking with almost the same voice no matter how much they actually differ. The clumsy and reckless wedge is achieving the opposite of what it was intended to achieve: instead of driving the Communist powers apart, it imposes on them a measure of unity. As at so many earlier stages, the cold war strategy defeats itself.

From what I have said, it is, I think, quite clear that all the characteristic misconceptions and delusions of the cold war are reproduced in Vietnam. Once again American policy is based on opposition to a genuine native revolutionary force. The Vietcong is backed in its struggle by an overwhelming majority of the Vietnamese peasantry, otherwise it would not have been able to hold its ground and extend its control over three-quarters of the country. No foreign power, no matter how formidable its weapons, can in the long run prevail against this kind of a revolutionary element.

The French have repeatedly found this both in Indo-China and in Algeria; and the British have found it in so many of their former colonies and dependencies. Unwilling to see this, the White House and the State Department are telling the world that the real culprit is once again a foreign communist power—North Vietnam, and, behind it, the malignant Chinese colossus. The logic of this argument requires, of course, that military blows be inflicted on North Vietnam and, at a further remove, on China. And once again provocation breeds counter-provocation. North Vietnam and China and perhaps even Russia may all be drawn into the fighting in South Vietnam.

Escalation works both ways. And the world listens with dismay to wild talk that the United States ought to use this opportunity in order to destroy the embryo of the Chinese nuclear industry. Can we take it for granted that this wild talk exercises no influence on official American policy? And that the American leaders understand that Russia cannot afford to watch passively any massive American attack on any of the vital centres of China? And that a Soviet Government that would try to remain passive might be overthrown within twenty-four hours?

In Vietnam not only American policy has reached an impasse. The whole Western cold war strategy, having for nearly two decades moved in a maze of misconceptions and miscalculations and amid the wreckage of so many illusions, now stands helplessly before the blind Vietnamese wall. It is perhaps time now to draw the balance of this long and terrible venture, to count its material, political, and moral costs, and to assess the risks. I am not setting my hopes too high. I do not see the approach of the great cease-fire that would end the cold war.

To some extent, as I have said at the beginning, this has been and is an unavoidable war. The antagonisms and the tensions between the powers cannot be suddenly conjured out of existence. The conflict between capitalism and communism, which some prefer to describe as a conflict between democracy and communism, is not nearing any solution. The hostility between colonialism or neocolonialism and the peoples of Asia, Africa, and Latin America will not soon die down. But if the stark realities of these multiple conflicts are likely to remain with us, it may yet be possible for all the forces involved to behave more rationally than they have behaved so far, to lift from these conflicts the hysteria and insanity of the cold war, the fog of myths and legends, and the suicidal intensity of the contest.

I still believe that class struggle is the motive force of history and that only a socialist world—one socialist world—can cope with the problems of modern society. But in our time class struggle has sunk into a bloody morass of power politics. On both sides of the great divide a few ruthless and half-witted oligarchies, capitalist oligarchies here, bureaucratic oligarchies there, are not only holding in their hands all the power of their nations; they have also obfuscated the minds and throttled the wills of their nations, and usurped for themselves the rôles of the chief protagonists in social and ideological conflicts. The class struggles of our time have degenerated into the unscrupulous contests of the ruling oligarchies.

Official Washington speaks for the world's freedom. Official Moscow speaks for Socialism. 'Save me from my friends!'—Freedom might say. 'Save me from my friends!'—Socialism must say. On both sides of the great divide the peoples have been silent for too long and have for too long identified themselves with their Governments and their policies. The world has come very close, dangerously close, to a division between revolutionary and counter-revolutionary nations. This to my mind has been perhaps the most alarming result of the cold war.

Fortunately things are changing in the Soviet part of the world, especially in Russia where the people have been shaking off the old discipline and the old conformism and have been regaining an independent mind and a critical attitude towards their rulers. Things are, I hope, changing here, in the United States too. I see a significant sign of the change in the determination of so many Americans to scrutinize and to argue out the assumptions of their Government's policy, assumptions which America has so long accepted without scrutiny and in virtual unanimity.

We may not be able to get away from the severe conflicts of our age and we need not get away from them. But we may perhaps lift those conflicts above the morass into which they have been forced. The divisions may once again run within nations, rather than between nations. We may give back to class struggle its old dignity. We may and we must restore meaning to the great ideas by which mankind is still living, the ideas of liberalism, democracy, and communism.

PART THREE

FROM A BIOGRAPHER'S
SKETCHBOOK

THE MORAL DILEMMAS OF LENIN[1]

LENIN often invoked the examples of Cromwell and Robespierre; and he defined the rôle of the Bolshevik as that of a 'modern Jacobin acting in close touch with the working class, as its revolutionary agent'. Yet, unlike the Jacobin and the Puritan leaders, Lenin was not a moralist. He invoked Robespierre and Cromwell as men of action and masters of revolutionary strategy, not as ideologues. He recalled that even as leaders of bourgeois revolutions Robespierre and Cromwell were in conflict with the bourgeoisie, which did not understand the needs even of bourgeois society; and that they had to arouse the lower classes, the yeomanry, the artisans, and the urban plebs. From both the Puritan and the Jacobin experience Lenin also drew the lesson that it was in the nature of a revolution to overreach itself in order to perform its historic task—revolutionaries had, as a rule, to aim at what was in their time unattainable, in order to secure what was attainable.

Yet, while the Puritans and the Jacobins were in their consciences guided by moral absolutes, Cromwell by the 'word of God', and Robespierre by a metaphysical idea of virtue, Lenin refused to attribute absolute validity to any ethical principle or law. He accepted no supra-historic morality, no categorical imperative, whether religious or secular. As did Marx, he regarded men's ethical ideas as part of their social consciousness, which often was a false consciousness, reflecting and veiling, transfiguring and glorifying certain social needs, class interests, and requirements of authority.

It was therefore in a spirit of historical relativism that Lenin approached questions of morality. Yet it would be a mistake to confuse this with moral indifference. Lenin was a man of strong principles; and on his principles he acted with an extraordinary, selfless dedication, and with intense moral passion. It was, I think, Bukharin who first said that the Leninist philosophy of historic

[1] *The Listener*, 5 February 1959.

determinism had this in common with the Puritan doctrine of pre-destination that, far from blunting, it sharpened the sense of personal moral responsibility.

Cromwell and Robespierre became revolutionaries when they were caught up by the current of actual revolution; neither of them had at the threshold of his career chosen to work for the overthrow of the established system of government. Lenin, on the contrary, deliberately entered the path of the revolutionary a full quarter of a century before 1917. Of the thirty years of his political activity, he exercised power in the course of only six years—for twenty-four years he was an outlaw, an underground fighter, a political prisoner, and an exile. During those twenty-four years he expected no reward for his struggle other than moral satisfaction. As late as January 1917 he said at a public meeting that he and men of his generation would probably not live to see the triumph of revolution in Russia. What, then, gave him, a man of political genius and of extraordinary ability in many other fields, the moral strength to condemn himself to persecution and penury in the service of a cause the triumph of which he did not even expect to see?

It was the old dream of human freedom. He himself, the greatest realist among revolutionaries, used to say that it was impossible to be a revolutionary without being a dreamer and without having a streak of romanticism. The enlargement of human freedom implied for him, in the first instance, the freeing of Russia from Tsardom and from a way of life rooted in age-old serfdom. Ultimately it implied the liberation of society at large from the less obvious but not less real domination of man by man inherent in the prevalence of bourgeois property. He saw in the contradiction between the social character of modern production and the unsocial character of bourgeois property the chief source of that irrationalism which condemns modern society to recurrent crises and wars, and makes it impossible for mankind even to begin to master its own destiny. If, to Milton, Englishmen loyal to the King were not free men, and royalism was moral slavery, then to Lenin loyalty to the bourgeois society and its forms of property was also moral slavery. Only that action was moral to him which hastened the end of the bourgeois order and the establishment of the proletarian dictatorship; for he believed that only such a dictatorship could pave the way for a classless and stateless society.

Lenin was aware of the contradiction inherent in this attitude.

His ideal was a society free from class domination and state authority; yet immediately he sought to establish the supremacy of a class,
the working class, and to found a new state, the proletarian dictatorship. He sought to resolve this dilemma by insisting that, unlike
other states, the proletarian dictatorship would have no need of any
oppressive government machine—it would not need any privileged
bureaucracy which, as a rule, 'is separated from the people, elevated
above it, and opposed to it'. In his *State and Revolution*, which he
wrote on the eve of the Bolshevik seizure of power, he described the
proletarian dictatorship as a sort of para-state, a state without a
standing army and police, a state constituted by 'a people in arms',
not by a bureaucracy, a state progressively dissolving in society and
working towards its own extinction.

Here, in this conception, and in its conflict with the realities of
the Russian revolution, was the source of the one truly great and
crushing moral crisis Lenin ever knew—the crisis at the end of his
life. He had often to face grave dilemmas, to submit his views to
the test of experience, to revise them, to retrace his steps, to acknowledge defeat, and—what was more difficult—to admit error; he
knew moments of hesitation, anguish, and even of nervous breakdown, for to the actual Lenin, not the Lenin of the Soviet icono-
graphy, nothing human was alien. He suffered the most severe
nervous strain whenever he had to confront old friends as political
enemies. Never till the end of his life did he overcome the pain that
his breach with Martov, the leader of the Mensheviks, had caused
him. He was profoundly shaken by the behaviour of the leaders of
the Socialist International in 1914, at the outbreak of the first world
war, when he decided to brand them as 'traitors to socialism'. Yet at
none of these and other important political turns did he experience
anything like a moral crisis.

Let me give you two further illustrations: in 1917 he had pledged
himself to convoke and uphold the Constituent Assembly. Early in
1918 he convoked it and dispersed it. Yet he had no qualms about
that act. His loyalty was to the October revolution and the Soviets;
and when the Constituent Assembly took up an attitude of irreconcilable opposition to both, it was in a mood of almost humorous
equanimity that he ordered its dispersal. In 1917, too, he had
pledged himself and his party to fight for world revolution and even
to wage a revolutionary war against Hohenzollern Germany. But
early in 1918, at Brest Litovsk, he came to terms with the Kaiser's

M

government, and signed with it a 'shameful' peace, as he himself put it. Yet he did not feel that he had broken his pledge: he was convinced that by concluding that peace he had secured a respite for the Russian revolution, and that for the time being this was the only service he could render to world revolution.

In this and in some other situations he held that *réculer pour mieux sauter* was a sound maxim. He saw nothing dishonourable in the behaviour of a revolutionary who retreats from his position before overwhelming enemy forces, provided that the revolutionary acknowledges the retreat as a retreat and does not misrepresent it as an advance. This, incidentally, was one of the important differences between Lenin and Stalin; and it is a moral difference, the difference between truthfulness and prestige-ridden, bureaucratic mendacity. It was precisely when he had to bow to expediency, and to act 'opportunistically' that Lenin was more than usually anxious to preserve in his party the sense of its direction—a clear awareness of the goal for which it was striving. He had brought up his party in an enthusiasm as ardent and a discipline as severe as were the enthusiasm and the discipline of Cromwell's soldiers. But he was also on guard against the excess of enthusiasm which had more than once led revolutionary parties to quixotry and defeat.

Guided by this astringent realism, Lenin was then for five years engaged in building the Soviet state. The administrative machine he created had little in common with the ideal model of it he had drawn in *State and Revolution*. A powerful army and an awe-inspiring political police came into being. The new administration reabsorbed much of the old Tsarist bureaucracy. Far from merging with a 'people in arms', the new state, like the old, was 'separated from the people and elevated above it'. At the head of the state stood the party's Old Guard, Lenin's Bolshevik Saints. The single-party system took shape. What was to have been a mere para-state was in fact a super-state.

Lenin could not have been unaware of all this. Yet for about five years he had, or appeared to have, a calm conscience, no doubt because he felt that he had retreated from his position under the overwhelming pressure of circumstances. Revolutionary Russia could not survive without a strong and centralized state. A 'people in arms' could not defend her against the White Armies and foreign intervention—a severely disciplined and centralized army was needed for that. The Cheka, the new political police, he held, was indispensable for the suppression of counter-revolution. It was impossible to overcome the devastation, chaos, and social disintegration consequent upon civil war by the methods of a workers' democracy. The working class itself was dispersed, exhausted, apathetic, or demoralized. The nation could not regenerate itself by itself—'from below'; and Lenin saw that a strong hand was needed to guide it from above, through a painful transition era of unpredictable duration. This conviction gave him what appeared to be an unshakable moral self-confidence in his course of action.

Then, as if suddenly, his self-confidence broke down. The process of state building was already well advanced, and he himself was nearing the end of his active life, when he was seized by acute doubt, apprehension, and alarm. He realized that he had gone too far, and that the new machine of power was turning into a mockery of his principles. He felt alienated from the state of his own making. At a party congress, in April 1922, the last congress he attended, he strikingly expressed this sense of alienation. He said that often he had the uncanny sensation which a driver has when he suddenly becomes aware that his vehicle is not moving in the direction in which he steers it. 'Powerful forces', he declared, 'diverted the Soviet state from its "proper road"'. He first threw out this remark as if casually, in an aside; but the feeling behind it then took hold of him until it gripped him completely. He was already ill and suffered from spells of sclerotic paralysis; but his mind still worked with relentless clarity. In the intervals between attacks of illness, he struggled desperately to make the vehicle of the state move 'in the right direction'. Again and again he failed. He was puzzled by his failures. He brooded over the reasons. He began to succumb to a sense of guilt, and finally, he found himself in the throes of moral crisis, a crisis which was all the more cruel because it aggravated his mortal illness and was aggravated by it.

He asked himself what it was that was transforming the Workers' Republic into an oppressive bureaucratic state. He surveyed repeatedly the familiar basic factors of the situation: the isolation of the revolution; the poverty, the ruin, and the backwardness of Russia; the anarchic individualism of the peasantry; the weakness and demoralization of the working class; and so on.

But something else now also struck him with great force. As he watched his colleagues, followers, and disciples—those revolutionaries turned rulers—their behaviour and methods of government reminded him more and more of the behaviour and the methods of the old Tsarist bureaucracy. He thought of those instances in history when one nation conquered another but then the defeated nation, if it represented a higher civilization, imposed its own way of life and its own culture on the conquerors, defeating them spiritually. Something similar, he concluded, can happen in the struggle between social classes: defeated Tsardom was in fact imposing its own standards and methods on his own party. It was galling for him to have to make this admission, but he made it: Tsardom was spiritually conquering the Bolsheviks, because the Bolsheviks were less civilized than even the Tsar's bureaucracy had been.

Having gained this deep and ruthless insight into what was happening, he watched his followers and disciples with growing dismay. More and more often he thought of the *dzierzhymordas* of old Russia, the gendarmes, the leaders of the old police state, the oppressors of national minorities, and so on. Were they not sitting now, as if resurrected, in the Bolshevik Politburo? In this mood he wrote his last will, in which he said that Stalin had already gathered too much power in his hands, and that the party would be well advised to remove him from the office of its General Secretary. At this time, towards the end of 1922, Stalin was sponsoring a new constitution which deprived the national minorities of many of the rights hitherto guaranteed to them, and which, in a sense, reestablished the 'one and indivisible' Russia of old by giving almost unlimited powers to the central government in Moscow. At the same time both Stalin and Dzerzhinsky, the head of the political police, were engaged in a brutal suppression of oppositions in Georgia and in the Ukraine.

On his sick bed, while he was struggling with his paralysis, Lenin decided to speak up and denounce the *dzierzhymorda*, the big brutish bully, who was in the name of revolution and socialism, reviving the old oppression. But Lenin did not absolve himself from responsibility; he was now a prey to remorse, which was extinguishing the feeble flame of life left in him but which also aroused him and gave him strength for an extraordinary act. He decided not merely to denounce Stalin and Dzerzhinsky but to make a confession of his own guilt.

On 30 December, 1922, cheating his doctors and nurses, he began to dictate notes on Soviet policy towards the small nations, notes intended as a message to the next party congress. 'I am, it seems, strongly guilty before the workers of Russia'; these were his opening words, words the like of which had hardly ever been uttered by any ruler, words which Stalin subsequently suppressed and which Russia was to read for the first time only after thirty-three years, after the Twentieth Congress. Lenin felt guilty before the working class of his country because, so he said, he had not acted with sufficient determination and early enough against Stalin and Dzerzhinsky, against their Great Russian chauvinism, against the suppression of the rights of the small nations, and against the new oppression, in Russia, of the weak by the strong. He now saw, he continued, in what 'swamp' of oppression the Bolshevik Party had landed: Russia was ruled once again by the old Tsarist administration to which the Bolsheviks 'had given only a Soviet veneer'; and once again the national minorities 'were exposed to the irruption of that truly Russian man, the Great Russian chauvinist who is essentially a scoundrel and an oppressor as is the typical Russian bureaucrat'.

For thirty-three years this message was to be concealed from the Soviet people. Yet I think that in these words: 'I am, it seems, strongly guilty before the workers of Russia'—in his ability to utter such words—lay an essential part of Lenin's moral greatness.

TROTSKY AT HIS NADIR

TROTSKY'S DIARY IN EXILE,[1] now published for the first time, was discovered in a 'forgotten valise' at his home in Mexico twelve years after his assassination. He wrote it in France and Norway in 1935. This is not, however, as the editors claim, the only diary he has written. Among his published and unpublished papers there are a few others, written at various times; it is surprising that Trotsky's literary executors should be so poorly informed about his literary heritage. But although the claim about its uniqueness is unfounded, this diary is of exceptional interest as a political and human document: Trotsky rarely, if ever, wrote about himself as intimately and self-revealingly as he does here.

'The diary is not a literary form I am especially fond of', he says in the first entry. '. . . . I would prefer the daily newspaper. But there is none available. . . . Cut off from political action, I am obliged to resort to such *ersatz* journalism. . . .' This unpromising introduction need not be taken literally. There is much more than *ersatz* journalism here, because Trotsky was in fact far more fond of this particular 'literary form' than he cared to admit. True, he usually resorted to it only during a lull in his political activity; but this was probably the only time when he could freely indulge in introspection.

The lull during which he wrote this diary was, for many reasons, his nadir. He had already spent two years in France, enjoying—if this be the right word here—the precarious asylum which the Government of M. Daladier had stingily granted him. Paris having been declared out of bounds for him, he had lived *incognito*, under police surveillance, in various places in the provinces. Every now and then his identity was discovered; and, amid an uproar in the press, pursued by crowds of reporters and photographers, hounded by numerous enemies on right and left, he had to escape hurriedly

---

[1] Translated by Elena Zarudnaya, (London 1959). This review was first published in *The Listener*, 16 July 1959.

from one place of residence, to look for another and reassume his *incognito*—until the next incident or accidental indiscretion compelled him to take to the road once again. The threat of expulsion from France hung over his head. Only because no other country would allow him to enter was he permitted to stay on, for the time being, in complete isolation at a small village in the Alps, not far from Grenoble. France was just then on the eve of the Popular Front; the Stalinists exercised increasing pressure on the Government; and so he had reason to fear final deportation—it could only be to a remote French colony like Madagascar.

In the Soviet Union this was the lull before the great purges, in all of which he was to figure as villain-in-chief. The Kirov affair was only a few months old. Zinoviev and Kamenev were once again imprisoned and, despite repeated recantations, accused of collusion with Trotsky, counter-revolutionary activity, treason, and so on; Trotskyism generally was under fire. Even from afar Trotsky felt the mounting fury of the terror Stalin was unleashing, although the precise facts were not yet known. Trotsky's family was already affected. His first wife Alexandra Sokolovskaya and his two sons-in-law had been, or were just being, deported to Siberia. He had already lost his two daughters, Zina and Nina—Zina had committed suicide; the orphaned grandchildren were all, except one, in Russia, at fate's mercy. Finally, there came the news from Moscow, ominously vague at first, of trouble with Sergei, Trotsky's youngest son, a promising scientist, who was utterly non-political and was not involved in the Opposition but was now falling victim to Stalin's vengeance. The tense expectation of definite news about Sergei and the anguish of his parents fill many a page in this diary.

For reasons of yet another order, this was for Trotsky a time of acute frustration. He had come to France in 1933, after nearly five years of exile in Turkey, with ambitious plans and sanguine hopes which were now at an ebb. He had been confident that in France he would be able to resume his political activity on a large scale. After Hitler's rise to power and the 1933 catastrophe of the German left— a catastrophe to which Stalinist policies had greatly contributed and of which Trotsky had been the unheeded Cassandra—he launched the so-called Fourth International. From personal experience I know how great were the hopes he placed on it. A group of his co-thinkers, to which I belonged at the time, warned him in vain that he was embarking on a futile venture. Soon indeed it turned out that the Fourth International was still-born. Trotsky nevertheless desperately tried to breathe life into it; and he had just instructed his followers to enter the Socialist Parties and there to try to recruit adherents for the new International.

In any case, Trotsky's presence in France had not made it easier for him to plunge back into political activity. In the turbulent events of the last pre-war decade, especially in those occurring outside the U.S.S.R., his role was that of the great outsider. 'For the very reason', he writes, 'that it fell to my lot to take part in great events, my past now cuts me off from chances of action. I am reduced to interpreting events and trying to foresee their future course'. Yet, his past which cut him off from chances of action did not allow him to remain inactive either: he, the leader of the October Revolution, the founder of the Red Army, and the inspirer of the Communist International, could not possibly reconcile himself to the role of the outsider.

If to all these circumstances we add his persistent ill-health, and something as humanly ordinary as a middle-age crisis, not to speak of difficulties in earning a living, we shall get an idea of his mood at this time. The recurrent and mysterious fever from which he had suffered for thirteen years now gave him spells of utter enervation and immobility. But although the strain on his nerves was severe, he still showed astonishing energy and vitality when critical events confronted him with a direct challenge. In the intervals he tended, not surprisingly, to succumb to hypochondria: he brooded over his advancing age and over death. He was only fifty-five, but repeatedly he recalled Lenin's or rather Turgenev's saying: 'Do you know what is the greatest vice? To be more than fifty-five years old.' Revolution is as a rule the business of the young; and professional revolutionaries age much more rapidly than do, say, British parliamentarians. Trotsky was as little reconciled to growing old as he was to being an outsider.

He had premonitions of his violent death at Stalinist hands. 'Stalin', he observed, 'would now give a great deal to be able to retract the decision to deport me. He will unquestionably resort to a terroristic act in two cases . . .: if there is a threat of war, or if his own position deteriorates greatly. Of course, there could also be a third case, and a fourth . . . We shall see. And if we don't, then others will.' At the same time he began to think of suicide, but the thought was to take a more definite shape only five years later, when he was to write his testament.

Even while his energy was sapped, he could not live in a country without reacting to the political events of the day; and he could not react otherwise than with the full force of all his militant instincts, his mighty passion, his anger, his irony. He watched the manœuvres and the shilly-shallying of the nascent Popular Front, was convinced that they would all end in disaster, and had a clear presentiment of the France of 1940. Without inhibition he expressed his contempt for the official leaders of the European Labour Movement—Blum, Thorez, Vanderwelde, the Webbs. On a few occasions he drew graphic and devastating thumb-nail sketches, of which one in particular makes piquant reading today—the sketch of M. Paul-Henri Spaak, the future Secretary-General of N.A.T.O., who in the early nineteen-thirties was something like Trotsky's disciple, diligently, yet apprehensively, submissive, and over-awed by the master.

However, the crux of this Diary is not in what Trotsky had to say on events and public figures or even on literature—he said it all more fully and much better in other writings. The diary is remarkable mainly because of the pages he devotes to the fate of his family, pages full of tragic pathos and nobility.

Trotsky's anxiety over his youngest son was all the more poignant because he feared that Sergei, in his political innocence and indifference to politics, would not be able to take the blow that fell on him; and in Trotsky's anxiety there was an admixture of a sense of guilt. Natalya Ivanovna, on learning about their son's imprisonment, said: 'They will not deport him under any circumstances; they will torture him in order to get something out of him, and after that they will destroy him'. The image of their tortured and bewildered son haunted the parents. (In truth, Sergei was not as bewildered as they feared he would be. Recently I have talked with a man who spent twenty-three years in Stalin's concentration camps and prisons and was, he thinks, the last person to share a prison cell with Sergei. Sergei stood his ordeal proudly and, facing death, he not merely refused to bear false testimony against his father, but found himself bound to him by new ties of moral solidarity, although even then Sergei was not a 'Trotskyist'.)

With sublime tenderness Trotsky watched his suffering wife, recollected various incidents of their common life—they had now lived together for thirty-three years; and he felt that he ought 'to fix her image on paper'. He did this with undisguised partiality, yet with truth. What he has sketched is in effect the image of the Niobe of our age, as true an exemplar of the countless and nameless martyred mothers of our time as, on a different level, Anne Frank is of the martyred children. Natalya Ivanovna was not to her husband the kind of political comrade that Krupskaya was to Lenin—she was far less politically minded and active than Krupskaya. 'Even though she is interested in the small daily facts of politics', Trotsky writes, 'she does not usually combine them into one coherent picture.' The loving husband could not express more clearly a doubt about his wife's political judgement. But this was not important: 'When politics go deep down and demand a complete reaction', he goes on, 'Natalya always finds in her inner music the right note.' Of this, her 'inner music', he speaks frequently; and, incidentally, when he described her it was mostly while she was listening to some music. He notes with gratitude that she never reproaches him for their son's misfortune, or else that she conceals her suffering even from him. Finally he relates:

Concerning the blows that have fallen to our lot, I reminded Natasha the other day of the life of the arch-priest Avakuum. [Avakuum was a seventeenth-century rebel against Greek Orthodoxy who had been deported twice before he was burnt at the stake.] They were stumbling on together in Siberia, the rebellious priest and his faithful spouse. Their feet sank into the snow, and the poor exhausted woman kept falling into the snowdrifts. Avakuum relates: 'And I came up, and she, poor soul, began to reproach me, saying "How long, arch-priest, is this suffering to be?" And I said, "Markovna, unto our very death". And she, with a sigh, answered: "So be it, Petrovich, let us be getting on our way"'.

And so it was to be with Trotsky and Natalya Ivanovna: the suffering was to be 'unto our very death'. Five years later, writing his testament, he suddenly lifted his head and saw 'Natasha approaching the window from the courtyard and opening it wider so that the air may come more freely into my room'; she made him think at this moment of the beauty of life and he 'fixed' this image of her in the last paragraph of his testament.

It is certainly no matter of chance that between his entries about Sergei, Trotsky, unexpectedly and seemingly out of context, tells the story of the execution of the Tsar and the Tsar's family. At this moment of anxiety and anguish over his own children, the innocent victims of his conflict with Stalin, Trotsky undoubtedly thought about those other innocent children, the Tsar's, on whom the sins of the fathers were visited. He records that he personally had no part in taking the decision about the Tsar's execution—the decision was primarily Lenin's; and that he was startled at first when he learned about the fate of the Tsar's family. But he does not record this to dissociate himself from Lenin. On the contrary, after seventeen years he defends Lenin's decision as necessary and taken in the interest of the revolution's self-defence. In the midst of civil war, the Bolsheviks could not leave the White Armies 'with a live banner to rally round'; the Tsar's children, he says, 'fell victim to that principle which constitutes the axis of monarchy: dynastic succession'. Any one of them, if left alive, would have served the Whites as rallying banner and symbol. The unspoken conclusion of this meaningful digression is clear enough. Even if one granted Stalin the right to exterminate his adversaries—Trotsky was far from granting him that—Stalin still had not a shred of justification for persecuting the children of his opponents. Sergei was not bound to Trotsky by any principle of dynastic succession.

Some critics, mostly ex-communists, have, in this connexion, commented on Trotsky's 'unteachability' and the 'arrogance' with which he asserted his communist convictions to the end. The criticism seems to me particularly ill-founded. If Trotsky had renounced his principles and beliefs from disillusionment, under the lash of persecution and defeat, this surely would not have testified to his intellectual integrity and moral stamina, or even to his 'teachability'. He would not have been himself if he had done this. At the lowest ebb of his fortunes he was indeed as unshaken in his philosophy of life as he had been at its height. In this I see his strength, not his weakness. When at last, in 1940, weighed down by illness, age, and so many cruel blows, he pondered the possibility of suicide, he was above all anxious that the world should not see the suicide as his moral capitulation and renunciation of principles. He wrote the testament to make it clear that if he were ever to take his life, he would do so from sheer physical inability to carry on the struggle, not from despair or doubt in his cause. He did not commit suicide however—the axe of an assassin smashed his brain. He penned his testament as he penned this diary, in a moment of all too human frailty; but even the frailty underlines his moral stature.

This is not to say that Trotsky's attitude was invulnerable. But his vulnerability lay not where the critics I have mentioned see it. He belonged to what he himself called the heroic epoch of the Russian revolution. An intense nostalgia for that epoch swayed him to the end of his days. Through its prism he looked upon all later events; and in his thought and imagination he constantly projected that epoch into the future.

The projection was at odds with the actual course of events, and never more so than in the nineteen-thirties. The processes of revolution, both within and without the Soviet Union, developed in forms very different from those of the 'heroic phase' of 1917-20, in forms which could not but be repugnant to the adherent of the classical Marxian tradition, in forms which marked indeed a degeneracy of revolutionary politics, in a word—in Stalinist forms. But basically it was still the revolution for which Trotsky stood that has assumed these forms. He considered it to be his mission to expose the 'degeneracy' and to create a new Communist Party which, he believed, would be capable of guiding the revolution towards renaissance. He overrated his capacity to achieve this; as he also overrated the potentialities of revolution in the West. On the other hand, he undoubtedly underrated the vitality of the new Soviet society, its inherent capacity for self-reform and regeneration, its inherent ability to overcome Stalinism eventually, and to go beyond Stalinism.

Yet, despite all his fallibility and his moments of weakness, Trotsky emerges even from this diary as one of the very few giants of this century. His nostalgia for the heroic period of the revolution, the Lenin era, would have been sheer quixotry if that era had been nothing but the dead past. Yet twenty years after Trotsky's death a new Soviet generation is looking back to that era almost as much as he did, and still seems to find some lessons to learn from it. And so Trotsky appears not merely as the nostalgic survivor of one epoch, a closed one, but as the great precursor of another, which is only beginning.

AN OBITUARY ON STALIN[1]

THE same illness which thirty years ago removed Lenin from the political scene has now removed Stalin from the command. Lenin lingered on his death-bed for twenty months, but 1923 marked the end of the Leninist era of Bolshevism. Similarly 1953 sees the end of the Stalinist era. If to outsiders Lenin's disappearance seemed an event of only local, Russian significance, Stalin's withdrawal is recognized as a landmark in world history. Unwittingly the anti-Communist world is thus paying a tribute to the dying man and to the legend hovering over his death-bed.

But how different the two men look on their death-beds. In his lifetime Lenin was not surrounded by any cult. Modest, unassuming, and above all soberly devoted to his ideals, he did not allow his followers to wrap him up in mist and legend. His successors were free to initiate the Leninist legend only when, struck down by illness, he became speechless. Lenin had to die before the Leninist cult could be born. Stalin has been surrounded by quasi-religious adulation for over a quarter of a century. The cult has grown old with him; and I doubt whether it can survive him for very long.

In a sense the Stalinist era may loom larger in history than the Leninist era. It has lasted much longer; and it has been crowded with world-shaking events. But the weakness of the Stalinist legend is that it is too strongly divorced from the realities of our time and that it is made up largely of that perishable stuff which bureaucratic machines produce.

Here is another contrast between 1923 and 1953: the men assembled around Lenin's death-bed and fighting for the succession were genuine historical characters: Stalin, Trotsky, Zinoviev, Kamenev, Rykov, Bukharin, each of them was of that flesh and blood, that will, and that thought of which makers of history are made. Their virtues and vices were known to all, and so were, by and large, their ideas and aspirations. Around Stalin's death-bed

[1] *Manchester Guardian*, 6 March 1953

only his shadows wrestle and wrangle over his mantle. His prospective successors, Molotov, Malenkov, Beria have no character, no mind, no political life of their own—they have all been Stalin's mere projections. How long can any shadow wear the mantle when the body is no longer there?

Yet in one respect there exists a broad similarity between 1923 and 1953. Both dates mark critical phases in the fortunes of the Russian revolution. Lenin was dying at a time when the revolution had reached a cross-roads and could no longer travel along the road on which he had led it. Stalin too is dying at such a cross-roads. But the two cross-roads are very different from one another.

Lenin had founded the Soviet State as a proletarian dictatorship but also as a proletarian democracy. He had denied freedom to the old ruling classes and their parties. But he had hoped that the working classes would enjoy the fullest possible economic and political liberty in the new State. He succeeded in accomplishing his negative task but was frustrated in his positive hopes. The proletarian dictatorship as it shaped itself after the civil war was not a proletarian democracy. It was rapidly evolving into an autocratic form of government. Courageously but hopelessly Lenin wrestled with the dilemma between proletarian democracy and autocracy speaking on behalf of the proletariat. Plekhanov once wrote that if there is an historical need for a certain function to be performed history produces the organ capable of performing it. Lenin was not the 'organ' suited for performing the functions of a quasi-Socialist autocrat. Stalin was.

In the Leninist era bolshevism lived on the hope of world revolution. By 1923 that hope had been dashed. By that year European communism had finally lost the impetus imparted to it by the First World War. An era of isolation had begun for the Russian revolution. The ideology of the Bolshevik party began to evolve from its early militant internationalism to national self-centredness, to 'peaceful co-existence with the capitalist world', and finally to the more extreme forms of Russian nationalism. For this metamorphosis, too, Lenin, the Marxist internationalist *par excellence*, was not suited. Somebody else had to guide his party in the new direction.

If Lenin had lived longer he would have had to become either a Stalin or a Trotsky, for these two men embodied two opposed solutions to the dilemmas of the 1920s. Yet Lenin could probably become neither a Stalin nor a Trotsky—in a sense both these characters were blended in him. Illness and death gripped him while he stood at a cross-roads at which he was incapable of choosing any of the roads that led ahead.

In one way or another, in part deliberately and in part empirically, Stalin chose his road. Untroubled by the scruples which beset Lenin and other Bolshevik leaders, he moulded the Soviet State into an autocracy. He turned his back on the internationalist tradition of Marxism and elevated the Russian Revolution's sacred egoism to a principle. This was the essence of his 'Socialism in one country'. To paraphrase a term now much in use, 'Socialism in one country' was the formula in which Stalin proclaimed Bolshevism's readiness for a self-containment to a world which was bent on containing it.

But history has now overtaken Stalinism as it once overtook Leninism. The chapter of self-containment is closed—it has been forcibly closed by the revolutionary processes generated by the Second World War. Conservative minds in the West see Stalin as the initiator and plotter of those processes because to the conservative mind revolution is always the outcome of the conspiracy and the plot. The historian will record that in the last decade of his life Stalin desperately and unavailingly clung to self-containment, that he tried to stem the rising tide of international revolution which threatened to wash away the rock of 'Socialism in one country' on which Stalin had built his temple.

At Teheran, Yalta, and Potsdam, when with Roosevelt and Churchill he delimited the spheres of influence, he was essentially still acting in the spirit of self-containment, although this was to be self-containment within an area somewhat expanded in agreement with his allies. He himself was hardly aware that victory over Germany and Japan would impart to his own State and party an expansive momentum which he would not be able fully to control. We know now from Tito himself that Stalin's conflict with Tito actually began when Stalin, pointing to his agreements with his war-time allies, was trying to curb Tito's hot expansionism, to divert him from Trieste, and to persuade him not to help the embattled Greek Communists. The Chinese Revolution caught Stalin completely unawares, as he admitted to Kardelj. To the end he urged Mao Tse-tung to come to terms with Chiang Kai-shek and to refrain from a final bid for power. He showered warnings and remonstrances on his Chinese disciple, satellite, and rival. Mao listened reverently, nodded approvingly, and then coolly ignoring Stalin's counsel of wisdom and caution, led Chinese communism to its triumph. Only when the tide of the Chinese Revolution swept forward, carrying every obstacle in its way did Stalin bow to it, thus saving his Communist reputation almost in the last minute.

Western statesmen and politicians have been puzzled by Stalin's rôle in these events. They have seen that Stalin inspired, supported, and even armed the satellite Communist parties. Like Stalin himself, they have assumed that he was in complete control of the satellites, and thus of the revolutionary ferment in the world. The assumption has been singularly devoid of any sociological, psychological, and historical sense! The magic wand which Stalin believed would allow him to control the elements of revolution in the world had long since broken in his hand; its fragments can be seen tossed about by the currents and waves of contemporary history. To the end Stalin pretended that he was still wielding that wand and that it was he that made the waves flow and ebb. He controlled the revolutionary elements to this extent only, that wherever they managed to assert themselves they did from self-preservation rally around Russia and accept the Stalinist cult. In a similarly paradoxical way, the Jacobin Republican elements in Europe once rallied around Napoleon's empire. But Stalinism as the expression of a definite phase of the Russian revolution, that of isolation and self-containment, has long since been dead. It fell to Stalin himself to make the funeral oration on it—this is what his last public speech at the nineteenth party congress amounted to.

Inside the Soviet Union, too, Stalinism had virtually outlived its day. It had come to life as the version of Marxism suited to a country in which barefoot *muzhiks* working their land with *sokhas*, wooden ploughs, formed the overwhelming majority. In Stalinism the Socialist ideal of Western European origin was blended with the backwardness and illiteracy of a semi-Asiatic country and with the native tradition of Tsarist autocracy. The Socialist ideal had its inner integrity and consistency. Tsarist Russia, too, possessed its own organic unity and outlook. The amalgamation of the two was bound to produce something as bizarre and as incongruous as Stalinism.

In the course of three decades, however, the face of the Soviet Union has become transformed. The core of Stalin's historic achievements consists in this, that he had found Russia working with wooden ploughs and is leaving her equipped with atomic piles.

He has raised Russia to the level of the second industrial Power of the world. This was not a matter of mere material progress and organization. No such achievement would have been possible without a vast cultural revolution, in the course of which a whole nation was sent to school to undergo a most intensive education.

Like everything in Stalinism, this cultural revolution, too, has been self-contradictory. It has been marked by the antics of the Stalinist cult, the despotic rule of dogma, the falsification of history and so on. All the same, under Stalinist tutelage the Soviet peoples have come or are coming of age culturally. They owe to that tutelage at least as much as they have suffered from it; and now they seem on the point of outgrowing it. This in the last instance accounts for that intellectual *malaise* and for that constant ferment of ideas of which the recent heresy hunts provide abundant negative proof or evidence. Through these heresy hunts Stalinism, that Marxism of the illiterate, is struggling to maintain its domination over the mind of a people which has emerged from illiteracy.

Stalin's death, like Lenin's, will thus coincide with the accumulation of many elements making for an internal crisis, a crisis in the long run much more important than the immediate jockeying for power in the Kremlin. The development of that crisis may for some time yet remain invisible to Western eyes. Just so a hundred years ago, during the rule of Nicholas I, the Iron Tsar, did the growth of a similar crisis remain hidden from Western observers, including the now fashionable and much-quoted but misleading Custine. Yet only a few years after the death of Nicholas I his successor, Alexander II, emancipated the Russian and the Polish peasant serfs and initiated a number of quasi-liberal reforms.

Let us sum up the elements of the crisis looming ahead. While Lenin was on his death-bed the revolution was evolving towards an autocracy and withdrawing into its national shell. While Stalin is wrestling with death the Soviet people seem to be sick with the autocracy, and the revolution has long since broken out of its national shell. It is impossible to prophesy how this crisis is going to be solved. Probably no rapid or startling developments should be expected in the near future. 'Stalin is dead—long live Stalinism!'— this cry will resound from Moscow in the next few months, regardless of the fact that Stalinism has been half-dead even before Stalin has died.

Eventually the crisis can be solved only in one of two ways:

N

through a democratic regeneration of the Revolution or through counter-revolution. Some statesmen and policy-makers of the West seem to bank on a counter-revolutionary development. Even if their hopes should come true this could only be an ephemeral solution, that is no solution at all. No revolutionary nation has ever made real peace with returned Bourbons or Stuarts and renounced its revolutionary heritage. The peoples of the Soviet Union may in due time shake off Stalinism, or rather the oppressive aspects of Stalinism. But there is no reason to suppose that they will ever genuinely and effectively renounce the Bolshevik Revolution. Any attempt to make them renounce it will only deepen the gulf between East and West and may even give new life and strength to the Stalinist legend.

WARSAW'S VERDICT ON
ROKOSSOVSKY

AT the beginning of last October[1] two well-known Polish politicians from Warsaw visited me in my home in England, to discuss the situation in Poland. This was shortly before the upheaval in Warsaw as a result of which Wladyslaw Gomulka was to return to power and Marshal Konstanty Rokossovsky was to be dismissed from the Polish Politbureau and Ministry of Defence. My guests, old acquaintances and pre-war comrades, described the inner alignments in the Polish Workers Party, the conflict in its midst between the Stalinists, the so-called Natolin group, and the anti-Stalinists, the attitudes of individual leaders, and the prospects of the approaching dénouement. They themselves belonged, of course, to the anti-Stalinist wing, and, firmly yet not without reservations, backed Gomulka. At one point of our discussion, I asked:

'And where does the army stand in this conflict? What do you think Rokossovsky is going to do? May he not throw his weight behind the Natolin group and stage a *coup* against you?'

'Rokossovsky?' my visitors were surprised by the question. 'No, we do not expect any difficulty from him. He will play no role at all in the coming crisis. He has kept aloof from the inner party struggle, as in his office he was bound to do, but he has indicated his anti-Stalinist feelings more than once. In any case, we can count on his absolute loyalty to the Central Committee, whose orders he will carry out; and in the Central Committee, the Stalinists are already an isolated minority. No, no, Rokossovsky is not the man to stage a *coup* . . .'

Yet a few days later, when the Central Committee met for its now famous session and when Khrushchev and colleagues suddenly

[1] 1956

descended on Warsaw, the danger of a military coup appeared quite real. Warsaw was astir with rumours about movements of Russian and Polish troops. Rokossovsky, far from playing no part in the crisis, found himself at its very centre. It was indeed over his re-election to the Politbureau rather than over Gomulka's return that the conflict between the Stalinists and the anti-Stalinists came to a head. To Gomulka's return the Natolin group had already reconciled itself; and 'Re-elect Rokossovsky!' was now its battlecry. Since the battle was joined over this the anti-Stalinists demanded his dismissal. After a most dramatic scene at the session Rokossovsky was indeed dismissed.

Yet my anti-Stalinist visitors, who assured me so confidently of Rokossovsky's sympathy with their attitude and of his loyalty, were not altogether mistaken. Rokossovsky was undoubtedly one of the most authentic anti-Stalinists in Poland, an anti-Stalinist of much longer standing than, for instance, Gomulka. Few could have stronger reasons for hating Stalinism than he had. Yet it was as a symbol of Stalinism that he was dismissed from all his posts and had to leave Warsaw. What accounts for this paradox?

The city from which he has been so ingloriously expelled is his birthplace. It was in Warsaw at the turn of the century, when Poland was ruled by a Tsarist Governor-General, that he spent his childhood and early youth. Only during the First World War did he find himself, together with many other Poles, in Russia. Since then, however, something like a curse seemed to debar him from his native city. At least three times when its fate hung in the balance he returned or attempted to return to it; and every time disaster lay in wait for him.

The October revolution of 1917 was to him, as to many left-wing Poles in Russia, the supreme act of liberation. In 1919 at the height of civil war, when Lenin's government was on the brink of defeat, the twenty-three-year-old Rokossovsky volunteered for the Red Army and joined the Communist Party. No problem of national loyalty was as yet involved. After about 150 years of Poland's incorporation in the Russian Empire, Poles were as often involved in Russian politics as Irishmen were in English affairs. Poles—it is enough to mention here Dzerzhinsky and Radek—played a prominent part in the Bolshevik leadership. And in 1919 Moscow did not yet think of re-annexing any of the territories of nations which had once been subjected by the Russian Empire. Instead, the ideal of the revolution was still annexing the hearts and the minds of foreigners.

A year later, however, in 1920, the young Rokossovsky was already marching with the Red Army on Warsaw. He marched with high hopes and enthusiasm, and there was still no question for him of any conflict of national loyalties. He believed himself to be fighting in an international civil war, not in a war of nations, and the Red Army's march on Warsaw had been preceded and provoked by Pilsudski's march on Kiev. It was, indeed, some of the left-wing Polish expatriates in Russia who urged Lenin to pursue Pilsudski's troops into the Polish capital and beyond, for they believed that the Polish workers and peasants would welcome the Red Army and would rise against the Polish landlords and capitalists. Lenin shared the hope, although Trotsky, the Commissar of War, and Radek, the most brilliant of the Poles in Moscow, were opposed to the offensive on Warsaw.

Poland spurned the invaders. She ignored their revolutionary slogans and internationalist appeals and saw in them only the successors to the old Tsarist armies of conquest. At the gates of Warsaw the Red Army was routed and forced to retreat. Among the retreating was the unknown Polish Red Army man Rokossovsky. His city and country had rejected him and his comrades. This was the remote prelude to his final humiliation in Warsaw thirty-six years later.

The young Rokossovsky was probably not unduly despondent. Like many of his comrades he must have told himself that 'history had not yet said its last word'. It seems that in the early 1920s he was for a short while back in Warsaw as a clandestine communist emissary; but this is not certain. In the middle 1920s he was posted to the Frunze Military Academy in Moscow where young commanders who made their mark in the civil war were trained. The Academy's presiding genius was Tukhachevsky, the Red Army's most brilliant and modern mind, the originator of the use of parachute troops, who saw in the tank and aircraft the decisive weapons of the next war. Tukhachevsky had led the Red Army on Warsaw; and he hardly ever gave up altogether the idea of repeating the march in more favourable circumstances, when he might be able to drop Polish communist parachute troops behind the enemy lines, to organize revolution there. Such ideas appealed to Tukhachevsky's Polish *élève*. Rokossovsky was also receptive to Tukhachevsky's 'ultra-modernistic', as they then seemed, conceptions of mechanized warfare and absorbed all that was valuable in his military teaching.

Tukhachevsky befriended him; and Rokossovsky, after he had, in 1929, graduated from the Academy, acted as liasion officer between Tukhachevsky, i.e. the Soviet General Staff, and the Polish section of the Comintern. The brilliant Russian Staff Officer remained a Polish communist dreaming of revolution in his country.

His closeness to Tukhachevsky, his Polish origin and Polish communist preoccupations made him suspect to Stalin. And so, when in 1937 Stalin ordered Tukhachevsky to be executed as traitor and the entire Polish Communist Party to be denounced as 'a gang of Trotskyists and Polish spies' and disbanded, Rokossovsky was thrown into prison and then deported to a concentration camp, where he spent four years. Even now he avoids talking about his experiences behind the barbed wire. Subjected to torture and thrown among ordinary criminals, he used all his willpower to keep himself mentally alive and to follow the trend of political and military events. He was less concerned with the personal injustice he suffered than with the harm the purges had done to the Red Army, in a most critical international situation. Lying on his prison bunk, he went through in his mind over and over again the complex strategic and operational games with which Tukhachevsky had occupied his Staff Officers. Since September 1939, he had no doubt that the Red Army would still need his services. He was familiar enough with the 'spirit' of Russian history to know that the distance between a Siberian concentration camp and G.H.Q. in Moscow may, on occasions, prove to be fantastically short. And indeed, in the summer of 1941 Rokossovsky, the 'traitor and Polish spy', was rehabilitated and hastily brought back to G.H.Q. In the autumn, when Hitler's armies approached Moscow and when, after the Soviet débâcle on the Dnieper, Stalin was compelled to dismiss the incompetent Voroshilov and Budienny from the highest military posts, he picked three officers for the most important commands: Zhukov, Vassilevsky and Rokossovsky.

There is no need to go here into Rokossovsky's record in the Second World War. Suffice it to recall that under Zhukov's orders he was the most important operational commander in the battles of Moscow and Stalingrad. What did he fight for? Certainly not for Stalin, his jailer and torturer. And certainly not for the Russian Empire. For military glory or fame? Perhaps. But what was the worth of glory and fame that could so easily be destroyed and turned into disgrace and infamy? To judge from his behaviour in various situations, Rokossovsky was not vainglorious. It is much more probable that the cause to which he gave his talents was still communism—a cause which he believed to be debased but not destroyed or invalidated by Stalinism. Whatever his motives, within a single year he rose to the status of one of the greatest commanders in the greatest of wars.

Yet his triumph was marred when, after an interval of nearly a quarter of a century, he was on the point of re-entering his native city. During the summer of 1944 he was in command of that Soviet army whose spearhead had reached the Vistula and one of Warsaw's suburbs, while across the river, inside the city, the Poles had risen in arms against the Wehrmacht. The insurgents, led by anti-communists, hoped to defeat the Germans without Soviet help and thus to forestall Rokossovsky. When this proved impossible, they appealed in despair for Soviet help. This might have been Rokossovsky's opportunity for a reconciliation with his native city. (Was this not the moment for dropping—at last!—his parachute troops behind the enemy's lines? . . .) He might have entered the streets of Warsaw as its triumphant liberator. But it was not given to him to accomplish the feat.

Stalin forbade him to succour embattled Warsaw. It was said that the general situation at the front and a full-scale Soviet offensive mounted farther to the south, in the Carpathians, did not allow Soviet forces to become engaged in Warsaw. Another version was that by the time the Polish rising flared up the Germans had dislodged Rokossovsky's troops from their forward positions on the Vistula and had thrown them back. The insurgents took a different view of the matter: they believed that Stalin had deliberately delivered them to German revenge and destruction because he did not wish the rising, inspired and led by anti-communists, to succeed. Amid the burning ruins of Warsaw, the insurgents fought and died, cursing the Soviet army. Rokossovsky could not view the agony of his native town with indifference. But Stalin's orders were clear and strict; and Rokossovsky, placed as he was, could not disregard them. When some months later he at last entered Warsaw, the city was a vast cemetery; and he could not find in it the streets and land-marks of his childhood.

Moscow, in its hour of victory, received its Polish defender with gratitude. On 24 June 1945, at the great Victory Parade in the Red Square, Rokossovsky led the Soviet Army in the march past. He galloped at the head of choice regiments and divisions as they swept the mud of Moscow with the innumerable banners and standards of Hitler's army, which they then threw at Stalin's feet.

But Stalin's favour did not last. He was jealous of the popularity of his Marshals and afraid of them. Vassilevsky, the nationalist and Great Russian, was perhaps the only one of them whom he trusted. The others he was anxious to send away from Moscow and relegate to obscurity. He ordered Zhukov to withdraw to Odessa, and he posted Rokossovsky to headquarters at Lignitza, in Upper Silesia, and then to Warsaw.

When, in 1949, Rokossovsky was appointed Polish Minister of Defence, the typical comment in the West was that as 'Stalin's man of confidence' he was to assure the subservience of the Polish communists to Moscow. Rokossovsky and those who knew his back-ground could only be sadly amused by such comment. For the hero of the battles of Moscow and Stalingrad—the Marshal who had led the great victory parade in the Red Square—to be eliminated from the Soviet army and appointed Minister in a satellite government was a humiliating degradation. Warsaw was for him the place of 'honorary exile'.

But not only the West saw Rokossovsky as Stalin's Polish viceroy. Polish opinion, too, looked on him in this way and refused to accept him as a Pole. His countrymen knew, of course, nothing about the suspicion which as a Pole he had drawn upon himself in Moscow, or about his ordeal in Stalin's prisons and concentration camps—no one dared to mention such things in those days. They saw him as Stalin's watchdog, a Russified Pole, and a Russifier. There was never, in truth, any lack of Russified generals in the Polish army, even before 1939—officers who were quite incapable of addressing their men in correct Polish. Such was, for instance, the 'national hero' General Zheligowski, who on Pilsudski's orders seized Vilno from the Lithuanians in 1921; and I remember my own general, who commanded a large Polish garrison in 1929-30, whose Polish was almost incomprehensible to those of his officers who did not understand Russian. Rokossovsky, despite his long service in Russia, had remained a Pole in character, manner and speech. He did not Russify the Polish army. He did not even put it into Russian uniforms, as Rakosy's men, among whom there was no Soviet Marshal, put the Hungarian army. Nor was it he who brought Russian advisers and instructors into the Polish commands—they had been there long before he arrived. And yet it was he who had to take the blame for their presence and who was to Poles the Muscovite and the arch-traitor. He became the victim of a reputation which circumstances rather than his own character created for him.

There were in Polish history men who much more than Rokossovsky deserved the reputation of traitors and who are yet celebrated as great patriots even by the most nationalist Polish historians. To mention one striking instance, Prince Adam Czartoryski was Foreign Secretary to Tsar Alexander I; at the Congress of Vienna it was he who represented the Russian Army against Europe and brought the rump of Poland, the so-called Congress Poland, under Russian rule, with the Tsar enthroned as Polish King. Yet the most anti-Russian writers have not ceased to extol Czartoryski's patriotic virtues. True, in feudal Eastern Europe of the early nineteenth century the Polish aristocrat could feel at home at the Court of St. Petersburg, for feudal kinship and solidarity were more important and alive than national consciousness and sentiment. But in the Moscow of the early days of the revolution communist solidarity also prevailed over national antagonisms. The historian may draw an analogy between Czartoryski and Rokossovsky, but he will hardly be able to charge Rokossovsky with having been, as Czartoryski was, among the grave-diggers of Poland's independence.

However, in October 1956 it was not a historical verdict that Warsaw was passing on Rokossovsky. It was the verdict of popular opinion and popular emotion aroused against Stalinist oppression. Circumstances now finally conspired to make of Rokossovsky's name the hated symbol of that oppression. Warsaw, we know, was astir with news and rumour of Russian and Polish troop movements designed to defeat Gomulka and reinstate the Stalinists. Who, the Poles asked, could be responsible for these movements if not Marshal Rokossovsky, the Minister of Defence? And so, in the critical days of 19 and 20 October, all Poland's political passion suddenly concentrated on him. To the overwhelming majority he was the villain of the piece, while to the retreating Stalinists he automatically became a hero; and they decided to fight their own rearguard battle over his re-election to the Politbureau.

Rokossovsky himself said not a word to advance or support his candidature. Had he had as much political sense as he had military ability, he would have himself withdrawn his candidature, disowned his backers, and rid himself of the odium. This he did not do. He appeared to be surprised at finding himself at the very heart of the passionate political controversy, embarrassed, and bewildered. He stammered, faltered and stumbled to his final humiliation.

Was he in fact responsible in any degree for the troop movements and the preparation of a pro-Stalinist *coup*? Only the historian with access to the archives will be able to give a conclusive answer. When, on 20 October, the question was raised at the session of the Central Committee, Rokossovsky at once volunteered an explanation. He said that there had been no significant movements of Polish troops about which he had not kept the Politbureau informed; and he was responsible only for Polish troops. Marshal Koniev was responsible for the movement of Soviet troops in Poland. On Politbureau instructions Rokossovsky had asked Koniev for an explanation and was told that the movements were ordinary autumn manœuvres; nevertheless he had asked Koniev, again on behalf of the Polish Politbureau, to stop the 'manœuvres'. Rokossovsky concluded his brief, peculiarly embarrassed, and ineloquent statement with a plain and apparently frank declaration of loyalty to the Polish Government and the Polish party leadership, i.e. to the new leader Gomulka, 'without whose orders not a single step is going to be made'. Not one of the party leaders denied the truth of Rokossovsky's words. All the same, public opinion received them with the greatest incredulity; and Gomulka, aware of Rokossovsky's personal tragedy and the comedy of errors which made of him a Pole in Russia and a Russian in Poland, could do nothing but dismiss him from all his posts.

The dismissal was primarily a symbolic act designed to testify to Poland's 'regained independence' and to soothe her offended pride. But even now Rokossovsky the real man cannot separate himself from the symbol he has become; and the ambiguity of his role continues to pursue him, this time in Moscow. There the Pole and exdeportee has been received with the honours due to the great military leader in whose person Russia and her Army have been offended and insulted; and he has been appointed Soviet Vice-Minister of Defence. Has he received these honours as a consolation for the disgrace he has suffered in Warsaw?

PART FOUR

HISTORICAL AND LITERARY ESSAYS

BETWEEN PAST AND FUTURE

In his Trevelyan lectures reproduced in *What is History?*[1] Mr. E. H. Carr presents a philosophical–historical credo. It is usually somewhat risky for a practising historian to come forward as philosopher of history; he may lack the necessary philosophical equipment; and/or he may reveal a divergence between his theory and practice. Mr. Carr's credo is, nevertheless, most impressive; in some respects it is the best statement of its kind ever produced by a British historian.

The vantage-point from which he approaches his theme lies on the borderline between British academic tradition and Marxism. Throughout his argument the interplay of these two influences is greatly in evidence. Much though Mr. Carr has absorbed from the Marxist conception of history, he does not identify himself with it and maintains a certain reserve towards it; and in spite of his explicit criticisms of the British tradition, especially of its empiricist strand, he is of it, even if not quite in it. Indeed, he picks up the threads of British philosophy of history where R. G. Collingwood left them, about a quarter of a century ago, in *The Idea of History*, a book which has had a strong and, one guesses, fairly recent impact on Mr. Carr. If he does not bring to his job Collingwood's philosophical sense and subtlety, he is greatly superior to his predecessor as both historian and political theorist.

He follows Collingwood in the reaction against the 'factological' and empiricist method and sees history as 're-enactment of the past in the historian's mind' and as 'dialogue between the past and the present' (or rather between the past and the future). 'The function of the historian is neither to love the past nor to emancipate himself from the past, but to master and understand it as the key to the understanding of the present.' Yet the historian, as he views bygone times, is immersed in his own epoch, its interests, preoccupations,

<hr>

[1] This review was first published in *The Times Literary Supplement* of 17 November 1961.

and ideas; and so in fact the present provides him with his key to the past. On the face of it we are confronted here with an insoluble contradiction between the present as key to the past and the past as key to the present. To Mr. Carr the contradiction is not insoluble; it represents rather a 'unity of opposites'. With the Hegelian and the Marxist Mr. Carr would probably say that in this lies the dialectics of the problem. Seen from another angle this is the wider and familiar unity of object and subject, the fabric of the past being the object and the historian's present-bound mind the subject.

Thus the historian's work is of necessity subjective, yet it can also be objective; re-enacting the past, he can give us its true image. But he has to 'navigate' between the Scylla of objectivism, which proclaims 'the unqualified primacy of fact over interpretation', and the Charybdis of subjectivism, where history is merely spun out of the historian's mind. At a few stages of his argument Mr. Carr, like Collingwood, comes perilously close to Charybdis. He asks, for instance, 'What is a historical fact?', and, demonstrating the fallacy of the view that 'facts speak for themselves', he asserts that they 'speak only when the historian calls on them'. The 'only reason', for instance, why we are interested in the battle of Hastings is 'that historians regard it as a major historical event'; and whether any social or political occurrence attains the rank of an historical fact depends on whether it is 'accepted by . . . historians as valid and significant'.

There is a flavour of the historian's professional egocentricity about these assertions. Surely events like the battle of Hastings, the discovery of America, the battle of Waterloo, the world wars, the Russian revolution, the extermination of millions of Jews by the Nazis, the first space flight, and so on are historic events regardless of the historians. From the circumstance that to posterity the historian is the only source of knowledge about them it does not follow that it is he who gives them their historic character. It is rather their historic character, i.e., their real impact on human affairs, that causes the historian to 're-enact' such events in his thought. Empiricism, for all its limitations, which Mr. Carr exposes so convincingly, is superior to the subjectivist schools in its understanding of this aspect of the problem. In spite of his subjectivist slips Mr. Carr is also conscious of it when he states with admirable lucidity: 'It does not follow that because a mountain appears to take on different shapes from different angles of vision, it has objectively either no shape at all or an infinity of shapes.' The shape and reality of the historic fact rise above all interpretation. 'It does not follow that . . . because no existing interpretation is wholly objective, one interpretation is as good as another, and the facts of history are in principle not amenable to objective interpretation.' Indeed, only the reality of the historic fact makes the search for historical truth meaningful, a search which like all cognition proceeds in asymptote-like manner.

What then renders one interpretation more valid than the other? Every historian is conducting the dialogue between past and present; yet some of the dialogues are significant and others futile. How much of the 'mountain' the historian sees, and how clearly he sees it, depends largely on his angle of vision, that is on his *Weltanschauung*, as it has been formed by his social background. Therefore, Mr. Carr says, 'study the historian before you study his history'.

We sometimes speak of the course of history as a 'moving procession'. . . . The historian is just another dim figure trudging along in another part of the procession. New vistas, new angles of vision, constantly appear as the procession—and the historian with it—moves along. . . . The point in the procession at which he finds himself determines his angle of vision on the past.

If he happens to find himself with 'a group or nation which is riding in the trough, not on the crest, of historical events', he is bound to get the wrong angle, the false vista, or no vista at all.

Hence the fogs of pessimistic conservatism, scepticism, anti-'historicism' and resignation that hang over so much of contemporary history writing. 'History was full of meaning for British historians so long as it seemed to be going our way; now that it has taken a wrong turning, belief in the meaning of history has become a heresy.' Mr. Carr concentrates the attack on Sir Lewis Namier, Professor Karl Popper and Sir Isaiah Berlin. He remarks on the paradox that Toryism has found its intellectually most aggressive historical mouthpiece in Namier, the naturalized Tory, because, unlike the typical English conservative who 'when scratched turns out to be 75 per cent. a liberal', Namier 'had no roots' in the Whig-Liberal tradition and in its optimistic belief in social progress. No one inhibited by that tradition could fully share Namier's delight

o

at the 'tired lull' (the lack of real argument) in British politics, could see in it 'a greater national maturity', and wish with Namier 'that it may long continue undisturbed by the working of political philosophy'.

In Professor Popper and Sir Isaiah Berlin the conservative aversion from political philosophy takes the form of extreme subjectivism, of a moralism which expects the historian to act as 'hanging judge' (especially *vis-à-vis* the leaders of the Russian revolution), of a bitter hostility towards the scientific treatment of history and towards every form and variety of determinism. On a more popular level these attitudes produce the naïve view that only 'individuals', as opposed to 'social forces', are the historian's proper theme. Mr. Carr aptly quotes Goethe's remark that 'when eras are on the decline all tendencies are subjective; but on the other hand, when matters are ripening for a new epoch, all tendencies are objective'.

What Mr. Carr says about the scientific approach to history, causality, and the problem of individual and society belongs to the most cogent arguments that can be found in the literature of the subject. In the chapter on 'History, Science, and Morality' he demonstrates how closely the methods of science and history have in recent decades moved towards each other, as science, learning to deal with events rather than facts, and with processes rather than static states, has itself become permeated with the historical spirit. It should perhaps be added in parenthesis that Mr. Carr's opinion about the obsoleteness of all 'laws' and their dismissal by modern science is less well founded than he assumes, witness the hesitancy which Broglie, Einstein, and others have experienced precisely on this point.

However, Mr. Carr is on firm ground when he asserts that 'the historian has some excuse for feeling himself more at home in the world of science today than he could have done a hundred years ago'. This is true even if philosophers of history, who are not quite at home either in science or in history, are unaware of it, and 'are so busy telling us that history is not a science . . . that they have no time for its achievements and its potentialities'.

Here and there, however, Mr. Carr's argument is philosophically somewhat shaky, especially when he deals with the principle of causation and the role of accident in history. His references to 'examples from ordinary life' are rather trivial, and he does not quite come to grips with his problem. Those, he says, who dismiss or belittle causality and dwell on chance or accident do so precisely because they ride in the trough and not on the crest of events. 'The view that examination results are all a lottery will always be popular among those who have been placed in the third class.' Yet Mr. Carr himself is by no means sure that examination results are not a lottery. The proverbial shape of Cleopatra's nose, the monkey bite that killed a king, the death of Lenin, he maintains, 'were accidents which modified the course of history'. He rejects in this point the contrary opinions of such determinists as Montesquieu, Marx, and Tolstoy, and concludes that 'it is futile to spirit [the accidents] away or to pretend that . . . they had no effect'.

He dismisses apodictically Trotsky's view that in history as in biology causality 'refracts itself through the accidental' and works through something like a 'natural selection of accidents'. But he makes no attempt of his own to correlate philosophically his acceptance of causation and his recognition of the important and possibly decisive role of the accident. Yet if accident does 'modify the course of history' ought not the historian to make full allowance for it? No, Mr. Carr answers; he is entitled to ignore accident because it does 'not enter into any rational interpretation of history or into the historian's hierarchy of significant causes'. But this surely is begging the question. In what sense is an interpretation that ignores a real and possibly decisive factor of history 'rational'? If accident does modify the course of events yet does not fit the historian's 'hierarchy of significant causes', is there not something wrong with that hierarchy? And may not the historian's causes be far less significant than he pretends? 'Accidental causes cannot be generalized', Mr. Carr adds; and so they are of no theoretical interest. But are then the historian's generalizations not arbitrary?

The strand of subjectivism which underlay an earlier part of Mr. Carr's argument comes here overwhelmingly to the fore. If it were indeed true that an event attains or fails to attain the rank of an historic fact according to 'whether it is accepted by historians as valid and significant', then the historian would be entitled to eliminate from his scheme of things any element he does not consider as significant, no matter what its real impact on events may have been. But his 'hierarchy of causes' would then be merely rationalistic, not rational—it would be spun out of his own mind;

the 'mountain' of history would then have no objective shape, but such shape only as the historian had chosen to give it; and he himself would rule from its top as autocratic master over an amorphous mass of facts. He would not be entitled, however, to rule in the name of 'objective causation' and determinism. Mr. Carr seems unaware of his philosophical inconsistency and of the extent to which he exposes his flank here to counter-attack from Professor Popper and Sir Isaiah Berlin.

Readers of Mr. Carr's *History of Soviet Russia* must be somewhat puzzled by this element of subjectivism, for the *History* is conceived in a predominantly empiricist style, bordering at times on factology—but this is evidently just another case in which the historian's practice diverges from his theory.

It is also odd to argue, as Mr. Carr does, for both the determinist and the teleological approach to history. ('Historical thinking', he quotes Huizinga approvingly, 'is always teleological.') The confusion may be due to careless handling of philosophical terms (of which the use of the term 'absolute' in Chapter V is another example). However, behind this particular confusion there is a real problem which Mr. Carr discusses with much originality. It is this: men act because they are impelled by certain causes; yet in acting they strive for definite aims and purposes. The causes are reflected in the aims; and the aims react upon the causes. The historian is no exception: he views the patterns of historic cause and effect through the prism of his aims and purposes—with his social ideal and his image of the future in his mind. In Namier's wise phrase, historians 'imagine the past and remember the future'; they summon history to serve their ideals.

The cognitive value of an historian's work depends therefore on the nature of his ideal. His understanding of the past gains force and depth from a social purpose which is in harmony with the realities of his own epoch and with the forward movement of his own generation. A reactionary purpose tends to close the historian's mind to the past as well as to the present. Hankering after bygone times, he cannot understand even those times. He cannot conduct fruitfully the dialogue between the past and the future, because with the future he has no contact.

To this reviewer at least the general truth of this reasoning appears undeniable. Yet a caveat may not be out of place here. The historian's conviction that he 'rides on the crest of the tide' may easily lead him to a sort of 'progressive' subjectivism and encourage him to treat history as a mere 'projection of the present on to the past', as it was once treated by the Liberal Croce and the Bolshevik Pokrovsky. Although as a rule the 'progressive' outlook is historically more fertile than the reactionary one, writers nostalgic for the past have sometimes been quicker in detecting the flaws of a newly established and forward-looking régime than have been its adherents—hence the effectiveness of 'feudal socialists', from Sismondi to Tolstoy, in their critique of the bourgeois way of life. On the other hand, the sense of riding 'on the crest of the wave' has turned Stalinist (and Khrushchevite) historians into utterly unscrupulous falsifiers and manipulators. The progressive *Weltanschauung* may indeed give the historian the key to the past; but how often does subjectivism or political arrogance strike it out of his hand!

With these reservations one willingly endorses Mr. Carr's statement that 'history properly so-called can be written only by those who find and accept a sense of direction in history itself'. His declaration of 'faith in the future of society and in the future of history' breaks like a strong and refreshing breeze into the stuffy air of intellectual despondency that has for so long prevailed in our philosophy of history.

Historiography is a progressive science in the sense that it seeks to provide constantly expanding and deepening insights into a course of events which is itself progressive. This is what I should mean by saying that we need 'a constructive outlook over the past'. Modern historiography has grown up during the past two centuries in this dual belief in progress, and cannot survive without it, since it is this belief which provides it with its standard of significance . . .

For myself I remain an optimist; and when Sir Lewis Namier warns me to eschew programmes and ideals, and Professor Oakeshott tells me that we are going nowhere in particular and that all that matters is to see that nobody rocks the boat, and Professor Popper wants to keep that dear old T-model on the road by dint of a little piecemeal engineering, and Professor Trevor-Roper knocks screaming radicals on the nose, and Professor Morison pleads for history written in a sane conservative spirit, I shall look out on a world in tumult and a world in travail, and shall answer in the well-worn words of a great scientist: 'And yet—it moves'.

The author is perhaps less explicit than he might have been

about his 'sense of history's direction'. He leaves the reader with
the impression that his image of the future, which must imprint
itself so strongly on his image of the past, is a somewhat precarious
common denominator of such disparate phenomena as the Soviet
planned economy, the anti-imperialist revolutions of Afro-Asia, the
welfare state, Keynesianism and the heritage of British radicalism.
And Mr. Carr may himself not have noticed that in closing his
argument on a triumphantly optimistic note he echoes in fact the
optimism of that nineteenth-century liberal view of history with
which he has dealt so severely at the beginning of the argument.
This is by no means accidental, for, to paraphrase Mr. Carr, he
too 'when scratched turns out to be 75 per cent. a liberal', one of the
most unorthodox, radical, and open-minded British liberals of his
generation.

THE MENSHEVIKS

I: GEORGE PLEKHANOV

THE Mensheviks are sometimes labelled the Girondins of the Russian revolution; but they are still waiting for their Lamartine, for the historian who would be willing to identify himself with their ideas, their experience, and their tragedy. So far the Bolsheviks have monopolized the historians' attention. There has been no lack, at least here in the West, of writers willing to embrace the Menshevik cause, and even to do so with some ostentatiousness. But those writers prefer to compose volumes of anti-communist polemics rather than to present us with any historical image of Menshevism. Meanwhile even as an émigré school of thought Menshevism has reached its end: its veterans are nearly all dead and even the *Sotsialisticheskii Vestnik*, its famous periodical, has ceased publication.

Any survey of Menshevism must offer an assessment of the stature and the role of George Plekhanov, whom his American biographer, Mr. Samuel Ho Baron,[1] describes, tritely but truly, as 'the father of Russian Marxism'. It is difficult to imagine the Russian revolution (or even Leninism) without Plekhanov's work. It was Plekhanov who made of the advance of Marxism into Russia a brilliant intellectual conquest. He was assisted by Paul Axelrod, Vera Zasulich, and Leon Deutsch; former Narodniks, Populists, who like himself had been compelled to leave Russia: with them he formed the so-called Group of the Emancipation of Labour in Geneva, early in the eighteen-eighties.

Beyond this tiny and poverty-stricken circle of propagandists, there was, for many years, almost no Marxism and no social democratic movement among the Russians. Plekhanov and his friends were the real vanguard of revolution, or rather the vanguard of

---

[1] *Plekhanov: the Father of Russian Marxism* (London 1964). This article was originally published in *The Listener* of 30 April, 1964.

a vanguard that was to come before the end of the century. Yet when, after twenty years of propaganda, in 1903, the movement which they had inspired split into factions, Plekhanov and his associates all became Mensheviks; not one of them turned into a Bolshevik.

Like all Narodniks, Plekhanov at first expected that the rural commune, which still seemed to be surviving in the Russia of the 1870s, would provide the base for a predominantly agrarian native socialism; and that the peasantry would rise to re-make Russian society. Bakunin was the formative political influence; the great anarchist, despite his bitter feud with Marx, conveyed to many young Populists a profound admiration for Marx and Marxism.

These pages in Plekhanov's biography take us back to the *milieu* of the Russian intelligentsia and to its intense ideological searchings, which it is now all too fashionable to view only through the prism of Dostoevsky's *The Possessed*. There is no question that in his savage satire Dostoevsky caught some real weaknesses and vices of the Populist movement; but he overlooked its virtues. The *milieu* of *The Possessed* is the *milieu* of the young Plekhanov: the landlord's son, and the student of the Mining Institute of St. Petersburg, might have rubbed shoulders with the Verkhovenskys, the Stavrogins, and the Shatovs. Moreover, the distance between the novelist himself and that *milieu* was sometimes negligible. Thus we see Dostoevsky, at the height of his fame and at the close of his life, and Plekhanov, at twenty and at the threshold of his political career, facing each other over the coffin of Nekrasov, the famous poet of the Populists. The scene might have been taken from Dostoevsky's own pages—and it is a pity that Plekhanov's biographer has made so little of it. The novelist was still in that slightly remorseful mood, in which the success of *The Possessed* at the Tsarist court had put him. He tried to show a little innocuous friendliness towards the radicals and revolutionaries. Nekrasov's funeral was a good occasion for that. At the poet's grave Dostoevsky compared him with Pushkin, a somewhat exalted and insincere comparison. Then Plekhanov spoke on behalf of a group of revolutionaries (who had come to the cemetery armed with revolvers and ready, if need be, to fight off the gendarmes). An altercation occurred, for Plekhanov objected to the comparison between Pushkin and Nekrasov, saying that Pushkin had done little more than 'sing of the toes of ballerinas'. The grim confrontation, the queer argument, the revolvers—how close we are to Varvara Petrovna's *salon* in *The Possessed*.

Yet the gulf between the old Dostoevsky and the young Plekhanov, though deep, was less wide than it appeared. Shortly after the encounter at the cemetery, Plekhanov was already breaking with Populism and attacking precisely those of its weaknesses and vices that Dostoevsky had stigmatized. In the famous dispute of the Norodnovoltsy, held at Voronezh in 1879, Plekhanov—still only twenty-two—carried the argument to a breach, because he objected to the Party's acting in isolation from the people, 'behind the people's back', and to its allowing itself to be carried away by terrorism. It was on the terrorism and the arrogant self-sufficiency of the revolutionaries that Dostoevsky had also dwelt so penetratingly, so obsessively, and so distortingly. But whereas Dostoevsky blamed the revolutionary idea for the faults of the revolutionaries, Plekhanov criticized those faults for the sake of the revolutionary idea. Dostoevsky called the revolutionaries to redeem their sinful souls through religion and mysticism. Plekhanov found an answer to their critical problems in–Marxism. Dostoevsky saw Russia's salvation in her *urodivyie*, her holy lunatics and cripples, capable of living in utter abnegation and true Christianity. The young Plekhanov himself stands as a living refutation of *The Possessed*: he symbolizes the self-regeneration of the revolutionary movement, its moral and political metamorphosis, its passage from terrorism and Populism to Marxism.

Plekhanov had left Russia early in 1880. He was to remain in exile for over thirty-six years, almost till the end of his life. He devoted his first years abroad to a diligent and fascinated first-hand study of Marxism. He also watched attentively the changes occurring in Russia's social structure. The rural commune was a crumbling anachronism on which nothing could be built, socialism least of all. He saw the peasantry succumbing to the market economy, to private property, and capitalism—these peasants, therefore, were to him no longer the force of elemental revolution idealized by the Narodniks, but the retrograde class, submerged in the 'rural idiocy' of which Marx spoke.

What then were the chances of socialism in Russia? In the bourgeois west the industrial workers were fighting for socialism. But in pre-industrial Russia there were very few urban workers, and even those few were only displaced peasants. How long would it take for modern industry and a socialist proletariat to grow up? Writing to Marx in 1881, Vera Zasulich wondered: 'If ... our rural commune were to perish, the socialist in Russia would have no alternative but to devote himself to . . . calculations designed to find out . . . *in how many centuries* Russian capitalism will perhaps attain a development similar to that of western Europe'. Here, in this suggestion of a centuries-long wait under capitalism, was perhaps the seed of the future Menshevik failure. Marx in his reply preferred to encourage even the utopian Narodnik hopes about the rural commune rather than to countenance the fatalistic prospect of 'centuries of capitalism'.

Plekhanov's prognostications were more complex and elastic than Zasulich's but he accepted the axiom that Russia must go through her own capitalist development to the end before she could even begin to move towards socialism. The coming revolution was to be bourgeois, not socialist. This was to be an article of faith with nearly all Russian socialists, Mensheviks and Bolsheviks alike, until the year 1917. Yet what was the socialists' role in a bourgeois revolution? What could fighters for the emancipation of labour strive for in an upheaval which could only establish a new mode of the exploitation of labour? Plekhanov answered that the workers must wrest their rights and political freedoms from Tsardom; that they should struggle, if possible, in alliance with the liberal bourgeoisie; and continue the struggle even after the revolution, if need be, against the bourgeoisie. The long-term dilemma, however, remained unresolved.

Plekhanov did not content himself with translating Marxism into the Russian idiom. He was one of the leading lights of European socialism as well, one of the foremost spokesmen of the newly formed International. At least since the death of Friedrich Engels, in 1895, if not even earlier, he was Europe's first philosophical exponent of Marxism. The interpretation of the economic-political aspects of the doctrine had fallen primarily to Kaul Kautsky, behind whom stood the authority of the most powerful and successful socialist party in the world. Plekhanov was the subtler and the more brilliant mind and he held the pride of place as the interpreter of dialectical materialism. He confronted Marxist theory with the philosophical currents of the time, as no one has done it since; and he used Marxism more systematically than either Franz Mehring or Antonio Labriola did as a tool of literary and artistic criticism. When the great controversy between the revisionists and the orthodox Marxists began in the late 1890s, Plekhanov at once moved into the fray as the most irreconcilable of the Marxists— only Rosa Luxemburg, who was much younger, was as uncompromising. He turned even against Kautsky when that official guardian of orthodoxy tried diplomatically to assuage the controversy. Incidentally, one should not judge the intellectual quality of that original debate against revisionism by analogy with the pidgin Marxism to which Moscow and Peking are treating us just now. As to Plekhanov: his biographer rightly remarks that here was a major paradox in his fortunes: the very success of his anti-revisionist campaign paved the way for Bolshevism and for his own defeat.

The relationship between Plekhanov and Lenin is of absorbing historical interest. Even in the heat of controversy, Lenin willingly acknowledged himself as Plekhanov's disciple. 'It is impossible', he wrote as late as in 1920, 'to become an intelligent and *genuine* communist without studying, precisely *studying, all* that Plekhanov has written on philosophy, for what he has written is the best that can be found in the whole international literature on Marxism.' Plekhanov, on the other hand, never quite freed himself of the sentiment with which he had first welcomed the young Lenin as his political descendant, who would not merely continue his work but bring it to fruition. This distinguishes Plekhanov's attitude to Lenin from that of all other Mensheviks. He did not in fact join the Mensheviks at once during the 1903 split. At first indeed, he, alone of all the leading Russian Marxists, stood with Lenin. Only later did he have second thoughts and begin to vacillate. Then he moved away from Lenin in 1905, during the great dress rehearsal for the revolution, when he already acted the ultra-Menshevik part that was to be his in 1917. He dogmatically insisted on the exclusively bourgeois character of the revolution; he demanded that the party accept the liberal bourgeoisie as its ally, as its senior ally. 'We should not have taken up arms' was the moral he drew from the Moscow insurrection of 1905. But afterwards he again moved closer to Lenin and co-operated with the Bolsheviks, when all Menshevik and intermediate groups boycotted them.

Even in 1912, when Lenin proclaimed his own faction to be *the* party and declared that the Mensheviks and whoever went with them placed themselves outside its ranks—even then Plekhanov still stuck to Lenin. He felt that Lenin was drawing the conclusions from his, Plekhanov's, premisses and theories. This was broadly true, except in one point: Plekhanov, ever since he had in the eighties turned to the industrial worker, put the peasant out of his mind, as it were. Lenin, having, with Plekhanov, turned to the industrial worker, then turned back to the peasant in order to win him as an ally for the worker, a junior ally. Plekhanov saw in this a relapse into the illusions of Populism, of which his own Marxism was the absolute negation. Lenin's Marxism, being somewhat further removed from Populism, was free enough to reabsorb much of the old Populist sensitivity to the peasantry and yearning for accord with the *muzhik*.

Only the outbreak of the First World War separated Plekhanov and Lenin finally and irrevocably. Lenin proclaimed it to be the socialist's duty to turn the imperialist war into civil war, while Plekhanov voiced without inhibition his social patriotism. In 1917, when he returned to Russia, he adopted so 'moderate' and anti-revolutionary a posture that even the most right-wing Mensheviks avoided having any connexion with him. This was a sad home-coming after thirty-six years. And it was the bitter irony of Plek-hanov's life that when, in September 1917, General Kornilov was staging his *coup d'état*—the *coup* that was intended to destroy Kerensky's Government and moderate socialism as well as Bolshev-ism—he wanted Plekhanov as a Minister in his Cabinet. Needless to say, the old philosopher was above such temptations. Intense though his bitterness against Lenin was, it knew limits. Plekhanov's bitterness was all the more intense the less he now understood the Bolsheviks: he castigated them as Bakunin's followers, as anarch-ists, destroyers of the Russian state, and as belated Narodniks who had abandoned Marxism for the old, discredited utopia of a peas-ant socialism. An exhausted and disillusioned man, he died shortly after the October revolution, on 12 June, 1918.

The relationship between Plekhanov and Lenin, so complex and ambivalent, recalls to one's mind the connexion between another intellectual inspirer of revolution and another revolutionary leader, Erasmus and Luther. Plekhanov is the Erasmus of pre-revolution-ary Russia, the Marxist Erasmus. 'Erasmus seems at times', writes Johan Huizinga, the Dutch historian, 'the man who was not strong enough for his age. In that robust sixteenth century it seems as if the oaken strength of Luther was necessary, the steely edge of Cal-vin, the white heat of Loyola. Not only were their force and their fervour necessary, but also their depth, their unsparing, undaunted consistency. . . .' The 'oaken strength' of Lenin, and the 'steely edge' of Trotsky, it may be said, accorded also better with the needs of 1917 than Plekhanov's ideas and character. His misfortune was that he had exhausted himself in the great intellectual labour through which he had prepared the revolution, just as Erasmus had spent himself in the work of criticism and enlightenment through which he had paved the way for the Reformation. Each performed his task within the limits that his time, his generation, and his historical situation set him. Neither was able to transcend those limits.

II: THE DÉBÂCLE OF 1917[1]

The Mensheviks never recovered from the shipwreck they suffered in 1917. It was not only the Bolshevik insurrection that defeated them—their own moral *débâcle* overwhelmed them as well. This had begun soon after the February revolution, while they seemed to be riding on the crest of the wave. Like other parties, they were at first thrown into disarray by the unexpected collapse of Tsardom. Most of their leaders were exiled or in prison. Their rank and file had been scattered by war-time mobilizations. Their political thinking was confused. Their organizations were disrupted. But whereas other parties, notably the Bolsheviks, presently overcame the confusion, the Mensheviks did not: with every month that passed their disarray grew deeper and deeper.

Not a single one of the great pioneers and historic figures of Menshevism played any role in the events of 1917. Plekhanov had exhausted himself in the great labour through which he had educated two generations of Marxists and prepared the revolution. He and his closest associates, Axelrod, Zasulich, and Deutsch, who, even as lonely mouthpieces of socialism, had held out with him for nearly forty years, were cruelly by-passed by the events. Nearly all of them now stood far to the right of the main body of the Mensheviks.

Martov and Potresov, the younger leaders and real initiators of Menshevism in 1903, were also in utter discord with their own party: Potresov was with Plekhanov far to the right of it, while

[1] First published in *The Listener* of 4 February, 1965.

Martov was far to the left. Dan, Tseretelli, Skobelev, Abramovich, and Lieber, these were now the official chiefs and spokesmen of Menshevism. They were far less known than Plekhanov and Martov; and they were far smaller in stature.

That the founders and inspirers of Menshevism had no common language with their party in 1917, and that second-raters replaced them at its head, was ominous enough. Worse still was the fact that Menshevism had become a loose agglomeration of disparate groups and individuals, lacking the cohesion and structure of a political party. No bonds of solidarity and no ties of discipline united the Mensheviks of the right and centre with those of the left and extreme left, and of all the intermediate splinter groups. Every one of the many political crises of that year deepened and accentuated the discord between the 'social-patriots' and the internationalists in their midst. And while the National Executive consisted of moderates, the Petrograd organization and its committee were in a most radical mood. To quote Sukhanov, the well-known chronicler of the revolution:

The Menshevik internationalists had in their hands the entire party organization of the capital. The Petersburg Committee consisted of Martov's followers. The branches in the working class districts . . . had long been demanding a formal break with official Menshevism. This affair dragged on; the demand was obstructed by the efforts of old and influential Mensheviks. But now Tseretelli and company, those Mensheviks of the right wing, had become unendurable . . . A mass exodus from the organization had begun. The example was set by Larin, a well-known Menshevik economist. In the first part of September, the strongest of our working class organizations split . . . the ferment spread to other districts and the provinces.

What a contrast all this formed with the state of affairs in Bolshevism! Among the Bolsheviks, too, there were various shades of radicalism and moderation, of right and left. A few moderates had indeed left the ranks soon after the February revolution. But ever since all the shades and groupings had been parts of a single whole, cohering into the disciplined party of which Lenin was the accepted leader. If the story of Menshevism in 1917 is one of ceaseless splitting and disintegration, the story of Bolshevism is, on the contrary, one of continuous integration and unification. All inner Bolshevik quarrels and rivalries and all *émigré* squabbles of pre-revolutionary years were as if overcome and forgotten. The *Otsovi-*

sty and *Vperiodovtsy*, the God seekers, the boycotters, and ultra-radicals, who had been at loggerheads with the Leninists for nearly a decade, were all returning to the fold; among them men like Lunacharsky, Pokrovsky, Manuilsky. On the other hand, Trotsky and a large galaxy of brilliant revolutionaries, former Mensheviks most of them, Yoffe, Uritsky, Volodarsky, Ryazanov, Karakhan, Yureniev, and others, were also entering the Bolshevik Party, not to speak of Alexandra Kollontai who had gone over to the Leninists even earlier.

In a way this contrast between Menshevik disintegration and Bolshevik integration offered a retrospective comment on the great debate that had given rise to the schism fourteen years earlier. That schism had originally turned on the formula defining the structure of the party. Lenin had advocated a clear-cut, strictly defined, massively built organization, consisting only of active and militant members. Martov had envisaged a much 'broader' party, accommodating well-wishers and fellow-travellers as well as full-time activists. In later years, after 1907, the controversy shifted to the question whether the party should abandon clandestinity and emerge into the open. The Bolsheviks insisted once again on the need for a tight, centralized organization working both underground and in the open, whereas most Mensheviks, 'the Liquidators', as Lenin labelled them, preferred to give up clandestine work and to give up the irksome disciplinarian rigidities of a centralized party. These theoretical differences were now, in 1917, reflected, and indeed exaggerated in the realities of the two parties, one closely knit, dynamic, and expansive, the other loose, lax, and falling asunder.

There were other, deeper reasons for the Menshevik *débâcle*. The Mensheviks struggled against the Bolsheviks with a guilty conscience. They were tortured by remorse and qualms. The following scene will illustrate this. It is related by Irakli Tseretelli in his posthumously published *Memoirs of the February Revolution*. The author, famous as socialist spokesman in the second Duma and a hard-labour convict, was in 1917 leader of official Menshevism and mainstay of the Liberal–Socialist coalition. He writes:

One evening we, the Socialist Ministers, reported at a meeting of Socialist leaders of the Petersburg Soviet about the government's decision to arrest Lenin and the other chieftains of the July rising.

Tseretelli refers here to the turbulent July demonstrations in

Petrograd, which the government suppressed, charging Lenin and his party with an attempt at an armed rising and high treason. It was then that Lenin was branded as a spy in the pay of the German army. Tseretelli goes on to say:

All those present were disconcerted. Mikhail Issakovich Lieber, the most impulsive of all, exclaimed in anguish: 'History will look u₁on us as upon criminals!' As he said this he suffered a nervous fit. Yet he was one of the most determined adversaries of the Bolsheviks; he had denounced them as traitors . . . and when he recovered from the fit . . . he took a most active part in the liquidation of their rising. If such was his first reaction to our decision to strike at the Bolsheviks, it is easy to imagine the mood among other comrades.

Tseretelli is out to prove that the February régime was defeated only because it was unable to form a 'strong government'. Other anti-Bolsheviks and leaders of the February régime, Kerensky, Chernov, and Abramovich, have offered other explanations, and concluded that if only they had had the courage to do what Lenin did, that is to take Russia out of the war and sign a separate peace, the October revolution would never have occurred. Each of these answers contains an element of the truth; but none comes to grips with the issue. Why then did the Mensheviks and their associates fail to create the 'strong' government? And why did they not have the courage to take Russia out of the war?

Here past and tradition must also be considered. It is customary to think of the Mensheviks as Russia's Social Democrats. This description, though correct in itself, is inadequate. Past and tradition set the Mensheviks apart from other Social Democrats. Until shortly before the revolution they and the Bolsheviks had nominally still belonged to the same party. They were still trying to re-create the unity of that party in the spring of 1917, while Lenin was on his way to Russia. Despite their abhorrence of clandestinity they had been, till Tsardom's last day, a clandestine party. They had lived with the Bolsheviks in places of deportation and had shared prison cells with them. Like the Bolsheviks, they were committed to Marxist orthodoxy, and treated this commitment more seriously than did almost any European Social Democrats. They had never been revisionists or reformists. They had never believed in that peaceful transition from capitalism to socialism that Edouard Bernstein and the English Fabians had preached. They had been proud of Plekhanov's repudiations of Millerandism and *possibilisme*. They had rejected, that is, the idea that a socialist party might be justified in entering a bourgeois coalition government. They had always been convinced that in such a government socialists could only prop up the bourgeois order. And now, in the middle of this great revolution, this was precisely what they, the Menshevik ministers, were doing in Prince Lvov's and Kerensky's governments: they were renouncing their own past and their own proud convictions.

Yet, in a way, they were still the slaves of an orthodoxy. They still believed in the apostolic truth that the task of the Russian revolution was to sweep away the rubble of feudalism, to establish a bourgeois-democratic régime, and on its basis to modernize Russia. 'Russia is not ripe for socialist revolution!'—this was their cry; and until recently this had been the Bolsheviks' axiom as well. When suddenly, in April 1917, Lenin called for the overthrow of capitalism and the establishment of proletarian dictatorship in Russia, the Mensheviks felt that they had every reason to resist his course of action in the name of Marxist principle. This was, of course, sheer rationalization; it concealed the Mensheviks' attachment to bourgeois democracy, or rather their yearning for it. All the same, their conviction that the Bolsheviks were in conflict with reason, Marxism, and socialism was sincere and passionate.

Yet they were unable to act wholeheartedly on that conviction. As educated, theoretically minded socialists, they had learned their lessons from the political history of western Europe and were steeped in the traditions of the great French Revolution, of 1848, and of the Commune of Paris. In this respect there was no difference between Mensheviks and Bolsheviks—both had an intense historical awareness, such as was rare among their western-European comrades. A little incident, related again by Sukhanov, speaks for itself. Sukhanov describes how in the Petrograd Soviet, Mikhail Lieber, the same who was so afraid that 'history would look upon the Mensheviks as criminals', inveighed against Lenin's party and called for severe reprisals. Suddenly there was an interruption from the floor. Martov jumped to his feet and shouted at the speaker: '*Versalets!*' The term, with its pejorative undertone, meant 'man of Versailles'. The interjection, which would hardly have been intelligible to a western-European audience, referred to Thiers, Gallifet, and their associates, who in 1871 had withdrawn to Versailles

P

and from there fought against the Commune of Paris, suppressing it in blood. In the Petrograd of 1917 there was no need to explain to a Soviet audience the meaning of Martov's exclamation. All Socialist Parties and groups felt deeply that they were involved in a drama of which the Commune of Paris had been one of the early acts. Newspaper articles were studded with terms such as 'our Cavaignacs', 'our Louis Blancs', and other allusions to 1848. The dead of all European revolutions and counter-revolutions had risen from their graves and now stood behind the backs of the living.

What the experience of all earlier revolutions told the Mensheviks was that nothing can be more degrading and pernicious for any party of revolution than to struggle against an enemy on the left. Had not Cromwell and the Puritans become corrupted by the suppression of the Levellers? Had not the Jacobins declined after they had guillotined the radicals and egalitarians among their own comrades? 'No, we have, and we can have, no enemy on the left' Martov and his friends concluded; and even the Mensheviks of the right felt strangely uneasy. Something of that uneasiness is still there in Tseretelli's sprawling *Memoirs*, although he wrote them in the course of three or four decades in exile, and broke them off abruptly in the middle of his story with a lament over the missing 'strong arm' that might have and should have, but has not, forestalled the October revolution.

It is not, of course, that there was never any hint of the 'strong arm' in 1917. Tseretelli himself was Minister of Interior in the government that ordered the arrest of Lenin and Zinoviev, and imprisoned Trotsky, Kamenev, Lunacharsky, and many others. The 'socialist Ministers' presided impassively over the *pogrom* of the Bolsheviks after the July days. But the strong arm could not remain raised against the enemy on the left for any length of time: presently a mortal danger—the Kornilov mutiny—arose from the right, which Kerensky and the socialist ministers could repel only with Bolshevik help. Once again, the Mensheviks realized that they could not afford fighting against their enemy on the left. Nor could they afford making peace with him. This was their double undoing.

One can say of the Mensheviks what Carlyle once said of the Girondins: 'Their weapons . . . [were] Political Philosophy, Respectability, and Eloquence. . . .' Of the Bolsheviks we may say that their weapons 'were those of mere Nature; Audacity and Impetuosity which may become Ferocity, as of men complete in their determination, in their conviction; nay, of men . . . who . . . must either prevail or perish.' Contrary to a popular misconception, it was not the Bolsheviks in 1917 but the Mensheviks who were the 'men of the Formula', the doctrinaires, who in the name of an abstract principle or constitutional dogma turned a deaf ear on life's realities: on the peasantry's cry for land and peace, and on the nation's war weariness. They exhorted the nation to go on bleeding itself white; and implored the peasants to have patience with the lords of the manors. 'So they perorate and speculate; and call on Friends of Law, when the question is not Law or No-Law, but Life or No-Life. Pedants of the Revolution. . . .' They were indeed, like the Girondins, 'men of parts, of philosophic culture, decent behaviour; not condemnable . . . but most unfortunate. They wanted a Republic of Virtues, wherein themselves should be head; and they could only get a Republic of the Strengths, wherein others than they were head'. And so they fell—yes, 'they fell, but not without a sigh from most Historians'.

III: EXILE AND DEBASEMENT[1]

The well-known Menshevik leader, Rafail Abramovitch, recollects how crestfallen his comrades were during the October revolution: 'We knew', he says, 'that the game was lost, that the Bolshevik rising had caught the government unawares, and that it was too late to try to organize serious resistance.'

Yet for a few moments the Mensheviks seemed to rally. Defeated, they tried to overcome their inner divisions and to draw together; for the first time in years they formed something like a united party. Martov again became their leader. His radical stance, unacceptable to them when they were in office, suited them quite well in opposition. Like everyone else, the Mensheviks were convinced that the Bolshevik government would soon, very soon, collapse; and that it would be remembered in history only as a strange, perhaps a tragic, episode, as the Russian revolution's brief utopian aberration. They had no doubt that it was they, the Mensheviks, who were riding the wave of the future.

This self-confidence could not last. As the months and the years were passing, and the Bolshevik régime was consolidating itself and

[1] First published in The Listener of 1 April, 1965.

transforming Russian society, the Mensheviks were shaken in their sense of values and of realities. Very early, Martov, who was magnificent at heart-searching and self-interrogation, began to wonder: was the October revolution really nothing more than a reckless adventure, a doomed premature essay in socialism? And even if it was only such a utopian aberration, should the Mensheviks assist the bourgeois Liberals, the right-wing Populists, and the White generals to bring that aberration to a speedy and bloody end? Or should they rather join hands with the Bolsheviks? Martov called for the restitution of political freedom and for the re-establishment of the Constituent Assembly which the Bolsheviks had dispersed. But already in May 1918 he proclaimed his party's solidarity with the Bolsheviks in their struggle against counter-revolution. And throughout the civil war he and his closest associates, whatever their mental reservations, were indeed on the Bolshevik side of the front, even though this estranged them from those right-wing Mensheviks who were on the other side.

However they acted, the Mensheviks were in one way or another at loggerheads with themselves. If, as Martov still claimed, the October revolution was a hopeless venture, if what Lenin and Trotsky were building was some sort of a socialist castle in the air, was it worth defending such a castle? Martov felt that he had to recognize the genuineness of the socialist aspirations and the historic legitimacy of the Soviet régime. In his so-called April Theses of 1920 he argued that although Russia was too backward to achieve socialism, the world at large, and the West in particular, were not; and so Russia was justified in producing her prelude to international socialist revolution. This was precisely what Lenin and Trotsky had argued.

However, Martov's belated acknowledgment of the legitimacy of the October revolution and even the services he rendered the Soviets during the civil war could not bridge the gulf between his party and the Bolsheviks. In the aftermath of the civil war the Mensheviks were eager to exploit any difficulty with which Lenin's government was confronted, as it struggled desperately with economic ruin and chaos. The Bolsheviks, frightened by famines, popular discontent, and widespread peasant risings, abandoned the idea of Soviet democracy, clung with a fresh and grim determination to their monopoly of power and turned it into the single-party system. They took to persecuting the Mensheviks with a panicky brutality, which was, however, tempered by cautionary historical reminiscences, scruples, and forebodings. Lenin did not wish to guillotine Russia's Girondins. There was no great purge of the Mensheviks, no execution of their leaders. Martov, Dan, Abramovitch, Nikolayevsky, and other lesser lights were allowed, or rather encouraged, to leave Russia and establish their political centre abroad. And now comes the long, melancholy story of Menshevism in exile. For a few years the *émigrés* managed to keep up contacts with friends in Russia; but they were unable to initiate any significant political action. The *émigrés* came to act as expert advisers on Soviet policy and communism to some of the European Social Democratic Parties. But their position was awkward and their influence slight. To their European comrades they still looked like Marxist doctrinaires and dogmatists: they were in fact still preaching the imminent advent of socialist revolution in Europe and called for proletarian dictatorship. On the other hand, even moderate Western Social Democrats, such as the English Fabians, suspected them of plotting against the Soviet government or, at least, of engaging in a clandestine anti-Bolshevik agitation.

Thus, suspected as almost crypto-communists by some and as underhand counter-revolutionaries by others, the *émigré* Mensheviks could do little or nothing in practical politics. They concentrated all their energies on the *Sotsialisticheskii Vestnik*, the *Socialist Courier*. This periodical, which Martov had founded in Berlin early in 1921, served as the forum for Menshevik ideas for forty-three years. No other *émigré* periodical survived for so long. Political earthquakes drove the editors from country to country, but the *Vestnik*, always carefully edited, appeared with incredible regularity. This was the Mensheviks' labour of love. As the editorial team was not fortified by influx of fresh blood, the paper was in the end written mostly by octogenarians. Its limitations were painfully obvious: it lacked vision, imagination, capacity to inspire. As a critic of Moscow's rulers, the *Vestnik* could not be compared with Trotsky's Bulletin *Oppozitsii*.

In exile Menshevism went on wrestling with the question that had beset Martov as early as 1918: what does Bolshevism represent? Was it—and is it—a malicious interruption of the legitimate trend of Russian history, a wasteful interval, a terrible hiatus? Or is it the legitimate product and the culmination of Russian history? With the years and decades the question was becoming anachronistic. The mere duration and the Protean vitality of the régime founded in 1917 seemed to have resolved it. Yet the controversy went on. The Mensheviks either had to try to keep abreast of all the immense events and upheavals, that is, to read the historical time aright; or else, if they were to persist in denying any positive value to Russia's historic movement, in denying even the very fact of that movement, then they would be smashing, as it were, all the clocks of history.

When Martov died in 1923, Dan and Abramovitch, the joint editors of the *Vestnik*, were committed to keep up the 'Martovist line'. Martov had sought to come to terms with the October revolution without surrendering to Bolshevism. Dan and Abramovitch lacked Martov's dialectical ability and the issues were getting more and more complex and difficult. Yet throughout the 1920s, and even the thirties, the Mensheviks still kept within bounds the conflict between their acceptance and their rejection of the revolution.

In the end, however, the Martovist tradition broke down, dissolving into its constituent parts; and each of Martov's two successors embraced a different aspect of it. Abramovitch came to repudiate all that the Bolshevik revolution stood for, while Dan proclaimed his acceptance of it. It was no matter of chance that this, the last schism in the old Menshevik Guard, occurred in the United States at the close of the last war; Russia's victorious emergence from the war, the defeat of nazism and fascism in Europe, and the growing Russo-American conflict called for a new view of the past and a new prospect for the future.

Both Dan and Abramovitch have left behind their books. The *Soviet Revolution* is little more than a re-hash of Abramovitch's articles published in the *Vestnik* over the years. Dan's work, published in Russian eighteen years ago, and only now in English, has more historical depth and is better written; yet it is also ill-proportioned, fragmentary, opinionated. Notorious in 1917 for his anti-Leninism, Dan speaks of the historically creative character of Leninism and of its ineffaceable and, on the whole, beneficial influence upon Russia's and mankind's destinies.

This is in effect an extraordinary Menshevik self-critique. He goes back to the roots of the Russian revolutionary tradition, delves into the origins of Bolshevism, re-examines Russia's social structure and the alignments of her social classes, and finds in these the causes of Bolshevik success and Menshevik failure. He tells his comrades, or ex-comrades, that it was their party, not Lenin's, that has misunderstood Russia's needs, the logic of the revolution, and the trend of events in the world. We Mensheviks, he says in effect, believed that Russia must go through two different revolutions: an imminent bourgeois one, which must proceed under bourgeois leadership; and another, a socialist one, which would be accomplished only in a more or less remote future by the working class.

Leninism had grasped from the outset that a poor and backward nation like the Russian could not advance and modernize itself otherwise than by revolution, and that the bourgeoisie was more likely to obstruct revolution than to promote it. It was the historic error of Menshevism that it relied on the Russian middle class to do what the French middle class had done in 1789. Writing some years before the victory of the Chinese revolution, Dan was very emphatic about the relevance of Leninism to the peoples of Asia and Africa.

Dan then goes on to say that Menshevism, having taken up a wrong attitude in a decisive historic situation, came into conflict with its own socialist principles, and so condemned itself to an ideological degeneration, which even Martov was unable to arrest. What he says about this runs parallel with Trotsky's familiar argument about the degeneration of Bolshevism. If the debasement of Bolshevism consisted, according to Trotsky, in the party's abandonment of the proletarian democracy and internationalism, then the degeneration of Menshevism, of which Dan speaks, consisted in its virtual renunciation of Marxism and socialism and its conversion to bourgeois democracy and liberalism. Such, says Dan, has been the paradoxical evolution of the two great currents of Russian socialism, that neither the Mensheviks nor the Bolsheviks of 1903 or 1905 would have recognized themselves in the images of themselves of the nineteen-thirties and the nineteen-forties.

Dan's extraordinary self-criticism becomes a historical apology for Bolshevism. In the end he excuses even Stalinism, with its violence and ideological prevarication. Of course, when Dan was writing some of these pages, the wartime tide of pro-Stalinism ran high in allied countries, especially in the United States. But he was a man of too strong convictions, too serious political an experience, and too high an integrity to be treated as a trimmer. The fact that Russia was emerging triumphantly from Armageddon, with the Third Reich prostrate at her feet, impressed him very deeply—was this not the supreme test and vindication of Bolshevism? He refused to consider the price of the Soviet victory, to ponder any alternatives to Stalin's policies, and to look critically at 'degenerate' Bolshevism. A dying man, he was escaping from debased Menshevism to depraved Bolshevism. And as he did so, he echoed Alexander Herzen's belief that 'whereas western Europe was approaching socialism through freedom, Russia could advance towards freedom only by way of socialism'.

Abramovitch's book is a most vehement rejection precisely of that belief. Russia, he says, has advanced nowhere since 1917. Nor has China made any progress since 1949. There is no merit in any communist revolution, even from the point of view of an underdeveloped country. 'This savagery', says Abramovitch, 'will never contribute to the cultural development or well-being of mankind . . . . this totalitarian rule is not so much anti-capitalist as it is antihuman.' But how and why has this huge black emptiness come over Russia? Abramovitch tries no historical explanation. If Dan sometimes carries objectivism to a grotesque extreme, Abramovitch's subjectivism is all too often absurd. He does not investigate; he castigates. He does not analyse the social character of Russia's régime; he indicts and condemns it. He declares the old Marxist criteria to be irrelevant: the issue is no longer between capitalism and socialism. 'Russia', he says, 'has succumbed to the new totalitarian version of the ancient oriental despotism.' Not surprisingly, he harks back to the pre-1917 era. 'The old Russia', he claims, 'was already well advanced on the path of evolution towards a modern democratic state.' In his eagerness to belittle all the revolutionary factors that had been at work in Russia, Abramovitch plays down the record even of his own party: he grossly exaggerates all the shifts to the right that had ever occurred in Menshevism. He draws a portrait of Menshevism which is as if designed to make it impossible for any American Congressional Committee to charge the Mensheviks with any past association with the Bolsheviks; and he does not seem to notice that what he has drawn is a malicious caricature of his own party. At the same time he presents the revolution as the combined product of accidental circumstances, clever Bolshevik unscrupulousness, and Lenin's craving for power. Unfortunately, his demonological conception of Bolshevism has not failed to exercise its influence on American sovietology.

He concludes his book with a peroration against the 'illusion of peaceful coexistence': 'Much as the peoples and governments of Britain, France, and the United States sincerely strive for peaceful coexistence with world communism, the communist movement continues on its aggressive path.' Russia herself 'is contending in bellicosity with more recent adherents to communism', with China in the first instance. To his last breath Abramovitch sounded this 'warning' in almost every one of his *Vestnik* articles. Before the appearance of the sputniks he expressed again and again the fervent hope that the United States would use its 'nuclear supremacy' to tame or destroy the Bolshevik evil once for all; and he did not hide his despair when he thought that America's rulers were failing to rise to their 'historic task'.

Thus Menshevism has ended its long career, driven into two ideological impasses: in one we saw the conscience-stricken Dan humbling himself before Stalinism; in the other we heard Abramovitch praying for the world's salvation by the Pentagon. What an epilogue this is to the story of Martov's party; and how Martov's ghost must be weeping over it.

RUSSIA AND THE WEST[1]

HISTORIANS have often described the futility and impotence of diplomacy in the epoch of the French Revolution and the Napoleonic Empire. The gulf between revolutionary France and conservative Europe proved too wide and deep for even the most adroit managers of international relations. No compact, no treaty, and no intrigue hatched in the chancelleries of Metternich, Castlereagh, or Talleyrand could resolve the antagonism of interests or subdue the vehemence of revolutionary and counter-revolutionary passions. France and her enemies had no common language in which to parley. They were unable to understand each other's motives and aspirations; and deep obsessive fears and suspicions turned almost every move made by one side into an evil conspiracy in the eyes of the other.

Our generation has re-lived this drama. It has seen the drama assuming a global scale and the passions and suspicions arming themselves with nuclear weapons. Once again the antagonists, Russia and the West, appear incapable of finding a common language in which to cope with the perpetual clash of their interests and ambitions. Each side is moving within the circle of its own preconceived ideas, prejudices, and fears. But quite a new fear has appeared, common to both camps, the fear of nuclear annihilation and self-annihilation. This curbs militancy but spurs on and magnifies mutual suspicion. More than ever any move made by one side assumes the most sinister aspect in the eyes of the other. Yet on both sides the moves and countermoves are carried out with trembling hands.

Is it at all possible for any of the antagonists to break out of his circle of preconceived ideas and fears? This is the question underlying George F. Kennan's *Russia and the West under Lenin and Stalin*. From the borderline of history and diplomacy Mr. Kennan

[1] Review of *Russia and the West under Lenin and Stalin* by George F. Kennan (London 1961) broadcast in the Third Programme, 21 September, 1961.

pleads for a new Western approach to Russia, an approach free of the misconceptions and errors of the past. He has made this plea earlier, in his Reith Lectures; but here he tries to give to it the depth of historical perspective. He surveys the record of relations between Russia and the West since 1917, and states:

There is, let me assure you, nothing in nature more egocentrical than the embattled democracy. It soon becomes the victim of its own war propaganda. It then tends to attach to its own cause an absolute value which distorts its own vision. . . . *Its* enemy becomes the embodiment of all evil. *Its* own side . . . is the centre of all virtue. The contest comes to be viewed as having a final, apocalyptic quality. If *we* lose, all is lost; life will no longer be worth living; there will be nothing to be salvaged. If we win, then everything will be possible; all problems will become soluble; the one great source of evil—*our* enemy will have been crushed; the forces of good will then sweep forward unimpeded; all worthy aspirations will be satisfied.

The warning against this 'absolutist' approach runs through the the whole of Mr. Kennan's volume. It comes from the man who at the start of the cold war pleaded for the 'containment' of the evil of communism. His present work may be regarded as an auto-critique of Western diplomacy, voiced by its most articulate representative—an auto-critique which in a way saves the honour of western diplomacy. But it is a melancholy thought that Mr. Kennan, once the State Department's policy planner and Ambassador in Moscow, should now, as Ambassador in Belgrade, find himself in a sort of honorary exile from the centres where American policy is made.

Mr. Kennan argues that the West's propensity to see itself as the embodiment of all virtue and the adversary as evil incarnate has imposed on Western, especially American, diplomacy, a rigidity of outlook which has been responsible for a long sequence of errors, miscalculations, unreal dilemmas, false decisions, and grave setbacks. The Western Powers have been unable to strive for the attainment of any limited objectives in any international conflict. Again and again they have had to aim at nothing less than the enemy's unconditional surrender. Under this banner of unconditional surrender, they have fought two world wars; and under it they are waging the cold war. This, Mr. Kennan believes, is the chief cause of the shrinkage of the Western influence in the world, despite all western victories and despite the West's material and moral superiority.

He argues that if the Allies had not fought the first world war *à outrance* and if they had not insisted that Russia, their ally, should also do so, there would have been no Bolshevik revolution—and no Allied intervention in Russia. The policy of unconditional surrender turned both Germany and Russia against the West, set the stage first for the Treaty of Rapallo and then for the Nazi–Soviet Pact of 1939, thus pre-determining the alignment of forces at the start of the Second World War. In that war again the Allies aimed at Germany's unconditional surrender, which they could not achieve without Russia's military power. They had therefore to look on helplessly and connivingly as Eastern and Central Europe passed under the domination of that power. They crushed one of their enemies, Hitler, only to assist in the triumph of the other, Stalin. The striving for absolute victory has invariably created ever worse predicaments for the West; and it does so in the cold war too. By waging the cold war *à outrance*, the West risks nuclear holocaust, and, at the very least, needlessly strengthens the bonds of Russo–Chinese unity, which, Mr. Kennan suggests, might otherwise loosen or even snap. He takes heart from the changes that have occurred in the Soviet Union since Stalin's death, and he views Khrushchev's Russia as a more 'reasonable' adversary or partner than Stalin's Russia had been. He castigates those 'Sovietologists, private and governmental, who seem afraid to admit to themselves and to others that Stalin is really dead.' He holds that American public opinion, in its response to Russia, 'has often been something like a decade behind the times. . . . Let us not repeat these mistakes. Let us permit the image of Stalin's Russia to stand for us as . . . a reminder of how much worse things could be and were—not as a spectre whose vision blinds us to the Russia we have before us today'.

Mr. Kennan's reasoning seems to me a curious tangle of right and wrong ideas. His conclusions evoke sympathy; and his critical thought commands respect. Mr. Kennan the diplomat who keeps his head above the flood of cold war emotionalism, and struggles to raise others above it, is a noble and moving figure. Yet Mr. Kennan the historian is somehow disappointing, for, despite all his perspicacity, he shows only little understanding for what has been going on outside the diplomatic chancelleries these last fifty years. He views history as being made primarily in the chancelleries. Outside these, he sees only the ugly turbulence of self-righteous democracies and fanatic revolutions, whose leaders so often have it all their own way because Presidents, Premiers, Ministers, and diplomats fail to keep cool heads and take the right decisions.

This bias makes his historical surveys largely unreal and unconvincing. There is, for instance, much that is sound in his critique of the policies of unconditional surrender. Yet he strains his argument when he projects unconditional surrender back into the First World War and makes it responsible *inter alia* for the triumph of the Bolshevik revolution. He fails to grasp that the revolution had its own vitality and momentum more powerful than the vicissitudes of war and the decisions of any diplomacy. In this he is not alone, of course—many Western writers hold the view that Lenin's party would have never won in conditions of peace. This view may have seemed plausible years ago; but has it not become untenable in the light of the Chinese revolution? Chinese communism won in the years 1948-1949, long after the conclusion of the Second World War. Its victory provides a retrospective commentary on the relationship between war and revolution in Russia and suggests that even if the First World War had ended, say, in the middle of 1917 or earlier, the Bolshevik revolution would still have triumphed, perhaps in 1919, 1920 or 1922.

Mr. Kennan also ignores the deep filiations between the October Revolution and the whole development of European socialism and class struggle, from the French revolution through 1848, the Paris Commune, the underground struggle of German socialism against Bismarck, and the general strikes of 1905. This makes it possible for him to say that in 1917, suddenly, 'the Western governments were faced on the Russian scene with a group of fanatics profoundly and incurably hostile to Western ideals and traditions.' Mr. Kennan's image of the revolution, a revolution almost devoid of its own momentum, coming into existence as the combined product of foreign diplomatic errors and of the fanaticism of a few Bolshevik leaders, is utterly unreal. He sees the greatest social upheaval of our century and indeed of all times as a freak of history.

His treatment of the Allied intervention in Russia is open to similar criticism. He is not a crude apologist of the intervention. He sees that it was useless and disastrous in its consequences. He condemns it. But he shows the Allies as embarking upon intervention in something like a fit of noble absent-mindedness; and he conjures out of existence any capitalist interest, any fear of socialist revolution and any counter-revolutionary design as the determining factors of Western policy. It is, of course, true that there was little premeditation and much absent-mindedness in the whole venture; and Mr. Kennan argues against the distortions of the Stalinist and Khrushchevite historians who present the intervention, and indeed the whole story of relations between the West and Russia, as a single premeditated, concerted, and powerful capitalist conspiracy against communism. To this Mr. Kennan replies that such a conspiracy never existed. I doubt whether it is the job of a serious historian to argue against the crudest Stalinist version of the events; and I would like to add that the Bolshevik writers of the Lenin era presented the story, even in the years of the intervention, without such simplifications and distortions. Lenin himself repeatedly emphasized that the Bolshevik régime would hardly have survived if it had been confronted with a coherent coalition of all capitalist interests determined to use all its strength in order to defeat the revolution. But it will not do to play down in Mr. Kennan's manner the intervention and its consequences. Unpremeditated, unconcerted, and relatively feeble though it was, its impact on a starving, exhausted, and disorganized Russia was devastating. Without the intervention and the Allied assistance to the White Armies there would have been no protracted and ferocious civil war, for on the eve of intervention the anti-Bolshevik forces had been utterly disheartened and demoralized by the total collapse of the *ancien régime*. And there would hardly have been the aftermath of the civil war, the famines, the paralysis of the economy, and the terror.

Somehow as a historian Mr. Kennan fails to live up to his own warning that the contrast between Russia and the West should not be viewed as the struggle between good and evil. As he moves on from the years of revolution and intervention through the interwar period to the Second World War, he does, after all, present the West as the embodiment of virtue, even if of virtue confused and fallible, and communism as evil itself, even if not as absolute an evil as that painted by the most obtuse propagandists. Again and again he makes a conscious effort to get away from his preconceptions; and this is when he produces his best pages, for instance his beautiful and touching tribute to the memory of Chicherin, the Bolshevik Foreign Secretary from 1918 till 1930. But again and again Mr. Kennan succumbs to deep-seated bias and prejudice. What, for instance, is one to make of a passage like this:

To be sure, Russia herself became inadvertently—despite Stalin's best efforts—involved in this war, lost some twenty million of her people, and had her economic progress set back by roughly a decade. But what are people in the philosophy of those who do not recognize the existence of the soul? . . . In the mathematics of a materialistic ideology, there is no suffering, however vast, which would not be justified . . . if it serves the interests of the adherents of that ideology.

These words follow Mr. Kennan's review of Stalin's mistakes on the eve and at the beginning of the last war, a review which does not differ significantly from my own analysis given in my study of *Stalin*. But was it necessary for Mr. Kennan to conclude that review with this moralistic and irrelevant tirade against the philosophy of Bolshevism? After all, the loss of twenty million of her people was inflicted on Russia by an enemy who did emphatically 'recognize the existence of the soul'. Has the faith in the existence of the soul prevented the governments of Europe from starting the slaughter of millions in 1914, long before the adherents of a materialistic philosophy were in power anywhere in the world? And how easy it would be to evoke Hiroshima and Nagasaki and then to turn Mr. Kennan's dictum against him and say that 'in the mathematics of a capitalist and Christian ideology, there is no suffering, however vast, which would not be justified. . . .'

Mr. Kennan is obviously torn between his search for truth and objectivity and his ideological fervour against communism; and this dichotomy in his own mind illustrates once again the depth of the great antagonism of our time and the immense intellectual confusion it generates.

Having said this I would like to do justice once more to the man who argues thus with his compatriots:

If we are to regard ourselves as a grown-up nation—and anything else will henceforth be mortally dangerous—then we must, as the Biblical phrase goes, put away childish things; and among these childish things the first to go, in my opinion, should be self-idealization, and the search for absolutes in world affairs. . . . When the ambivalence of one's virtue is recognized, the total iniquity of one's opponent is also irreparably impaired. . . . A world in which these things are true is, of course not the best of all conceivable worlds; but it *is* a tolerable one, and it *is* worth living in. I think our foremost aim today should be to keep it physically intact in an age when men have acquired, for the first time, the technical means of destroying it.

Yet I cannot approve the note of intellectual and moral weariness on which Mr. Kennan concludes his plea, quoting Bismarck of all men: 'Let us leave a few problems for our children to solve; otherwise they might be so bored.'

Our children will surely be occupied by many new problems of their own; and the fewer are our unresolved problems that we bequeath to them the more grateful will they be. But forces other than diplomacy will have to cope with these problems and resolve them.

THE IRONY OF HISTORY
IN STALINISM[1]

How many people, I wonder, can still remember all the sound and fury that were once aroused by Stalin's doctrine of 'socialism in one country'? For nearly a quarter of a century, from the middle 1920s to the late 1940s, this was the sacred canon of the Soviet Communist Party and of the international communist movement. The great ideological controversy raged in the middle of the 1920s, but once it had been concluded no doubt about the canon was tolerated; and innumerable Bolsheviks and foreign communists suffered the Stalinist anathema, or paid with their lives, for the slightest deviation from it. The second quarter of this century has, indeed, entered the annals of communism as the era of socialism in one country.

Mr. E. H. Carr is therefore justified in giving to the second part of his *History of Soviet Russia* the title *Socialism in One Country*. He proposes to deal with this subject in three volumes, of which the first has just appeared. The book has all the merits which one has come to expect from Mr. Carr's work: acute analysis and interpretation, clarity of exposition, and a massive and severe structure of historical facts. It is a searching examination of the main circumstances and trends which found their epitome in Stalin's doctrine.

What were those circumstances? The isolation of the Russian revolution; the frustrated Bolshevik hopes for the spread of communism in the west; Russia's inherited backwardness and poverty; the legacy of world war, revolutionary turmoil and civil war; the collapse of an old social structure; the desperate slowness with which a new structure was taking shape; the weariness and exhaustion of all social classes; and, above this convulsive chaos of a nation, the Bolshevik machines of State and party strug-

[1] Review of *Socialism in One Country 1924-1926*, Vol. I, by Edward Hallett Carr (London, 1958), broadcast in the Third Programme on 3 November, 1958.

gling to come to grips with the chaos, to order it and mould it.

Underneath there unfolded, in Mr. Carr's words, 'the tension between the opposed principles of continuity and change' which forms 'the groundwork of history'. The October Revolution marked a deep and dramatic break in Russia's destinies:

> Never had the heritage of the past been more sharply, more sweepingly or more provocatively rejected; never had the claim to universality been more uncompromisingly asserted; never in any previous revolution had the break in continuity seemed so absolute . . .
> But presently tradition begins to unfold its power as the antidote to change . . . tradition is something which remains dormant in uneventful times . . . of which we become conscious mainly as of a force of resistance to change . . . Thus in the development of the revolution the elements of change and continuity fight side by side, now conflicting, now coalescing, until a new and stable synthesis is established . . . Broadly speaking the greater the distance in time from the initial impact of the revolution the more decisively does the principle of continuity reassert itself against the principle of change.

From this angle Mr. Carr surveys various aspects of postrevolutionary Russia such as family life, the position of the Greek Orthodox Church, currents in literature, legal institutions, the mechanics of government, party and class, and the economic and social background at large. Everywhere he demonstrates the force of the resistance to further revolutionary change in that particular period. Everywhere past and present, tradition and revolution, Marxism and native Slavophile and Populist ideologies, socialist ideas and Messianic Russian aspirations interpenetrate and coalesce, until they form a curious amalgam in Stalinism and socialism in one country.

Now, this tension between change and continuity or revolution and tradition undoubtedly permeates all of Russia's recent history. I do not intend to question this—I myself have devoted considerable attention to this problem in my studies of Stalinism. But what is the balance between change and continuity? This surely is the crucial issue. To which of the two sides of the equation the historian is inclined to give greater weight of emphasis depends, of course, on the standpoint from which he approaches his subject. The pseudo-revolutionary doctrinaire will treat it differently from the Marxist realist; and the Marxist realist from the conservative.

Broad-minded and sympathetic to the revolution though Mr. Carr's approach is, his premises are, to my mind, essentially conservative. He tends to overstate the element of continuity, just as Tocqueville or Sorel, whom he quotes frequently, overstated it in their treatment of the French Revolution.

Tocqueville and Sorel, however, dealt with a revolution which only substituted the bourgeois form of property for the feudal one; and private property, however changed in form, made for the continuity between pre-revolutionary and post-revolutionary France. The Russian Revolution has uprooted private property at large, first residual feudal property, then bourgeois property, and finally peasant property as well. The impulse for social change has been accordingly deeper and stronger. Mr. Carr therefore seems to me to overstate his case when he says that 'once the revolution has . . . enthroned itself in the seats of authority a halt has to be called to further revolutionary change'. Soviet society, I suggest, underwent its most drastic upheaval, the forcible collectivization of farming, only in the years between 1929 and 1932, long after the revolution had 'enthroned itself in the seats of authority'. Nor is it necessarily a law of history that 'the greater the distance of time from the initial impact of the revolution, the more decisively does the principle of continuity reassert itself against the principle of change'. That this principle reasserted itself with extraordinary force while Soviet Russia was both isolated and under-developed is, of course, true. But is it still true today? Should we still assume that 'the greater the distance in time from the October Revolution' the more strongly does continuity reassert itself against change? Is the dynamic force of the Russian Revolution spending itself in the same way as that of the earlier revolutions did? I do not think so.

If the spread of communism in the last years of the Stalin era, especially its triumph in China, and the domestic Russian developments of the post-Stalin years are any pointers to the future, then the opposite seems to be true: the further we move from the October Revolution, the stronger is its impact. Far from having spent itself, the dynamic of the revolution seems to be growing; and after a period during which it was indeed overlaid by the patterns of Russian tradition it reasserts itself all the more powerfully —industrialization and mass education have shattered the very foundations of the old Russian tradition. One can hardly say of

Russia today: *plus ça change, plus c'est la même chose*; it is rather: *plus c'est la même chose, plus ça change.*

However, while one may argue about Mr. Carr's general historical perspective, he is certainly right in underlining the predominantly conservative mood of the Russia of the middle 1920s. Continuity, a revulsion against revolutionary change, and a kind of Soviet isolationism were indeed the keynotes of that period; they all went into the making of the doctrine of socialism in one country. The Bolshevik reaction against the internationalist revolutionary aspirations of the Lenin era found its expression in Stalin's idea. 'While the Bolshevik leaders,' says Mr. Carr, 'were absorbed in a vision of a progressively expanding revolution' they became 'in defiance of their intentions the wielders and defenders of Russian State power, the organizers of what was in all but name a national army, the spokesmen of a national foreign policy'. This 'laid the psychological foundations of "socialism in one country"', which sought to disguise a traditionally Russian *raison d'Etat* in socialist terms. The resurgence of traditionalism and nationalism was stimulated by the weakening of the proletarian element in the Russian body politic and by a temporary, yet significant, strengthening of the peasantry. This was the hey-day of the so-called bloc between Stalin and Bukharin, when the Bolshevik party was committed to a pro-*muzhik* policy and when even an ideologue like Ustryalov spoke of the peasant as becoming 'the sole and real master of the Russian land'. The peasant's horizon, Mr. Carr rightly observes, 'did not extend beyond the limits of his own economy . . . "Socialism in one country" . . . was a conception which fitted in perfectly with his . . . aspirations'.

Here, however, the Hegelian *List der Geschichte*, the sly irony of history, comes into its own. Circumstances force men to move in the most unforeseen directions and give their doctrines the most unexpected contents and significance. Men and their doctrines thus serve purposes sometimes diametrically opposed to those they had envisaged. Socialism in one country had, in opposition to Trotsky's permanent revolution, proclaimed the self-sufficiency of the Soviet Union—its self-sufficiency within a social framework of which the private and even capitalist farmer was to remain an essential element. Trotsky questioned the idea of self-sufficiency and pointed to the approaching conflict between the collectivist State and the individualistic farmer. Stalin prevailed against Trotsky; but presently he found himself to be carrying out, in his own way, some of the major policies expounded by his defeated enemy. Stalin had put socialism in one country on his banner because this seemed to 'fit in perfectly with the peasant's interests and aspirations' and because the essence of his policy allegedly lay in a lasting accommodation between the collectivist State and the property-loving peasantry. Yet it was under the same banner, the banner of socialism in one country, that Stalin set out to destroy the *kulak* as a class and to uproot peasant property. The revolution, so Stalin presently concluded, could not achieve self-sufficiency, nor even survive, within the social framework of the 1920s. He smashed that framework by a stroke of unparalleled violence.

In industrial policy, too, socialism in one country stood originally —in 1925-26—for resistance to change, for the cautious and moderate tempo of development, and against the 'primitive socialist accumulation' and the rapid industrialization advocated by Trotsky and Preobrazhensky. However, five years later, by 1929-30, socialism in one country had changed its content—what it had come to mean was precisely primitive accumulation and forced industrialization.

The supreme feat of history's irony, however, came only shortly before the close of the Stalin era. The party which had accepted socialism in one country as its canon played for international safety. It shunned world revolution and extolled the Soviet Union's sacred egoism. In every act of his policy and in every fibre of his being Stalin was the embodiment of that egoistical, self-sufficient and self-centred Soviet Union. Yet after the second world war Stalin, still waving the flag of socialism in one country, found himself carrying revolution into half a dozen foreign countries, carrying it on the point of his bayonets, and exporting it in the turrets of his tanks. He out-Trotskyed Trotsky, as it were, who had never thought of spreading revolution in this manner. And finally, in his last years, the author of socialism in one country viewed with incredulity, and not without misgiving, the rise of Chinese communism. The era of socialism in one country was at an end.

Looking back on this closed chapter, one may well ask again what was the meaning of Stalin's doctrine. I recollect the gravity with which thirty years ago in Moscow and in the European communist movement we argued this issue as a purely theoretical proposition: is it indeed possible to achieve socialism in a single and isolated country? No, said the old Leninists, to whom socialism meant a classless and Stateless society, an international society based on international division of labour. To those old Leninists the Soviet Union was a nation *in transition* from capitalism to socialism. They held that no matter what progress the Soviet Union might make in various fields, it would remain in that state of transition at least as long as it was isolated. The Stalinists and the Bukharinists argued that the Soviet Union would achieve fully-fledged socialism, even if it were to remain isolated for an indefinite time. They were indeed half-convinced that the Soviet Union was destined to become something like a laboratory of socialism in a single country.

Who was right? The answer which events have given is by no means clear-cut; it is certainly far more complicated than those who tried to anticipate it over thirty years ago could expect. Has socialism in one country justified itself as a theoretical proposition and a forecast of events? Did the Soviet Union achieve socialism while it stood alone? Even in the early thirties Stalin proclaimed that it did. This is still the orthodox view in Moscow today; and we are told that Soviet society is now making its passage from socialism to communism. But what is socialism? If it were simply the wholesale nationalization of industry, then Russia would have achieved socialism as early as the first year of the October Revolution and the whole great controversy of the 1920s would have been irrelevant. The mere fact that the controversy went on indicates that its participants had a rather different conception of socialism. To all of them socialism still meant a highly developed classless society, free, at the very least, from glaring social inequalities and political coercion. By this standard Stalin's—and indeed Khrushchev's—Soviet Union can hardly be said to have achieved socialism. Soviet society is still engaged in the transition from capitalism to socialism. It is far more advanced on the road than it was twenty or ten years ago, but it is still far from its goal; and in its social relationships it still contains strong elements of the bourgeois way of life. Moreover the Soviet Union which Stalin left behind had also ceased to be the 'single and isolated country' to which the controversy had referred. History has, as it were, refused to make of the Soviet Union the laboratory of socialism in one country; and so it has confined to limbo the once so passionately debated doctrine.

But if socialism in one country has, as an abstract theoretical proposition, remained meaningless, it has nevertheless played an outstanding part as a modern myth and an ideology. The myth helped to reconcile the Soviet masses to the miseries of the Stalin era; and the ideology helped to discipline morally both the masses and the ruling group for the almost inhuman efforts which assured the Soviet Union's spectacular rise from backwardness and poverty to industrial power and greatness.

STEPS TO A NEW RUSSIAN
LITERATURE[1]

MOST of the western discussions on commitment in literature and art would probably appear irrelevant to Soviet writers and would be quite incomprehensible to their readers. Whatever currents and cross-currents there are in post-Stalinist literature, whatever idols are smashed, and whatever old aesthetic truths are rediscovered, the notion that the writer is of necessity *engagé* continues to be taken for granted. It is too deeply embedded in the Russian tradition to be affected by the present ideological flux. Belinsky's maxim that 'art without ideas' (*i.e.*, philosophical and socio-political ideas) 'is like a man without a soul: it is a corpse' has dominated Russian thought for more than a century. Every giant of Russian literature paid his tribute to it with his work: Tolstoy, Dostoevsky, Turgenev and Chekhov, each, whatever were his particular views on politics, was *engagé*; each was deeply and passionately concerned with the way Russian society developed, or failed to develop. The Parnassians have filled only a small and pale page in the history of Russian letters, pale in comparison not only with the heritage of the committed Russian literature but also with the achievement of western Parnassian schools. (What is Balmont compared with Verlaine?)

An attitude of non-commitment can crystallize and become accepted only in a stabilized society where the foundations of national existence are generally taken for granted and where social conflict runs at a tension so low that it fails to communicate itself to art. Russia was, in the course of a century, pregnant with revolution; then came the birth and its pangs; then the post-natal fevers, which have lasted several decades; and now at last appear symptoms of recovery—or are they perhaps only portents of further disorders? Artistic sensitivity could not remain uninvolved in so many convulsions of the national life.

[1] *The Times Literary Supplement*, 16 August, 1957.

Yet this is a critical time for the idea of commitment, after it had for so long been grossly and brutally misused and perverted in the interest of the Stalin cult. Every noteworthy piece of writing in recent years has brought a protest against this perversion; and now in the voluminous almanac of Moscow's writers, the *Literaturnaya Moskva* for 1956, the protest has assumed the force of a *cri de cœur*. No wonder that those who have a vested interest in defending the literary practices of the Stalin era have singled out this almanac for attack. The editors of *Literaturnaya Moskva* have met the attack with a stubborn silence which speaks louder than any rejoinder or plea of defence; and no amount of prodding and cajoling has so far induced them to break the silence and retract the *cri de cœur*.

Yet both the attackers and the attacked have referred to the writer's duty to society, to communism, and Marxism–Leninism; but while the official propagandists refer to it in order to exact ideological obedience, the writers of *Literaturnaya Moskva* seek to rescue the idea of commitment from Stalinist distortions and to restore to it its original broad meaning. They insist that commitment must not be confused with immediate political utility or with political subservience which constricts the writer's artistic impulse and his urge for innovation. This is, for instance, how A. Kron, a talented critic, puts it:

Any cult is organically hostile to Marxism–Leninism, the scientific *Weltanschauung* of the working class. Wherever there is cult, scientific thought must retreat before blind faith, creativeness before dogma, and public opinion before arbitrariness. The cult generates a hierarchy of its own servants . . . it is incompatible with criticism . . . it is essentially anti-popular. The cult humiliates the people and makes it view as a gift sent from above that for which the people has paid a full price in its own toil and blood. Even the cult of the People (with a capital P) has its obverse side—it degrades the individual. The Leader was supposed to be the People's servant. But when millions of masters had to rise to their feet at the mere mention of their servant's name, there was in this something profoundly alien to the democratic traditions in which the revolution and our social order have brought us up. . . . Literature and art could not escape the destructive impact [of the cult]. Artistic creation is inseparable from social initiative and from the striving for the new. Yet an innovator, in whatever epoch he lives, is always somehow ahead of the understanding of his contemporaries. . . . With one's head bowed down, one cannot look ahead.

From this and many similar statements it is clear that malignantly though Stalinism travestied the idea of commitment, using it as a convenient screen for keeping literature in bondage, it has not succeeded in discrediting it. The October revolution remains to most Soviet writers their life's inspiration. The deeper they had been influenced by it and the more intimately they identified themselves with communism, the less did they fit in the climate of the 'cult', with its rigid conventions and rituals and its all-pervading sycophancy. It was in the nature of things that the chief sufferers from Stalinism should have been those writers and artists who had once stood closest to the Bolshevik Party—the names of such writers who perished in the purges of the 1930s would fill columns. And it was perhaps not a matter of chance that the officially most celebrated authors of the Stalin era, at least since Gorky's death, were Alexei Tolstoy and Ilya Ehrenburg, who had both met the October revolution with hostility, who were *émigrés* during the heroic period of Bolshevism, and who made their peace with the Party only at the time of its moral debasement. It is almost a rule that the more genuinely and deeply a writer has been committed to communism the less could he feel at ease under Stalinism, though none, not even the worst sycophant, could have felt quite at ease. The rejection of Stalinism has therefore entailed for many writers a search for the significance and implications of their commitment to communism.

In this respect the climate of literary-political opinion in Russia differs greatly from that in Poland or Hungary. True, in Moscow as in Warsaw and Budapest, the writers have suffered from the traumatic shock of Stalinism and have been in the 'vanguard' of de-Stalinization. But this is perhaps the only similarity, and the dissimilarities may be of greater significance. In Hungary and Poland, the poets and the novelists have reacted against Stalinism from offended national dignity and pride—as much against an external imposition as against the ideological aspect of foreign conquest. De-Stalinization there has been an act primarily of national emancipation, or at least a promise of it; and only in the last instance, if at all, has it been a search of communism itself for its 'lost soul'. Both Hungary and Poland have lived under Stalinism for only about a decade; and so literary-political opinion in these countries is still to a large extent shaped by men of the pre-war generation unmistakably hankering after the pre-revolutionary way of life and pre-revolutionary standards of values.

To Russian writers the problem of the Stalinist legacy presents far greater complexities and difficulties. In their revulsion against the 'cult' there is and there can be no room for emotions of offended nationalism. They are aware of the dual role Stalinism has played in Russia's life, degrading her morally and enslaving her but also transforming her into a modern, industrial and educated nation, pioneering for a new social order. To the Russian this legacy must be a source of pride as well as of humiliation. This has tended to make the Russian reaction against Stalinism slower, more hesitant, less spectacular, but perhaps deeper than the Polish and the Hungarian reactions. Simple and wholesale 'rejection' provides no answer here. What is rejected cannot be regarded as something external to Russian life—an imposition from without. The Russian must, on the contrary, cope with Stalinism as with a Russian phenomenon rooted in the revolution and deeper down in the subsoil of the Russian tradition. Nor does nostalgia after the pre-revolutionary epoch make itself perceptibly felt. Not one but four decades separate the Russia of today from that epoch—a span of time which would probably be sufficient to make any nation forget the ideological fleshpots of its *ancien régime*.

This is not to say that there have been no stirrings of nostalgia of any kind. Writers, artists and critics do cast round for broken threads of a tradition which might be picked up; but they look for them this side of 1917. 'We have a gap of thirty years to fill' is a revealing phrase which occurs very often. It is revealing because it shows that the object of Russian nostalgia is not the last pre-revolutionary decade, the era of Merezhkovsky, Balmont, Andreyev and Artsybashev, but the first post-revolutionary decade, the era of Blok, Mayakovsky, Essenin, Pilniak, Babel, and Meyerhold, a decade of restless innovation and high controversy, in which the Russian writer wholeheartedly accepted the idea of commitment, but refused to accept any single interpretation of it. The 1920s were also years of sophistication and broad-mindedness in Bolshevik literary policy: Lenin then dismissed the *Proletkult's* ambition to foster a 'proletarian culture'; Trotsky, fresh from the battlefields of the civil war, was Russia's leading literary critic and appeared in Moscow's artistic clubs to argue with young poets as with equals; Lunacharsky, the great Commissar of Education, produced his poor plays, the butt for the jokes of the literary and theatrical fraternities, but also his luminous essays in philosophical and literary criticism; Bukharin conducted a fascinating controversy with Pavlov on the philosophical implications of reflexiology; and all sorts of modernistic schools proliferated, each with its own galaxy of stars. During the Stalin era it was 'crimethink' to refer to this decade, of which only a few Mohicans survived; and so this forgotten decade appears now in retrospect as the golden age of Soviet literature and art.

However, the 'spirit' of the 1920s cannot be conjured up from the rare and faded files of old periodicals and brought back to life. It belonged entirely to its epoch; and it fed on a continuous intellectual and artistic tradition. The subsequent break and the deadening effect of the Byzantinism of the 1930s, 1940s, and early 1950s cannot easily be made good. One of the great liabilities of the Stalinist legacy is a terrible devastation of talent and an impoverishment of the soil and subsoil of literature. True enough, the poems and the novels published in recent years, and quite especially those which appear in *Literaturnaya Moskva*, are infinitely superior to the literary output of the Stalin era (with the exception of the work of Sholokhov and Pasternak); but they are sadly below the traditional standards of Russian writing.

Lamentable illustrations of the decline are found in the writings of authors who belong to Ilya Ehrenburg's generation and of Ilya Ehrenburg himself. Involuntarily, one thinks of a character in Ehrenburg's *The Thaw,* the painter Pukhov, who wasted and destroyed his artistic personality through sheer opportunism and constant adaptation to official requirements. It is enough to compare *The Thaw* with some of Ilya Ehrenburg's own early writings to sense the autobiographical element in this character: the painter Pukhov is Ehrenburg's own projection.

The fate of poets like Nikolai Tikhonov and Marietta Shaginian and others, who have spent what should have been their best creative years in the oppressive aridity of Stalinism, has not been much better. Shaginian has perhaps best expressed their predicament. In a tribute to Seyfulina she underlines the integrity of that talented and once very popular novelist who died recently almost forgotten, because her 'inner organic resistance to any lie' had compelled her to keep silent during most of the Stalin era. As if in self-exculpation, Shaginian, who could not bring herself to make such a sacrifice, writes that one 'does not necessarily become a liar by uttering certain kinds of lie'.

I am speaking about the special form of lie which is bred by the necessity to dissemble, to make oneself inconspicuous, to ensconce oneself—the kind of lie which has infected . . . many, many of us, writers. That lie is essentially a defensive mask which the imperfection of social relations . . . may force one to wear until it grows into one's face. . .

(In a similar tribute to Seyfulina, Ehrenburg adds that Seyfulina's truthfulness was a high achievement, for 'we do not find truth scattered under our feet on the highroads of our literature'.) It is the tragedy of authors like Shaginian and Ehrenburg that now when they try to tear off the masks and recover their faces they cannot recover them.

These more than middle-aged frustrated writers—Russia's angry old men and women—are playing their part in the present literary revival, such as it is; and the frankness and intensity of their frustration have a positive value of their own. But Russia's 'angry young man' is also coming to the fore; and his predicament is that he has no face yet. His anger, unlike that of his British counterpart, is well focused : he knows against whom he is bitter—against the bureaucracy, its corruption, its lack of culture, its despotic narrow-mindedness, and its tutelage over Russia's intellectual and artistic life.

Yet, curiously enough, the fact that his anger is so sharply focused and that its object is so well defined does not make the Russian 'angry young man' artistically more effective than is his British counterpart; on the contrary, it makes him less so. Sociological certitude is all too often allied to artistic platitude. Witness Dudintsev's *Not by Bread Alone*, which has achieved the same sort of celebrity as *The Thaw* enjoyed a few years earlier and which is politically equally symptomatic but artistically equally undistinguished. Incidentally, Dudinstev's and Ehrenburg's novels are not at all the best of their kind. V. Kaverin's *Searchings and Hopes* (published in *Literaturnaya Moskva*) and Galina Nikolayeva's *A Battle en Route* (serialized in the April, 1957, issue of *Oktyabr*) are works of the same social significance but of much higher literary merit, even though they have gained far less popularity. (Kaverin, a writer of the middle generation, is a novelist with a remarkable subtlety and economy of expression.) Yet, in none of these novels have the writers broken through certain limitations which derive not just from lack of artistic capacity, but which are inherent in the writers' attitude or, more broadly, in the present phase of de-Stalinization. In all these novels, and partly also in the much-debated short stories of Nikolai Zhdanov and Alexander Yashin, there recurs the same motif and even the same pattern of events, situations, characters and conflicts. In all we are shown the man of integrity and imagination, the innovator and pioneer, who is victimized by bureaucratic tyranny yet fights on against incredible odds and in the end—the end invariably comes some time after Stalin's death—wins the day.

The pattern is too simple to be convincing and artistically fruit-ful. The writers appear to be almost as narrowly committed to anti-Stalinism as they, or some of them, were until recently to Stalinism. The new hero is certainly more attractive than was the hero of yesterday, the unflinching orthodox Party man; but his character is almost equally predictable. This is even truer of the new villain, the insensitive bureaucrat who, one feels, all too often takes the place which the 'wrecker' and 'imperialist agent' held in the standard novels and plays some years earlier. The Soviet writer, even in his break with Stalinism, is still governed by the condi-tioned reflexes which Stalinism had formed in him. It is not his partisanship, his commitment, that is at fault, but his lack of realiza-tion that partisanship of the highest order is based in literature, as elsewhere, on objectivity of the highest order and strives for truth in all its unpatterned complexity and contradictoriness.

To say this is not to cast aspersion on the sincerity of most recent Soviet writing or on the passionate militancy shown by writers in exposing evils which are still only half overcome at best. Nor can one doubt the genuineness of the thrill which the new version of the struggle between good and evil gives the Soviet public, if only because this new version does away with the taboos of the Stalin era, or at least turns them upside down. A novel like *Not by Bread Alone* finds such wide popular response because it offers to masses of readers *relief from awe*. This is a salutary relief; it may be the essential prelude to the release of Russia's cramped spiritual ener-gies. But it is painfully obvious that it is only a prelude. The Russian writer still approaches his work with an eye on its immediate politi-cal utility; and even though the new kind of utility is preferable to the old and promises eventually to free literature from narrow preoccupation with utility, it still militates against imaginative innovation.

It may perhaps be too early yet to expect any genuine innovation. What Russian literature appears to be in urgent need of is a spell of apprenticeship. To put it bluntly: Russian writers have to re-learn to write. This is a sad conclusion to reach about the state of this literature less than half a century after Tolstoy's and Chekhov's departure. But this is the conclusion at which Moscow's most aspiring literary critics arrive in *Literaturnaya Moskva*; and it is most emphatically stated by M. A. Shcheglov, whose premature death, at the age of thirty, is now lamented in Moscow's literary circles and whose posthumously published essays written in the Belinsky tradition are indeed the work of a highly courageous and original mind.

Yet it is an odd experience to read Shcheglov and the other critics of *Literaturnaya Moskva* and to see what great gifts of exposition and what resources of literary erudition they marshal for nothing more than giving novelists and playwrights a few lessons in elementary aesthetics and recalling certain old truisms about the art of writing.

For all that the outlook for Russian literature is not at all bleak. What it needs is a continuation of the 'thaw' to free it still further from administrative restraints and to allow it to rid itself of ruinous conditioned reflexes. Once it has rid itself of these, a literature so rich in tradition as the Russian will hardly need a long time to recover its lost ground and to recapture its genius. Waiting for its genius are the untapped resources of Russia's national experience in this century, an experience unique in dramatic grandeur, in intensity of suffering and despair and of achievement and hope; an experience which could not but enlarge the nation's mind and give a new and unfathomable depth to its emotions, the ultimate sources of great literature and art. Perhaps the well of Russia's experience and emotions is too deep and still too agitated for contemporary literature to draw from it—it took more than half a century for the epic of 1812 to find its artistic expression in *War and Peace*. But sooner or later Russian literature is bound to draw from this well; and when it does so the world may hold its breath.

PASTERNAK AND THE CALENDAR
OF THE REVOLUTION[1]

I

THE most striking characteristic of Boris Pasternak's *Doctor Zhivago* is its archaism, the archaism of the idea and of the artistic style alike. The book has been received, in the West, as part of the recent Russian revulsion against Stalinism and as its most consummate literary expression. Yet *Doctor Zhivago* is nothing less than that—it is scarcely related to the Russia of the 1950s and to the experiences, troubles, and heart-searchings of the present Soviet generation. It is a parable about a vanished generation. Pasternak, now approaching his seventieth year—his formative period fell in the last decade before the October revolution—might have written this book in 1921 or 1922. It is as if his mind had stopped at that time, after the traumatic shock of the revolution; and as if nearly all that his country has since gone through had remained a blank. His sensitivity has remained unaffected, almost untouched, by the great and grim, yet not unhopeful drama of Russia's last three decades. The actual story of *Doctor Zhivago* ends in 1922. Pasternak brings it artificially 'up to date' in two brief and hurried postscripts, 'Conclusion' and 'Epilogue', the first covering thinly the years from 1922 to 1929, till Zhivago's death, and the second jumping straight into the 1950s. The postscripts have almost none of the better qualities of the work but show all its weaknesses and incongruities.

Much of the climate and local colour of *Doctor Zhivago* and many of its ideas can indeed be found in the poems and prose of Andrey Belyi, Zinaida Gippius, Evgenii Zamyatin, Marietta Shaginian, and other writers of the 1920s, who were once polemically described as 'internal *émigrés*'. They were so called because they lived and worked (and published their works) under the Soviet

[1] First published in the *Partisan Review*, Spring 1959.

régime, but in some measure shared the ideas and moods of the actual anti-Bolshevik *émigrés*. Some, like Gippius and Zamyatin, eventually went abroad and there voiced their opposition to the revolution without inhibition. Others adjusted themselves, assumed the postures of 'fellow-travellers', and eventually became Stalin's court poets—Shaginian, for instance, was a Stalin Prize Winner. Pasternak was not an 'internal *émigré*'—he was one of the genuine 'fellow-travellers' of the revolution. Yet in *Doctor Zhivago* it is as if he had spoken with the voice of an original, authentic 'internal *émigré*', equally unshaken in his hostility towards Bolshevism and his deep, physical and poetic, attachment to Russia. His perception, his emotions, and his imagination have remained as if closed to the many deep changes that have transformed his country beyond recognition and to some of the storms that have raged over it in the meantime. This testifies to the organic strength of his character but also to an extraordinary rigidity and limitation of his sensitivity.

II

Doctor Zhivago is a political novel *par excellence*; and so its appraisal must include an analysis of its political message. The author puts the message into the mouth of his chief character, who is largely his own projection, and into the mouths of the other figures who all talk at great length about their attitude towards the revolution. They dwell on the revolution's failure, on its inability to solve any problems, on the violence it has done to the human personality, and on the disillusionment it has brought in its wake. The plot is designed to bear out this critique. Nearly all the characters are driven to misery, despair and death; and love and humanity are defeated and destroyed by the 'politics of revolution'. In the background there is Russia, shown as convulsed and tormented to no purpose, unless in mystical expiation of sin. Christianity remains the hope and refuge, a Christianity which need not be clearly defined but is recognizable in its humanitarian outlook, its humility, its acceptance of history, and its refusal to try to remake man's earthly destiny. It is from this quasi-fatalistic Christianity that finally springs Pasternak's ethereal note of reconciliation even with the revolution, the unexpectedly optimistic note on which the novel ends. It may be, the author suggests, that the great expiation has

R

been accomplished and the deluge is over: its few survivors can already sense a 'presage of freedom in the air' and a 'silent music of happiness'; and they feel a peaceful joy for this 'holy city' of Moscow.

A message of this kind is a matter of faith and hardly lends itself to rational discussion. With nothing but these beliefs and convictions, Pasternak's characters are from the beginning outsiders to the revolution, lacking all point of contact with it, and psychologically static. The author evidently feels this and seeks to animate them, to take them 'inside' the revolution, and invest them with something like dilemmas. He presents Doctor Zhivago as almost a revolutionary at first, or, at any rate, a man sympathetic to the revolution, who suffers disillusionment and disintegrates in despair. In the same way he tries to complicate other characters like Strelnikov, the Red commander, and Lara, Strelnikov's wife and Zhivago's mistress. In every case, however, he fails. He tried to square a circle. From Christian rejection of the October revolution it might be possible for a Russian writer to produce perhaps a new version of Chateaubriand's *Génie du Christianisme*, but not a true, coherent, and convincing image of the revolution and of the human beings who have made it or experienced it.

How does Pasternak arrive at the rejection? Is his (and Zhivago's) profession of sympathy with the origins of the revolution mere pretence? Certainly not. He is the victim of a genuine and in a sense tragic confusion. He himself reveals this when he describes Zhivago's, that is his own, state of mind shortly before October, 1917: 'Here too were his loyalty to the revolution and his admiration for it, the revolution in the sense in which it was accepted by the middle classes and in which it had been understood by the students, followers of Blok, in 1905.' The revolution accepted by the middle classes in 1905, it should be recalled, had as its ideals either a Tsardom reformed into a constitutional monarchy or, as an extreme, a Liberal–Radical bourgeois republic. That abortive bourgeois revolution was implicitly opposed to the proletarian revolution of 1917. Pasternak-Zhivago is unaware that his 'admiration and loyalty' to the former must necessarily bring him in conflict with the latter.

The confusion goes even deeper: the Zhivago of 1917 is as if unaware that even this his 'loyalty to the ideas of 1905' is by now only a fading memory. 'This familiar circle', Pasternak goes on, 'also contained the foretaste of new things. In it were those omens and promises which before the war, between 1912 and 1914, had appeared in Russian thought, art, and life, in the destiny of Russia as a whole and in his own, Zhivago's.' The allusive reminiscence would convey to a Russian, if he could read it, far more than it can possibly convey to a Western reader. 'Between 1912 and 1914' Russia's middle classes, the bourgeoisie, had definitely turned their backs on their own radicalism of 1905, had taken their distance from the revolutionary underground movement, and were seeking salvation exclusively in a liberalized Tsardom. The mildly socialistic and radical intelligentsia, encouraged by a slight softening of the autocracy, spoke of the 'liquidation of the illusions and methods of 1905'; and the Bolsheviks were already virtually alone in upholding the tradition of revolutionary action—outside their ranks only Plekhanov and Trotsky, and their very few followers, did the same. This then is the climate of opinion which Pasternak-Zhivago recalls in 1917, reflecting that 'it would be good to go back to that climate once the war was over, to see its renewal and continuation, just as it was good to be going home'. Thus, even at this stage, on the eve of the October insurrection and well before his disillusionment had begun, Zhivago's 'loyalty and admiration for the revolution' is nothing but a transfigured and glorified nostalgia for pre-revolutionary Russia.

Latent and unconscious at the beginning, this nostalgia comes into its own and bursts to the surface later. 'I can still remember a time when we all accepted the peaceful outlook of the last century', says Lara to Zhivago. 'It was taken for granted that you listened to reason, that it was right and natural to do what your conscience told you. . . .' she adds (as if Russia had not lived in serfdom for most of that golden age, 'the last century', and in semi-serfdom for the rest of it!). 'And then there was the jump from this calm, innocent, measured way of living to blood and tears, to mass insanity. . . . You must remember better than I do the beginning of disintegration, how everything began to break down all at once—trains and food supplies in towns, and the foundations of home life and conscious moral standards.'

'Go on,' Zhivago interjects. 'I know what you will say next. What good sense you make of it all! It's a joy to listen to you.'

Pasternak's recital of the broken pledges of October is thus based on a false premise: The October revolution had never promised to satisfy his nostalgia and to 'go back to the climate' of 1912-14, let alone to that of the nineteenth century. He rests his case on the fact that the October revolution was not a bourgeois revolution or rather that it did not content itself with a mildly reformed version of the *ancien régime*. Of all the charges that have ever been levelled against Bolshevism, this is surely the most archaic one. When it was voiced around 1921 it was still the echo of a fresh controversy. In 1958 it comes to us like a voice from the grave.

III

'*Comme* La Guerre et la Paix, *le* Docteur Jivago', writes François Mauriac, '*ne restitue pas seulement des destinées particulières, mais l'histoire politique qui nait d'elles et qui, à son tour, les infléchit et leur donne une signification.*'

Mauriac naturally finds himself in the warmest sympathy with Pasternak's Christianity. But has he also based his opinion on a consideration of *Doctor Zhivago's* merits as a novel? Even though Pasternak himself, through various imitative details of composition and style, evokes *War and Peace*, it is difficult to see how any novelist can make the comparison seriously. Tolstoy's huge canvas is alive and crowded with a magnificently full blooded, richly individualized yet organically integrated, social milieu. In *Doctor Zhivago* a mere fragment of a milieu comes only partly alive, and this only in the opening chapters—the milieu of the pre-revolutionary intelligentsia, Platonically faithful to 'the ideas of 1905' but well adjusted in fact to the *ancien régime* and leading a smug existence on the fringes of the upper and middle bourgeoisie and of the Tsarist bureaucracy. After 1917 this milieu disintegrates and disperses, as it was bound to do; and—as nothing takes its place—its *membra disjecta*, as individuals, are whirled furiously into a social vacuum, from which they hark back to their lost felicity. No *histoire politique* emerges therefore from their private destinies, certainly not any *histoire politique* of the Bolshevik epoch.

Tolstoy takes the characters of *War and Peace* straight into the centre of the great events of their time. He throws them right into the stream of history, which carries them until they are overwhelmed or come on top. Pasternak places his characters in the backwoods and backwaters. They do not participate in any single important event; nor do they even witness any such event. Yet, what would *War and Peace* have been without Austerlitz and Borodino, without the fire of Moscow, without the Tsar's Court and Kutuzov's headquarters, and without the retreat of the Grande Armée, all reproduced by Tolstoy's epic genius? What significance would the *destinées particulières* of Pierre Bezukhov and André Bolkonsky have had without their deep and active involvement in these events? The drama of 1917-21 was at least as great as that of 1812; and it is far more momentous in its consequences. Yet Pasternak never manages to give us a single glimpse of its main theme, of its central occurrences, and of its significant actors. It is not only that he lacks the gift of epic narration and has no eye for the historic scene. He runs away from history, just as all the time his chief characters flee from the scourge of revolution.

We barely hear in *Doctor Zhivago* a grotesquely remote echo of the stormy prelude of 1905. Then, during the World War until September 1917, Zhivago serves as an army doctor in a God-forsaken Carpathian village and a Galician townlet on the Hungarian frontier, hundreds and hundreds of miles away from the centres of the revolutionary upheaval. He returns to Moscow almost on the eve of the October insurrection and stays there during the insurrection. What he sees, experiences, and has to say about it consists of a few flat and meaningless sentences which do not add up to half a page. Throughout the rising, which in Moscow lasted much longer and was much bloodier than in Petrograd, he stays in his rooms. His child has a cold, his friends come, talk about the fighting outside, get stuck at the Zhivagos' for three days, after which they go home at last. 'Yuri had been glad of their presence during Sasha's illness and Tonya forgave them for adding to the general disorder. But they had felt obliged to repay the kindness of their hosts by entertaining them with ceaseless chatter; Yuri felt exhausted by it and was glad to see them go.' This is all we hear or learn of the upheaval: not a single person appears that participates in it. On the next page we are told abruptly that Zhivago was 'shaken and overwhelmed by the greatness of the moment and the thought of its significance for centuries to come'. We must believe the author upon his word; we have seen no one 'shaken and overwhelmed'. Zhivago did not even look at the event, so full of 'significance for centuries to come', through the window of his flat or even through the chinks of his shutters. The revolution had only added to the 'general disorder' in his household and exposed him to the 'ceaseless chatter' of his friends.

There follow a few thin and incoherent pages in which we are shown how the revolution adds further to the 'general disorder' in the household. Then, Moscow succumbs to starvation, epidemics, cold; Zhivago himself falls ill with typhus and recovers. By now the author and his hero have began to brood over the breakdown of civilized life and the calamitous deterioration of human nature. 'In the meantime the Zhivagos were tried to the limits of endurance. They had nothing and they were starving. Yuri went to see the party member he had once saved, the one who had been the victim of a robbery. This man helped him as far as he could, but the civil war was beginning and he was hardly ever in Moscow; besides he regarded the privations people were suffering in those days as only natural, and himself went hungry, though he concealed it.' And so the Zhivagos pack up and leave for the Urals, hoping to recoup there and to enjoy some quiet well-being on what used to be their family estate.

Thus we have left behind the famished, tense, and severe Moscow of the early months of civil war, without getting as much as a hint of the issues agitating it: war and peace, Brest Litovsk, the German threat to Petrograd, the move of Lenin's government from Petrograd to Moscow, the attempts of the counter-revolution to rally, the hopes for the spread of revolution in Europe, the uprising of the Left Social Revolutionaries, the final dissolution of the old army, the emergence of the new one, not to speak of the distribution of land among the peasants, workers' control over industry, the beginnings of socialization, the attempt on Lenin's life, the first outbreaks of the Red terror, etc., all occurring during the months of Zhivago's stay in Moscow. We get no inkling of the severe pathos of these months, of the mass enthusiasms and the soaring hopes, without which the shocks to the hopes remain meaningless. We are hardly able to guess that Moscow is already being cut off by the Whites from food and fuel bases in the south: and so famine and chaos appear as the results of an apocalyptic breakdown of moral standards.

By coincidence I have read simultaneously with *Doctor Zhivago* the manuscript of memoirs written by an old worker who, himself an anarchist, took part in the Bolshevik uprising in Moscow. Without literary pretensions, very plainly, he describes the same period with which Pasternak deals; and he too is now bitterly disillusioned with the outcome of the revolution. But what a difference between the two pictures of the same city (even the same streets!) seen at the same time. Both writers describe the famine and the sufferings. But the old anarchist draws also unforgettable scenes of streets which, as far as he could see from a crossroads, were filled with Red workers, hastily arming themselves, and even with war cripples begging for arms; and then—the same streets changed into a battle-field; and he brings alive the inspired and tense heroism of Moscow's working class, an atmosphere of which Pasternak conveys not even a whiff. Again, it is as if Tolstoy had brought Pierre Bezukhov to burning Moscow only to let him bemoan the hunger and the ruins, without letting him (and us) feel how the great and tragic conflagration illumines Russia's past and present. To Tolstoy the fire of Moscow and the cruel deeds and sufferings of 1812 are no mere atrocities—if they had been, Tolstoy would not be himself, and *War and Peace* would not be what it is. To Pasternak the revolution is primarily an atrocity.

Zhivago's resentment swells in him during his long and weary journey to the Urals. He travels in an overcrowded goods train, packed with human misery. Here are some of Pasternak's best descriptive pages. The scenes and episodes are true to life—the literature of the 1920s is full of similar descriptions. Zhivago's chief preoccupation is still with his and his family's well-being, although he tries to 'defend the revolution' in a brief and rather lifeless dialogue with a deported anti-Bolshevik politician. He is finally overcome by disgust with the new régime, and with his time at large, in the Urals, when his expectation of satiety and quietude on the old family estate is disappointed, when he is torn between loyalty to his wife and love for Lara; and when eventually the Red partisans trap him on a highway, abduct him to their forest camp, and force him to serve them as doctor.

The picture of the Forest Brotherhood is forcefully drawn. There is in it a sense of space, Siberian space, of the cruelty and mercy of nature and man, and of the primordial savagery of the fight. Still, we touch here only a remote periphery of the civil war, a forlorn and icy corner of Mother Russia. (Pasternak himself spent those years in the Urals.) The types or rather situations he depicts here are convincing, and at times (for instance the doings of the witch in the Forest Brotherhood) even fascinating; but they are marginal.

They represent the anarchic fringe of the Red Army which by now fights its battles against Kolchak, Denikin, Yudenich, and Wrangel—elsewhere, mostly far to the West, in European Russia. There the human element, the problems, and the situations were different from those encountered in this Forest Brotherhood, although the civil war was savage and cruel everywhere. The Forest Brotherhood, at any rate, forms, even in fiction, too slender a basis for any *histoire politique* of this period.

It is there, in the partisans' camp, that Zhivago's final 'break' with the revolution occurs. Abducted from the highway, he explodes in anger over the violation of his rights as an individual, the insult to his human dignity, and the breakdown of all moral standards. After eighteen months in captivity, during which at moments he feels almost closer to the Whites than to the Reds, he manages to escape. If this were all, one could say that the story has its psychological and artistic logic and that the author has 'taken it from life'. But Pasternak does not content himself with this. Not relying on narrative and portrayal, he incessantly idealizes his hero, his own projection, and leaves us in no doubt that he shares Zhivago's thoughts and emotions and all his indignation. (Nearly all his characters do the same; the author does not manage to set up any real contrast or counter-balance to Zhivago!) Politically and artistically Pasternak thus involves himself in a self-revealing inconsistency. Zhivago, we know, had, as doctor, spent several years in the Tsarist army; and all those years he behaved extremely meekly, never making any fuss over his sacred rights as individual and his offended dignity. Implicitly, he thus acknowledges the right of the *ancien régime* to press him into service—he denies that right only to the Red partisans. Yet they do exactly what the old army had done: they make the doctor look after the wounded. Unlike the Tsarist army, they had not sent him call-up papers by mail but had kidnapped him—they had not yet had the time to build up a military machine which would mobilize doctors and others in a 'civilized' manner. Surely from the angle of Pasternak–Zhivago's morality this should have been an irrelevant detail: at any rate, to the idealistic and humanitarian doctor it should not have made so great a moral difference whose wounded soldiers he cured, those of the Tsar, of the Whites, or of the Reds. Why then does he only now feel so deeply insulted in his human dignity?

The juxtaposition of these two situations in Zhivago's life is significant in other respects as well. Near the Carpathian front, that cemetery of the Tsarist army, Zhivago had seen blood, suffering, death, and countless atrocities. Pasternak sparingly describes a few of these but he does not dwell on that side of Zhivago's early experience. He presents as an almost uninterrupted atrocity only that part of the story which begins with the revolution. Nostalgia for the *ancien régime* here too colours his entire vision, determines for him his horizon, and dictates even the composition of the novel.

Unintentionally, Pasternak portrays his hero, the sensitive poet and moralist, as the epitome of callousness and egotism—unintentionally, because otherwise he could hardly have so insistently identified himself with Zhivago and lavished on him all the lachrymose love with which the novel overflows. The egotism is physical as well as intellectual: Zhivago is the descendent not of Pierre Bezukhov but of Oblomov, Goncharov's character who, though not worthless, had spent all his life in bed, as symbol of the indolence and immobility of old Russia. Here is Oblomov in revolt against the inhumanity of a revolution that has dragged him out of bed. Goncharov, however, conceived Oblomov as a grand satirical figure; Pasternak makes of him a martyr and the object of an apotheosis.

IV

With the archaism of the idea goes the archaism of the artistic style. *Doctor Zhivago* is extremely old-fashioned by any standards of the contemporary novel; and the standards by which, being what it is, it has to be judged are those of the old-fashioned realistic novel. The texture of its prose is pre-Proust, nay, pre-Maupassant. It has nothing in it of the experimental modernity of Pilniak, Babel and other Russian writers of the 1920s. Obsolescence of style is not a fault in itself. The point is that Pasternak chooses deliberately his mode of expression which is the mode proper to the *laudator temporis acti*.

In his diary Pasternak-Zhivago thus expresses his artistic programme: 'Progress in science follows the laws of repulsion—every step forward is made by reaction against the delusions and false theories prevailing at the time. . . . Forward steps in art are made by attraction, through the artist's admiration and desire to follow the example of the predecessors he admires most.' This is not quite the truth. In art as well as in science progress is achieved by a combination of 'repulsion' and 'attraction' and the tension between these two forces. Every step forward, as Hegel knew, is a continuation of tradition and at the same time a reaction against tradition. The innovator transcends the heritage of the past by rejecting some of its elements and developing others. However, Zhivago's reflections have some relevance to Pasternak's literary conservatism.

This is Pasternak's first novel, written at the age of about 65, after he had been a poet all his life. His main formative influences had been the Russian Symbolist school, which flourished early in the century, then for a short time the pre-revolutionary Futurism, and finally, the 'Formalism' of the early 1920s. These schools enriched the idiom and refined the techniques of Russian poetry, but often they also weakened its *élan* and narrowed its imaginative range. Within the Symbolist and the Formalist traditions Pasternak has achieved almost perfection. His virtuosity of form has made of him Russia's most eminent translator of Shakespeare and Goethe. As far as I can judge from his poems, of which some are not easily accessible and others have remained unpublished, virtuosity rather than vigorous, inventive, and creative mastery distinguishes Pasternak. Yet as a poet too he is curiously antiquated compared with Mayakovsky and Yessenin, his contemporaries.

What prompted him to write his first novel at so advanced an age was the feeling that his poetry, or poetry at large, could not express adequately the experience of his generation. There is a touch of greatness in this admission and in the poet's effort to transcend his limitations. However, for any writer whose gifts had, for nearly half a century, been attuned exclusively to lyrical poetry, it would, in any case, have been risky to try his hand at a realistic and political novel. Pasternak's poetic tradition has proved an insuperable obstacle to his literary metamorphosis. He has not been able to jump the gulf between lyrical symbolism and prose narrative.

This accounts for the incongruity between the various elements that make up *Doctor Zhivago*: on the one side, lyrical passages, noble, richly imaginative, refined, and fastidiously polished; and on the other the core of the novel itself, flat, clumsy, laboured, and embarrassingly crude. It is as if the book had been written by two hands: the virtuoso-poet of 65 and a beginning novelist of 16.

Scattered like jewels over the pages of *Doctor Zhivago* are Pasternak's exquisite descriptions of nature or rather of mood in nature which serve him as keys to the moods and destinies of his hero. There is richness and delicacy in his images of forest, field, river, country road, sunrise and sunset, and of the season of the year. The realistically painted landscape is shot through with a mystical symbolism, which selects a bush torn by a storm or a frozen tree as omen or token. The writing on the wall is the writing on the face of nature itself. Even in these passages, which would by themselves make an impressive anthology of Pasternak's poetry in prose, his range is limited—he rarely succeeds, for instance, in the drawing of an urban scene; and not infrequently there is a note of affectation and preciosity in his manner of pressing on the reader the symbolical meanings 'hidden' in landscape or mood. All the same, Pasternak the image-maker and word-polisher shows himself at his best.

Unfortunately, a novel aspiring to the large and realistic scale cannot be built around such lyrical fragments. The author's attempts to do so only show up the perplexing contrast between his sophisticated word-mastery and his ineptitude as a novelist. His plot is, from the beginning to end, a jumble of absurd and assiduously concocted coincidences. The *deus ex machina* jumps incessantly before our eyes. Without his help the author simply does not manage to establish any connexion between the characters, to bring them together, to separate them, and to evolve and resolve their conflicts. He fails in this because he does not manage to develop and bring alive the characters themselves. Even Zhivago is little more than a blurred shadow. The psychological motivation of his behaviour is incoherent. The author substitutes for it exalted lyrical and symbolic allusions; and he speaks for Zhivago and on his behalf instead of letting the personality speak for itself. 'Everything in Yuri's mind was mixed up together and misplaced and everything was sharply his own—his views, his habits, and his inclinations. He was unusually impressionable and the freshness and novelty of his vision were remarkable.' 'The vigour and the originality of his poems made Yuri forgive himself what he regarded as the sin of their conception for he believed that originality and vigour alone could give reality to a work of art. . . .' 'Shyness and lack of simplicity [were] entirely alien to his nature.' The superlatives which the author heaps on his hero and the subtle poetic aura by which he surrounds him cannot give reality or depth to the figure. Zhivago's attitudes towards his wife and mistress, and towards his many children born of three women, are strained or never assume verisimilitude: not for a single moment does the father come alive in him (and none of his children has any individuality). Not only the author sings his hero's praises—nearly all the characters do the same. Nearly all are in love with Yuri, adore him, approve his ideas, echo his deep reflections, and nod their heads at whatever he says.

The other characters are altogether puppet-like or *papier mâché*, much though the author exerts himself to make them move of their own accord, or to make them look 'unusual', enigmatic, or romantic. Even more than in the case of Zhivago, lyrical patches, naïve and stilted dialogues, and affected superlatives have to stand for the portrayal of character and of actual relationships. This, for instance, is how the intimate concord between Lara and Zhivago is described:

Their low-voiced talk, however unimportant, was as full of meanings as the Dialogue of Plato.

Even more than by what they had in common, they were united by what separated them from the rest of the world . . .

They loved each other greatly. Most people experience love, without noticing that there is anything remarkable about it. To them—and this made them unusual—the moments when passion visited their doomed human existence like a breath of timelessness were moments of revelation, or of even greater understanding of life and of themselves.

In this *histoire politique* of the epoch the author makes no attempt to draw a single Bolshevik figure—the makers of the revolution are an alien and inaccessible world to him. He underlines that his revolutionaries are not party men. They are primitively picaresque types or wholly incredible eccentrics, like Klintsov-Pogo-revshikh, the deaf-mute instigator of rebellions in the Tsarist army, Liberius, the chieftain of the Forest Brotherhood, and the most important of them, Strelnikov, Lara's husband. Of Strelnikov we learn that he 'had an unusual power [how Pasternak loves this adjective!] of clear and logical reasoning, and he was endowed with great moral purity and sense of justice; he was ardent and honourable'. From disappointment in family life—apparently his only motive—he plunges into revolution, becomes a legendary Red commander, the scourge of the Whites and of the people at large; but eventually falls foul of the Bolsheviks—we do not know why and how but presumably because of his 'moral purity and sense of justice'; and he commits suicide. A few workers appear fleetingly in pale episodes, and are either half-wits or servile post-seekers. We do not see the Whites at all, apart from one remote and evanescent apparition. One could not even guess from this grand cross-section of the epoch who were the men who made the revolution, who were those who fought the civil war on either side, and why and how they lost or won. Artistically as well as politically the epoch-making upheaval remains a vacuum.

V

Yet despite this void, and the unctuous moralizing and all the falsettos, there is in *Doctor Zhivago* a note of genuine conviction. The suggestive indictment of the revolution must make its impression on the reader who is unfamiliar with the background of the years 1917-22 but is vaguely aware of the horrors of the Stalin era. Confusing the calendar of the revolution, Pasternak projects those horrors back into the early and earliest phases of the Bolshevik rule. The anachronism runs through the entire novel. In the years 1918-21 Zhivago and Lara are already revolted by the tyranny of the monolithic régime which in fact was not formed until a decade later:

They were both equally repelled by what was tragically typical of modern man, his shrill text-book admirations, his forced enthusiasms, and the deadly dullness conscientiously preached and practised by countless workers in the fields of art and science in order that genius should remain extremely rare.

It was then that falsehood came into our Russian land [Zhivago and Lara agree]. The great misfortune, the root of all evil to come was the loss of faith in the value of personal opinions. People imagined that it was out of date to follow their own moral sense, that they must sing the same tune in chorus, and live by other people's notions, the notions which are being crammed down everybody's throat.

I do not know [says Zhivago] of any teaching more self-centred and farther from the facts than Marxism. Ordinarily, people are anxious to test their theories, to learn from experience, but those who wield power are so anxious to establish the myth of their own infallibility that they turn their back on truth as squarely as they can. Politics mean nothing to me. I do not like people who are indifferent to the truth.

Zhivago-Pasternak goes on in this vein without any substantial contradiction from any other character. Yet, the 'forced enthusiasms', the deadly uniformity in art and science, the 'singing of the same tune in chorus', and the degradation of Marxism to an infallible Church—all this fits the fully-fledged Stalin era but not the years in which these words are spoken. Those were years of *Sturm und Drang*, of bold intellectual and artistic experimentation in Russia, and of almost permanent public controversy within the Bolshevik camp. Does Pasternak-Zhivago confuse the calendar of the revolution or is he confused by it? Whatever the truth, only this confusion enables him to make his case. He could not have actually argued in 1921 the way he does. Yet readers familiar only with the atmosphere of the latter-day Stalinism are all too likely to believe that he could. It may be objected that the author need not concern himself with historical chronology, and that he has the right to compress or 'telescope' various periods and so reveal the evil embedded in the thing itself. Where then are the limits of the compression? And does not historical and artistic truth come out mangled? Pasternak, at any rate, establishes most carefully, almost pedantically, the chronology of the events which form the background to Zhivago's fortunes; and so he should be expected to demonstrate the 'spirit of the time', on which he dwells so much, in accordance with the time.

To be sure, the deadly uniformity in art and science, the disregard and contempt of personal opinion, the infallibility of the ruler, and so many other features of the Stalin era evolved from germs which had been present in the early phase of the revolution; but they evolved in continuous and inexorable conflict with that phase. No great artist could possibly have missed, as Pasternak has, the colossal tragedy inherent in this chain of cause and effect and in the tension between the early and the late phases of the revolution and of Bolshevism. What Pasternak does is not merely to blur the contours of the time—he pulverizes all the real aspects of the revolution and dissolves them into a bloody and repulsive fog. Art and history alike, however, will re-establish the contours and make their distinction between the revolution's creative and its irrationally destructive acts, no matter how entangled these may have been, just as, in the case of the French Revolution, posterity, with the exception of extreme reactionaries, has drawn its distinction between the storming of the Bastille, the proclamation of the Rights of Man, and the rise of the new and modern, be it only bourgeois, France,

on the one hand, and the nightmares of revolution and the gods
that were athirst, on the other.

Pasternak hardly ever alludes (even in his 'Conclusion' and
'Epilogue') to the great purges of the 1930's. Yet he constantly uses
their black hue for his picture of the earlier period—this indeed is
the only respect in which he draws for his writing on any significant
social experience of the last three decades. His silence about the
great holocaust of the 1930s is not accidental. This was tragedy
within the revolution; and as such it does not concern the outsider,
let alone the internal *émigré*. What is striking here is the contrast
between Pasternak and writers like Kaverin, Galina Nikolaeva,
Zorin, and others, whose post-Stalinist novels and plays (unknown
in the West and some of them virtually suppressed in the Soviet
Union) have centred precisely on the tragedy within the revolution,
the tragedy which they also see from within. In Pasternak's pages
the transposed horrors of the Stalin era exist mainly as the source
of his own moral self-confidence, the self-confidence he needs for
his critique of the revolution at large. We have said that he might
have written *Doctor Zhivago* in the early 1920s; but he could not
have written it then with his present self-confidence. At that time,
with the 'heroic' phase of the revolution still fresh, the internal
émigré laboured under the sense of his moral defeat. After all the
experiences of the Stalin era, he now feels that he has morally recovered; and he flaunts his self-righteousness. This is a spurious
recovery, however; and it is helped along by a *suggestio falsi*.

Pasternak traces back Zhivago's ideas and his Christianity to
Alexander Blok. In Blok's *Twelve*, Christ walked at the head of
armed workmen, tramps, and prostitutes, leading them, in the
blood-red dawn of October, towards a greater future. There was a
certain artistic and even historic authenticity in this daring symbol.
In it were merged primitive Christianity and the elemental revolutionary élan of the Russia of the *muzhiks* who, chanting Prayer
Book psalms, burned the mansions of the aristocracy. The Christ
who blessed that Russia was also the Christ of primitive Christianity, the hope of the enslaved and the oppressed, St. Matthew's Son
of Man, who would sooner let the camel go through the eye of a
needle than the rich man enter into the Kingdom of God. Pasternak's Christ turns his back on the rough mob he had led in October
and parts company with them. He is the pre-revolutionary self-
sufficient Russian intellectual, 'refined', futile, and full of grudge

and resentment at the abomination of a proletarian revolution.

VI

Pasternak has been hailed in the West for his moral courage; much is written about his poetry as a 'challenge to tyranny' and his stubbornly non-conformist attitude throughout the Stalin era. Let us try and disentangle facts from fiction. It is true that Pasternak has never been among Stalin's versifying sycophants. He has never bowed to the official cult and observance; and he has never surrendered his literary integrity to powerful taskmasters. This alone would have been enough to earn him respect and to make of his writing a startling phenomenon.[2] His poetry stands out sharply against the grey background of the official literature of the last thirty years. Against that lifeless and unendurably monotonous background even the old-fashioned quality of his lyricism could appear and has appeared as a thrilling innovation. One may therefore speak of him as of a great and even heroic poet in that semi-ironical sense in which, according to some, the Bible speaks of Noah as a just man only 'in his generation', a generation of vice. Pasternak stands indeed head and shoulders above the poetasters of the Stalin era.

However, his courage has been of a peculiar kind—the courage of passive resistance. His poetry has been his flight from tyranny, not his challenge to it. To this he has owed his survival in a generation in which the greatest poets, Mayakovsky and Yessenin, committed suicide, and most of the best writers and artists, Babel, Pilniak, Mandelstam, Kluyev, Voronsky, Meyerhold, and Eisenstein, to mention only these, were deported, imprisoned and driven to death. Stalin did not allow some of Pasternak's poems to be published; but he spared their author and, by the despot's benevolent whim, even surrounded him with care, protecting his safety and well-being. Stalin knew that he had little to fear from his poetry. He sensed a threat to himself not in the archaic message of the man who harked back to pre-revolutionary times, but in the work of those writers and artists who, each in his own way, expressed the ethos, the *Sturm und Drang*, and the non-conformity of the early years of the revolution—there Stalin sensed the genuine challenge

---

[2] In asserting this I had forgotten that Pasternak did pay his poetic tribute to Stalin in the 1930s.

to his infallibility. With those writers and their message Pasternak has been in implicit conflict; and it would be unjust to their memory to hail him as the most heroic and authentic spokesman of his generation. Moreover, their message, even though it, too, belongs to its time and can hardly meet the needs of our day, has certainly far more relevance to the experience and the aspirations of the new Russia than have the ideas of *Doctor Zhivago*.

When all this has been said, one cannot react otherwise than with indignation and disgust to the suppression of *Doctor Zhivago* in the Soviet Union, and to the spectacle of Pasternak's condemnation. There exists no justification and no excuse for the ban on his book and the outcry against it, or for the pressure exercised on Pasternak to make him resign the Nobel award, the threat of his expulsion from the country, and the continuing witch-hunt. The Writers' Union of Moscow and its official instigators or accomplices have achieved nothing except that they have given proof of their own obtuseness and stupidity.

What are Pasternak's censors afraid of? His Christianity? But the Soviet State Publishers print in millions of copies the works of Tolstoy and Dostoyevsky, every page of which breathes a Christianity far more authentic than Pasternak's. His nostalgia for the *ancien régime*? But who, apart from a few survivors of the old intelligentsia and bourgeoisie, people of Pasternak's age, can share that nostalgia in the Soviet Union today? And even if younger people were to experience it vicariously—what possibly could the Soviet Union fear from that? It cannot and it will not go back to the past, anyhow. The work of the revolution can no longer be undone or reversed: the huge, formidable, and ever growing structure of the new Soviet society will hardly stop growing. Can perhaps a poet's eye, turned inwards and backwards, and wandering over the wastes of his memory, cast an evil spell? Zhivago still represents a powerful force, frequently felt and heard, in Poland, Hungary, Eastern Germany, and elsewhere in Eastern Europe; but in the Soviet Union he is the survivor of a lost tribe. In the fifth decade of the revolution it is time to view him with detachment and tolerance and to let him mourn his dead.

Pasternak's censors, too, are evidently confusing the calendar of the revolution. They have broken away from the Stalin era, or have been wrenched out of it; but somehow they still imagine themselves to be living in it. They are still superstitiously seized by old

S

and habitual fears and resort to the customary charms and exorcisms. Above all, they distrust their own, modern and educated, society which is growing mightily above their heads as well as Pasternak's.

Time does not stand still, however. Ten years ago *l'affaire Pasternak* would not have been possible. Pasternak would not have dared to write this novel, to offer it for publication in Russia, and to have it published abroad. If he had done this, Stalin's frown would have sent him to a concentration camp or to death. Despite all the present witch-hunting in Moscow, however, Pasternak's personal freedom and well-being have so far remained undisturbed; let us hope that they will remain so to the end. He might have gone abroad and in the West enjoyed fame, wealth, and honour; but he has refused to 'choose freedom' in that way. Perhaps he does indeed hear that 'silent music of happiness', of which he says, in the last sentence of *Doctor Zhivago*, that it spreads over his country, even if he does not quite understand that music. Slowly yet rapidly, painfully yet hopefully, the Soviet Union has moved into a new epoch, in which the mass of its people is seizing anew the sense of socialism. And perhaps, perhaps in ten years' time another *affaire Pasternak* will also be impossible, because by then the fears and the superstitions of Stalinism will have been dispelled.

TWO AUTOBIOGRAPHIES

I

THE present volume of Ilya Ehrenburg's *Memoirs*[1] is an eye-witness account of two crowded and stormy decades in Soviet and European history. For the Soviet Union the period began with the aftermath of the Civil War; it was to end with the Nazi invasion. In between lay the close of the Lenin era, the rise of Stalinism, the upheavals of industrialization and collectivization, the suppression of literary and artistic freedom, the Great Purges, and the Stalin–Hitler Pact of 1939. Within the same span of time bourgeois Europe recovered from the revolutionary shocks of 1918-21, enjoyed a spell of semi-illusory stabilization, and succumbed to the Great Depression and to fascism and Nazism, until it was engulfed by the Second World War.

Of the Russian scene Ehrenburg gives us only intermittent glimpses; he concentrates on the events, personalities, and political climate of Western Europe. He lived most of the time in Germany, France and Spain; he was little more than a tourist in his native country. Even while active as a propagandist for the Kremlin, he felt more at home in the cafés of Montparnasse than within earshot of the Kremlin bells. The topsy-turvy Berlin of the early twenties, the Rome of the time of Matteoti's assassination, the Paris of the Popular Front, and the Barcelona and Valencia of the years of the Civil War come more easily to life in his pages than does either Moscow or Leningrad. Nevertheless, his is a Russian writer's view of Western Europe, for he has been ever sensitive to the winds blowing over Russia and the moral pressures they bear. He always feels and makes us feel Russia's spiritual and political presence in Europe—most often he portrays Russian personalities against French or Spanish backgrounds. His pages are crowded with character sketches of Frenchmen, Spaniards, Italians, Poles, Czechs

[1] *Memoirs 1921-1941* (World Publishing Co. 1964). Reviewed in *The Nation*, 21 December 1964.

and Jews. The pen portraits, to mention only those of Antonov-Ovseenko, the hero of 1917, who represented Stalin in Barcelona in 1936; and Durutti, the Spanish anarchist of legendary fame; Ernst Toller, the German revolutionary playwright; Julian Tuwim, the Polish poet; and Peretz Markish, the Yiddish poet, are extremely well drawn and even moving. (Though I knew most of these men and my images of them differ somewhat.)

It is easy to see why these Memoirs must have excited and thrilled Soviet readers, especially the young ones: Ehrenburg has revealed to them a world which they had not been allowed to know, a world doom-laden yet magnificent, decadent yet still creative and capable of heroism. Western readers too will find this book instructive and pleasant to read, for Ehrenburg's style is easy, fluent and at times imaginative.

Yet his defects are not less evident here—the defects which once caused the tolerant and generous Lunacharsky to remark: 'Ehrenburg is the *best* type among the *worst* of our fellow-travelling literati.' Ehrenburg's writing is indeed too easy and too fluent. One feels as if one met the author in one of his favourite Montparnasse cafés and listened to an immense, rambling *causerie*, a *causerie* which never ceases to be vivid and intriguing, but is often superficial and less than candid. He would like us to accept his book as a weighty testimony but he wonders himself whether he is not asking too much. 'I said at the beginning that . . . I wanted to write a confession: I probably promised more than I can fulfill. . . . Having come to my adult life, I pass a great deal over in silence, and the more I advance the more often I have to omit events in my life about which it would be difficult for me to speak even to an intimate friend.'

'Yet in spite of this,' he insists, 'my book is still a confession.' Obviously, a 'confession' in which a great deal is 'passed over in silence' arouses distrust. If all that the author omitted were incidents of his private life or intimate emotions, one would not mind. Unfortunately, his silences cover many important events of public interest; not delicacy of feeling but political shrewdness dictates his discretion.

Repeatedly Ehrenburg deals with Soviet critics who long ago (in the twenties) used to reproach him for his 'scepticism' or 'nihilism'. In the rather congenial atmosphere of the post-Stalin era he is not really embarrassed by these labels. 'Of all the apostles,' he says with a touch of solemnity, 'doubting Thomas seems to me the most human'. He is quite glad to be described as a 'romantic ironist'. No doubt, these labels suited in some measure the young Ehrenburg, the author of *Julio Jurenito* and *Thirteen Pipes*, books of his that were already famous forty years ago. But the point is that the 'sceptic' or 'romantic ironist' of those years was subsequently eclipsed by a very different character, the Stalinist sycophant of the 1930s and the Stalin Prize-winner of the 1940s. And, of course, in the last ten years or so Ehrenburg has been the reputed herald of de-Stalinization, the author of *The Thaw*, the champion of artistic freedom. In the *Memoirs* it is this last Ehrenburg who 'defends' his 'sceptical' and 'ironical' self of the early twenties as if to make us forget the Stalinist hack and toady of the middle years. We are given to understand that the youthful 'doubting Thomas' somehow survived intact and unharmed in the veteran memoirist of today.

One would like to believe this. Yet as one ponders Ehrenburg's reminiscences one cannot help being aware of the hidden and wretched presence of the Stalinist hanger-on, eager for self-exculpation. This book has in it much of the ambiguity that has been inherent in the whole process of de-Stalinization, the ambiguity which derives from the fact that de-Stalinization has so far been the work of men who were once Stalin's underlings and accomplices. In this respect Ehrenburg's writing has been the characteristic literary pendant to the politics of Khrushchevism.

'Ehrenburg lifted the iron curtain that concealed the past from the present everywhere,' says Louis Fischer, himself an ex-admirer of Stalin. '. . . he is restoring to human life and dignity . . . the martyred men and women of Russia,' writes an innocent young American Sovietologist. Yet another critic speaks of these *Memoirs* as a 'feat of courage, a near-revolutionary act'. How easily a legend can be launched!

Far from lifting any iron curtain over the past, Ehrenburg lifts only that corner of it that others, those in office, have already raised. Of the truth about events and men he never offers us more than a licensed dose. He does not, for instance, tell us anything about the Great Purges that Khrushchev and other party leaders had not said. To 'human life and dignity' he 'restores' only those of the 'martyred men and women' who had already been officially rehabilitated. With a remarkable presence of mind he does not allow the name of a single unrehabilitated victim to slip into his narrative. He devotes warm-hearted, even sentimental passages to Tuchachevsky, Antonov-Ovseenko, Isaac Babel and others; and he conveys to us a chilling whiff of the terror-stricken Moscow of 1938. But he has nothing to say about the Great Trials of that time. Their defendants, Bukharin, Trotsky, Radek, Rakovsky, Kamenev, Zinoviev and the others—most of whom he knew well—still remain 'unpersons'. His capacity for remembering the past corresponds to the twists and turns and the tempo of the official de-Stalinization with startling precision. One may wonder why he never refers to someone like the now rehabilitated Krestinsky, an outstanding Bolshevik, whom he must have known in Berlin as Soviet Ambassador. The answer is simple: Krestinsky's rehabilitation was brought to public notice just after Ehrenburg had completed writing his *Memoirs*. This is only one of many possible illustrations.[2]

What is worse, Ehrenburg still vents something of the old rancour against the as yet unrehabilitated victims of the Stalinist terror. In his description of the Civil War in Spain one looks in vain for any hint at the terror the G.P.U spread there, at the suppression of P.O.U.M., the abduction and assasination of its leader, Andres Nin, and of other anti-Stalinists. One need only compare Ehrenburg's Spanish recollections with Orwell's *Homage to Catalonia* to grasp the meaning of such omissions. Or take his recollection of André Gide, who in 1936 went to Russia as a sympathizer but returned disgusted with the Stalin cult, which he denounced in a memorable little book *Retour de l'U.R.S.S.* Ehrenburg's comment: 'I do not know what affected him. Another man's heart is a dark continent.' He admits that he slandered Gide at the time; but even now, after 'calm reflection', he still compares the change in Gide's political attitude with the 'erratic flutterings of a moth'; and like a provincial Philistine, he cannot contain his indignation, almost horror, at the thought that Gide, going to Russia, had intended to raise with Stalin himself (!) the question of the legal position of homosexuals in the Soviet Union. ('Although I was aware of Gide's abnormality, I did not immediately grasp what he meant to speak to Stalin about.') He is similarly still quivering with malice towards

---

[2] The nimbleness with which Ehrenburg moves between the ghosts of the 'rehabilitated' and the limbo of the 'unpersons' was evident in the first volume of the *Memoirs*, in his description of the editorial team of *Nashe Slovo*, a Russian revolutionary (non-Bolshevik) *émigré* journal published in Paris during the First World War. He managed to describe in loving detail almost every member of that team, without mentioning even once its editor and moving spirit—Trotsky.

Panaït Istrati, the pathetic 'Gorky of the Balkans', as Romain Rolland described him, because Istrati had vehemently rejected the Stalin cult. These, by no means exceptional, examples of old Stalinist spite stirring in the *Memoirs* contrast curiously with the eulogies for such Western European stooges of Stalin as Marcel Cachin, Dolores Ibaruri, and their like.

Explicitly or implicitly, Ehrenburg is justifying Stalin's major policies in Europe. True, he often pleads ignorance of politics as a mitigating circumstance for himself, a strange plea for someone who has been so prominent as a political propagandist. But he is not so modest as to refrain from passing political judgements and verdicts. He blames Leon Blum (and his 'stupid bleatings') for the defeat of Republican Spain, but has nothing to say about Stalin's share in that defeat. He presents the French and Spanish Popular Fronts as heroic epics; he does not seem to suspect even now that those fronts brought about their own undoing, because they were, on Stalin's promptings, all too eager to appease the Western bourgeoisie and to curb the revolutionary energies of the French and Spanish workers and peasants. He describes with justified sarcasm the cowardice and the surrender of the German Social Democrats in the face of Nazism. But he makes no mention of the perverse Stalinist policies which had done no less to paralyse German labour in the early 1930s. Did he not, as an eye-witness, watch the *Rote Volksentscheid*, that infamous plebiscite in which, two years before Hitler became Chancellor, the Communists marched with the Nazis against the Social Democrats and called for the '*national* and social liberation of Germany'?

Only when he comes to the Nazi–Soviet Pact of 1939 does the author of the *Memoirs* put aside pretence and make-believe and describe convincingly the shock, the humiliation and the horror with which that act of 'Soviet–German friendship' had filled him. (He seems to suggest that some repercussions of that act are felt even now in the U.S.S.R.) Here, evidently, his deep and wounded Jewish emotion gets the better of him; and instead of the slick raconteur, a suffering and frightened human being speaks to us.

What is one to make of this strange *mélange* of sincerity and cant? Ehrenburg relates that a young Russian, listening to his tale of the Stalinist terror, asked him: 'How is it that you have survived?' 'I shall never know,' he replies, '. . . I lived in times when the fate of men was not like a game of chess but like a lottery.'

But this is surely not the truth of the matter. The fate of those of Ehrenburg's countrymen—and they were many—who had the courage to oppose Stalin was not at all like a lottery: none of them survived. Life was a lottery to quite a few Stalinists, however, for even Stalin's servants and flatterers could not be sure of their fate; many of them were disgraced and perished. In some cases—Ehrenburg's is one—a man's fate was rather like a strange combination of 'a lottery' and 'a game of chess'; these *Memoirs* occasionally show how the author played his hand at the game.

Should he on this account be condemned beyond redemption? In quite a few countries and in many ages thinkers and writers, from Galileo to Goethe and Pushkin, bowed to the despotism of rulers and paid a moral ransom in order to save themselves as scientists and artists and to get on with their work. Posterity, which honours heroic fighters against oppression, does not invariably condemn those who have bowed to a *force majeure*. Supreme heroism is rare, and its absence need not in itself be a vice.

Ehrenburg's misfortune was not so much that he lacked the character to resist Stalinism, but that he submitted to it so completely and even zealously that he thereby corrupted his own work and nearly destroyed himself as novelist and poet. He himself refers ruefully to his 'hastily written' and 'badly constructed' propagandist novels. He resembles in this the chief character of his own *Thaw*, the painter Vladimir Pukhov, who through opportunism and servility wasted his artistic personality. The writing of the *Memoirs* was for Ehrenburg an opportunity to cleanse himself, test his wasted talent, and regain artistic quality. To a very limited extent he has succeeded. He might have succeeded more genuinely and fully if he had not tried to impress us with his moral courage; if he had given up his posturing, his attempts at self-exculpation and his old rancour; if he had told us as much of the truth about the Stalin era as he knows instead of deliberately purveying half-truths.

Yet, Ehrenburg's role in the Russian 'thaw' has been considerable —not for nothing have the crypto- and neo-Stalinists attacked him repeatedly. But it is not easy to assess his role, for it bears on the complex relationship between half-truth and truth. I am not speaking here of the Truth of the metaphysicians, but of historical truth, which bases itself on ascertainable and undeniable facts. Soviet society needs that truth as much as it needs air to breathe. Without a genuine knowledge of the record of the Stalin era, it cannot over-

come its present ideological confusion and cannot advance. Ehrenburg's *Memoirs*, like Khrushchev's revelations, offer a lot of clues to
the record. But the clues are not the record. A half truth may sometimes be a useful introduction to the truth; it may even represent an
instalment of the truth and stimulate a creative ferment in minds
avid for knowledge. But all too often a half-truth can divert such
minds from the truth or block access to it, depending on the maturity or immaturity of the public.

Ehrenburg's *Memoirs* are undoubtedly exercising a dual and ambivalent influence. They represent a transient phase in the development of a new social consciousness in the U.S.S.R. the phase in
which Soviet thinking has painfully outgrown the Stalinist mythology but is still shrinking from perceiving the realities of the
recent past and of the present.

II

E. Yevtushenko's *Premature Autobiography*[3] contrasts somewhat
ironically with Ehrenburg's tardy and timid *Memoirs*. A slim book,
written hastily during the author's brief stay in Paris. is was published originally in French, and is still banned in Russia; The
author has even paid for it with a spell of disgrace. The reason is
not far to seek: in his account of his life there are none of the
diplomatic silences and evasions at which Ehrenburg excels. What
Yevtushenko tells us about men, events, and the spiritual state of
Soviet society boldly exceeds the licensed dose of truth; he exposes
large patches of the social and moral background to Soviet politics
which Moscow's rulers would still prefer to keep concealed. He even
begins his reminiscences with an attack upon the purveyors of reticent confessions and half-truths:

> Some people boast that they have never lied. Let them have a look at
> themselves in the mirror and tell us not how many times they have
> purveyed untruth, but how often they have preferred the comfort of
> silence. . . . I know that these people have an alibi . . . silence is
> gold. My answer is that their gold cannot be pure and that silence is
> a fraud. . . .

Yevtushenko's position has been easier, of course, than that of
almost any writer of Ehrenburg's generation: he did not have to

[3] *Autobiographie Précoce* (Julliard, Paris, 1963).

endure the terror and the moral pressures to which others had been subjected; he did not have to make the compromises with conscience which caused them to lose their self-respect. At the time of the Great Purges he was only four or five years old; he was only eight when Hitler attacked the Soviet Union; and he was not yet twenty when Stalin died. His mind is not contorted by guilt and craving for self-exculpation. He speaks for a generation that does not shrink from the full truth about the Stalin era but is eager to get at it and face the consequences.

Yevtushenko says of himself:

People in the West have tried to present me as an exceptional figure, detaching itself like a bright spot from the grey background of Soviet society. But I am nothing of the sort. Very many Soviet people detest the things against which I am struggling just as passionately as I do. . . . The new ideas and sentiments that are found in my poems were there, in Soviet society, well before I had begun to write. True, they had not then received a poetic form; but if I had not expressed them, someone else would have done so.

Yevtushenko's anger and disgust with Stalinism spring from his loyalty to the revolution and to communism, a loyalty which takes itself for granted. What he says about this has a more convincing ring than have Ehrenburg's declarations of ideological allegiance. He describes himself as 'half-intellectual and half-peasant' and says that 'revolution has been the religion of my family': 'We never pronounced the word 'revolution' with any official solemnity; we uttered it calmly, tenderly, and almost austerely.' One of his ancestors, a peasant, was deported to Siberia for setting fire to a landlord's mansion. A grandfather, also a semi-illiterate peasant, fought in the revolution and civil war, distinguished himself, was brought from Siberia to the Military Academy in Moscow, studied, and rose to the rank of general. 'Even in his imposing uniform, with all the insignia of rank [and all his medals] on his chest, he remained a simple peasant.' Not surprisingly, he perished in the purges. The poet recollects a last childish glimpse of the grandfather as he lulled him to sleep with songs of the civil war on the very night when he was to be arrested for 'high treason'. A similar fate befell another grandfather, a mathematician of Lettish origin. But of all this the grandson was to learn only many years later. In the meantime my parents would take me to workers' demonstrations at the Red Square and I would beg my father to lift me high above his shoulders so that I could see Stalin. Hoisted . . . over the heads of the immense crowd, I waved vigorously my little red flag and believed that Stalin himself looked at me and answered me.

In his devotion to the revolution, in the innocence with which he practised the Stalin cult, having imbibed it from childhood, and in the force of his reaction against it, Yevtushenko is representative of many—should one say most?—of his contemporaries. His occasional *naïvetés* are hardly surprising. When he tries, for instance, to define the difference between Lenin and Stalin, he says that Lenin wanted communism to be for the good of the people, whereas Stalin held that the people were there only to serve communism. What a euphemism! He echoes also some of the most threadbare banalities of 'Soviet patriotism' and sees in Khrushchev the real promoter and guarantor of de-Stalinization, progress, and artistic freedom. More puzzling than lack of political sophistication is a certain crudity of literary taste, which allows the poet to admire Stalin's style and to describe the latter's bizarre quasi-ecclesiastical 'Oath to Lenin' as a 'prose poem'. But in these illusions and *naïvetés* there is indeed an innocence which is altogether lacking in the writings of the old disillusioned opportunists posturing as martyrs. (Yevtushenko reminds us that even Pasternak, whom he adores as a poet and as a man, produced in his time some rhymed eulogies for Stalin.[4])

Yevtushenko is, of course, the 'citizen poet' and the fighter and drummer of the revolution in Nekrasov's and Mayakovsky's tradition. He turns his 'Poet's Corner', wherever it happens to be, into a barricade. On 'the other side' are, of course, the revolution's external enemies, but also 'Stalin's heirs', the privileged bueaucrats, corrupters of communism and anti-Semites, who are still conspiring against Russia's freedom. The author of *Babyi Yar* offers here a gloss on that poem of his. He continues to defy the anti-Semites: 'It

---

[4] Yevtushenko's remarks on the Pasternak of *Doctor Zhivago* are worth quoting: 'Those in the West who have tried to use his name in their cold war campaign have committed a veritable crime. Similarly, I shall never forgive some of our writers who have seized this pretext in order to try and wipe off Pasternak's name from our literature. . . .' 'Pasternak considered many events of our Soviet life as if he viewed them from the other bank of the river of time. . . . His isolation resulted in his . . . remoteness . . . from the struggle and the great changes occurring in the world. Boris Pasternak once said of himself that he was a kind of milestone between two historic epochs. Nothing could characterize him better than this. Therein lies the force and also the tragedy of this poet of genius.'

is false and even absurd to pretend that anti-Semitism is inherent in the character of the Russian people; it is as alien to them as it is to any other people. It has always and everywhere been artificially fostered in order to promote the basest of vested interests.'

He describes vividly how from his adolescence he had to wrestle spiritually with a friend, 'the young poet K.', a member of the Communist Youth and an anti-Semite, who sought to persuade him that all evil stemmed from the Jews. ('Were not most of those that split the workers' movement, from the *Bund* to Trotsky, members of that suspect race?')

After one such discussion K. stayed overnight in my flat. Next morning I was awakened by his shouting and jumping. Still in his pants, he performed something like an African joy dance and brandished a morning paper. On its first page the paper carried a long communiqué about the discovery of the conspiracy of the 'white coats' and the arrest of the doctors who had tried to poison Stalin. 'Well', K. shouted in exultation, 'who has been right all along? They are Jews, all of them.'

It did not then occur to Yevtushenko that the accusation of the Kremlin doctors might be false; he believed it and was depressed by the affair; but he refused to swallow the racialist moral of the story.

The same evening I went with my friend K. to see an old film. . . . By chance they showed a pogrom of Jews that occurred in Odessa in Tsarist times. On the screen criminals and shopkeepers filed past and with all the strength of their lungs shouted the old hate slogan : 'Kill the Jews and save Russia!' With blood stained batons they hit little Jewish children on their heads. . . . 'All the same [Yevtushenko said] you would not like this to happen again?' K. answered coldly: 'Listen, Zhenya, we are dialecticians; we must not repudiate the whole of our past.' His voice had a strange metallic sound; his eyes flashed with hatred worthy of a young Nazi. Yet in his buttonhole there glittered a Communist Youth badge. I looked at him with fright.

Like no other Soviet writer so far, Yevtushenko has brought into focus this latent but deep political cleavage, the tense tug-of-war between reaction and progress, in Russia. He insists that behind the reactionary moods and ideas were—or are—the privileged and corrupt groups of the bureaucracy.

More than once the poet K. used to reproach me for my lack of revolutionary vigilance. He was mistaken. I was vigilant in my own way—I watched him and his like. I was horrified to see how they built new houses for themselves and wallowed in luxury right in the centre of Moscow, where in overcrowded blocks many families usually shared one apartment. I kept a sharp eye on the members of that bureaucratic *élite* who gloated over the writings with anti-Semitic accents . . . which were appearing in our journals more and more often. And I saw how they grabbed their privileges under the very noses of underpaid workers.

This testimony is all the more remarkable because it is based on empirical observation rather than on any theoretical thesis. And the bluntness of this and similar statements was enough to ensure that this *Premature Autobiography* be placed on the Index in Moscow.

However, the most dramatic pages in this short book are those which describe the impact of Stalin's death and funeral on the author and the people around him. Most of them, he recollects, accustomed to the idea that Stalin was thinking for all of them, felt lost without him and were stunned. 'Russia wept. She wept with genuine tears, perhaps with tears of fear for the future. I too wept.' What follows is an unforgettable description of grim catastrophe at Stalin's funeral. On a frosty winter morning tens of thousands of men, women, and children moved from all ends of Moscow towards the House of Soviets, where the dead dictator lay in state. (The breath of the marchers was freezing in the air, forming a cloud overhead and settling on naked trees.) Suddenly the processions advancing from all sides merged into a terrible human avalanche, pouring down the slope of a street leading to the House of Soviets. The avalanche crushed women and children against lamp-posts and other obstacles on its way and moved over their mangled bodies. No one seemed able to halt it. Will-less and horror-struck, the crowd swept on.

The torrent carried me too all the time. Suddenly I felt something soft under my feet. It took me a moment to realize that I was trampling on a human body. I jumped up in terror and became suspended in the crowd which was still descending down the slope. For a long while I did not even try to walk on my feet again. It was my size that saved me. Smaller people suffocated in the throng before they were crushed underfoot. And finally we were caught in a trap. Military trucks, tightly lined up narrowed the road and barred our passage. Human waves broke against them with furious momentum. 'Take away the trucks, move the trucks!' the crowd screamed in terror. A young fair-haired police officer looked on, tears in eyes: 'I cannot help it, I haven't got any orders!' he in his turn began to scream. The edges of his lorry were already stained with blood. But men and women were still being hurled against it and crushed under the officer's eyes. Before dying they only heard his words: 'I haven't got any orders!'. All of a sudden I felt exploding within me a savage hatred of this incredible stupidity, of the docility that had produced this 'I cannot help it, I haven't got any orders!' For the first time now all this hatred was turned against the man whom we were about to bury, for I realized at last that it was he who was responsible, that it was he who had produced this bloody chaos, that it was he who had inculcated into human beings this mechanical and blind obedience to orders from above.

Over a hundred and thirty years earlier Adam Mickiewicz in a great poem depicted a similar scene that had taken place in the St. Petersburg of the Tsars in the middle of a magnificent military parade. There is much poetic power in Yevtushenko's description, which may enter literature, and the history books, as a shocking eye-witness account and as a condensed symbolic presentation of an entire epoch. Yevtushenko's resounding anger with the docility induced in his countrymen by Stalin's rule takes us far away from the half-truths of official de-Stalinization. Through him young Russia is crying out against the shame and the suffering of her fathers and grandfathers.